ZOMBIE TALES

OBLIVION

ROSS RICHIE
chief executive officer

ANDREW COSBY
chief creative officer

MARK WAID
editor-in-chief

ADAM FORTIER
vice president,
publishing

CHIP MOSHER
marketing director

MATT GAGNON
managing editor

Zombie Tales: Oblivion — published by BOOM! Studios. Zombie Tales is copyright © 2009 Boom Entertainment, Inc.
BOOM! Studios™ and the BOOM! logo are trademarks of Boom Entertainment, Inc., registered in various countries and
categories. "Zaambi," in illustrated form, is copyright © Terry Morgan and Chris Morgan and Boom Entertainment, Inc.
Based on the short story "Zaambi" copyright © 2005 Terry Morgan and Chris Morgan. All rights reserved. The characters
and events depicted herein are fictional. Any similarity to actual persons, demons, anti-Christs, aliens, vampires,
face-suckers or political figures, whether living, dead or undead, or to any actual or supernatural events is coincidental and
unintentional. So don't come whining to us.

Office of publication: 6310 San Vicente Blvd Ste 404, Los Angeles, CA 90048-5457

A catalog record for this book is available from the Library of Congress and on our website at www.boom-studios.com on
the Librarian Resource Page.

First Edition: October 2008

10 9 8 7 6 5 4 3 2 1
PRINTED IN KOREA

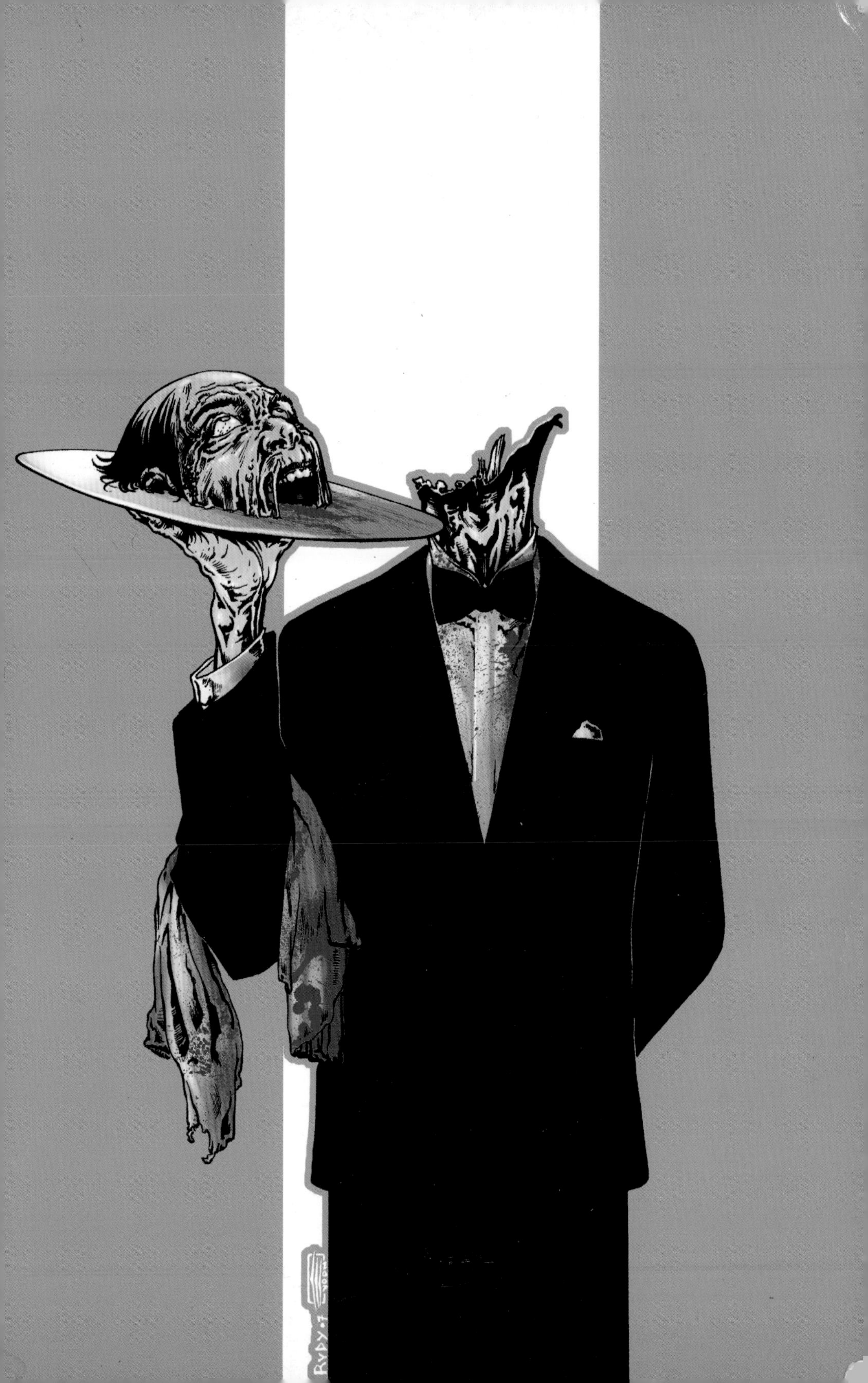

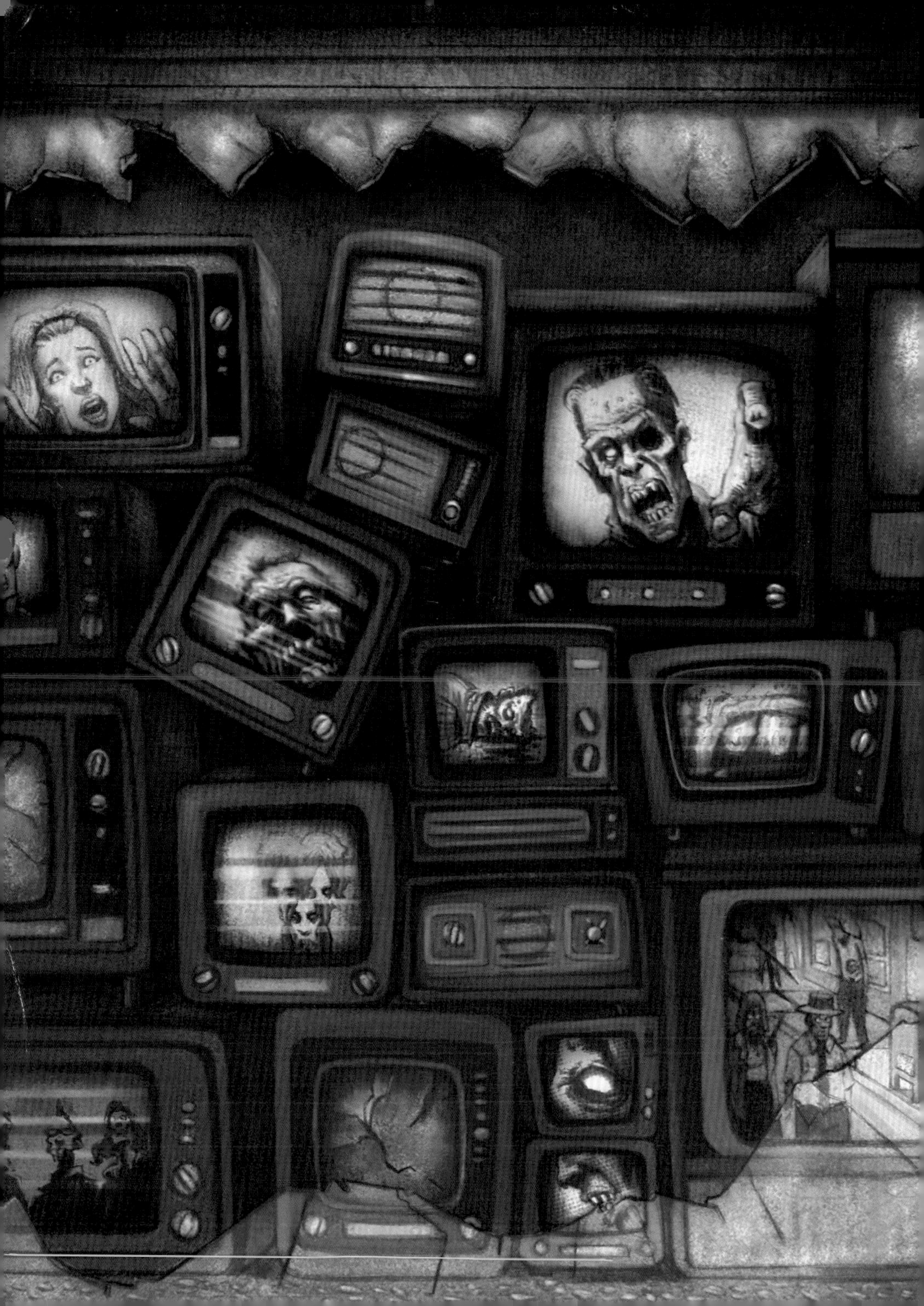

THE WAR AT HOME
Part One
Story: JOE R. LANSDALE
Art: EDUARDO BARRETO

PEOPLE PERSON
Story: STEVE NILES
Art: DANIEL LAFRANCE

SPRING 2061
Story: KIM KRIZAN
Art: JON REED

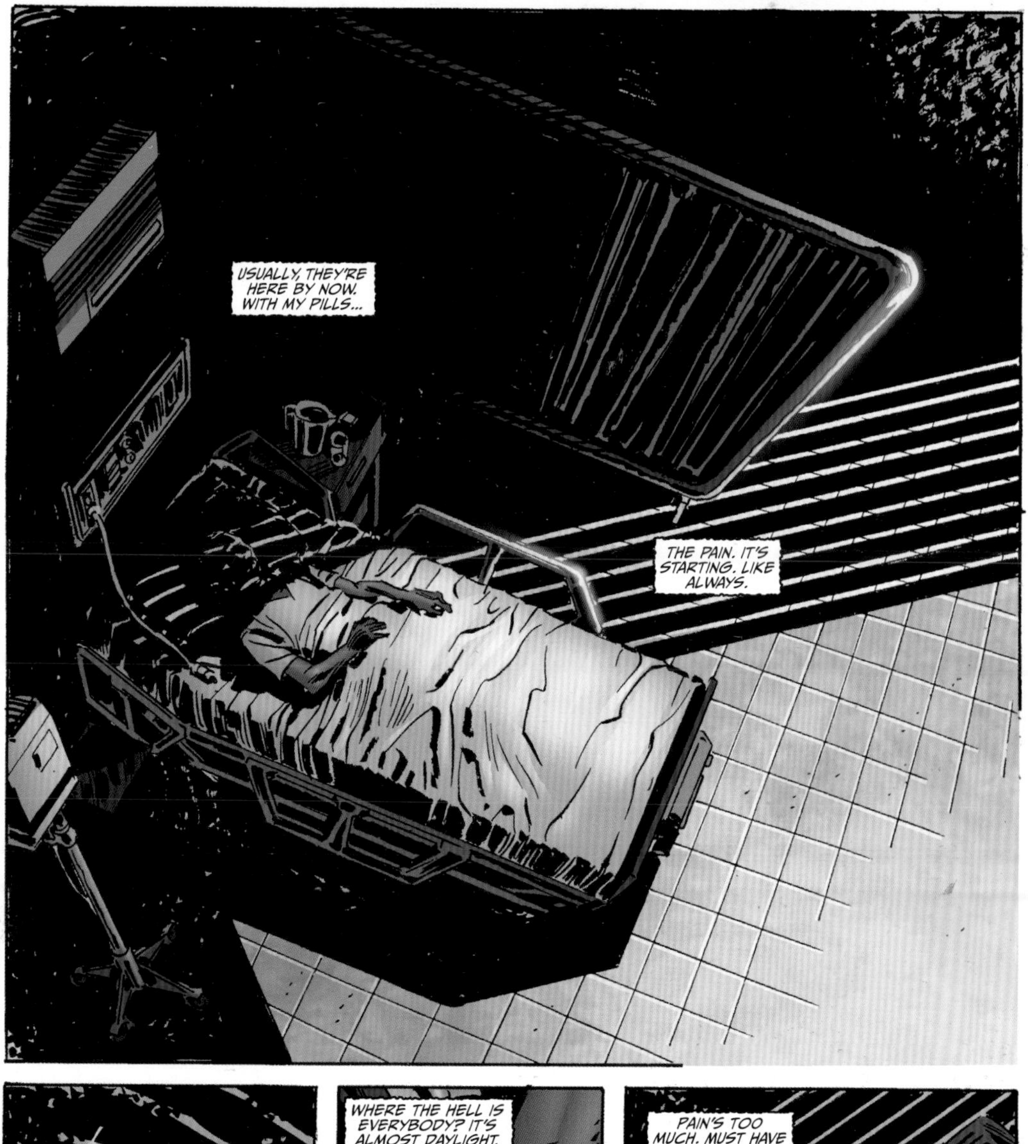
USUALLY, THEY'RE HERE BY NOW. WITH MY PILLS...
THE PAIN. IT'S STARTING. LIKE ALWAYS.

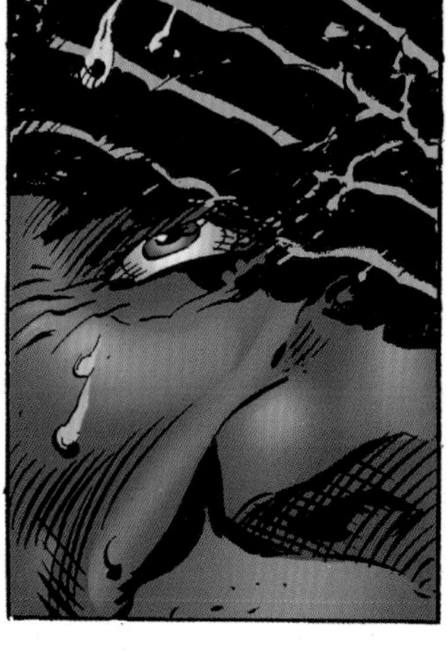

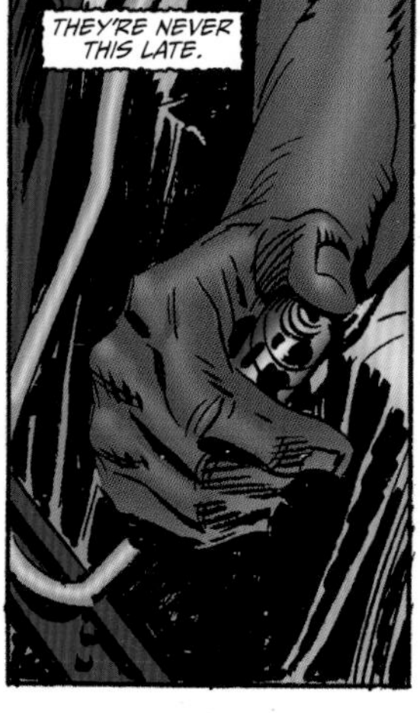
WHERE THE HELL IS EVERYBODY? IT'S ALMOST DAYLIGHT.
THEY'RE NEVER THIS LATE.

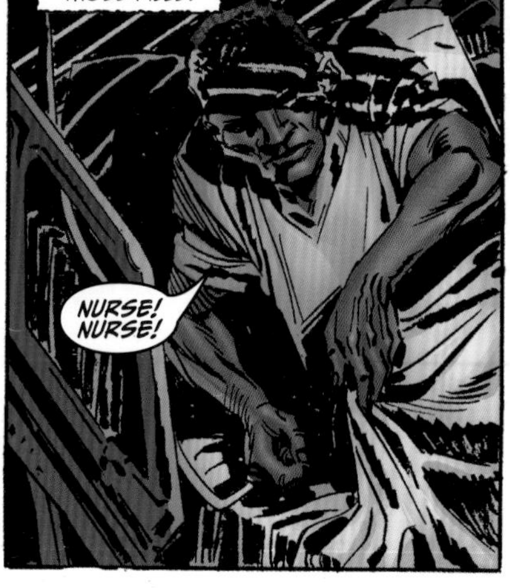
PAIN'S TOO MUCH. MUST HAVE THOSE PILLS.
NURSE! NURSE!

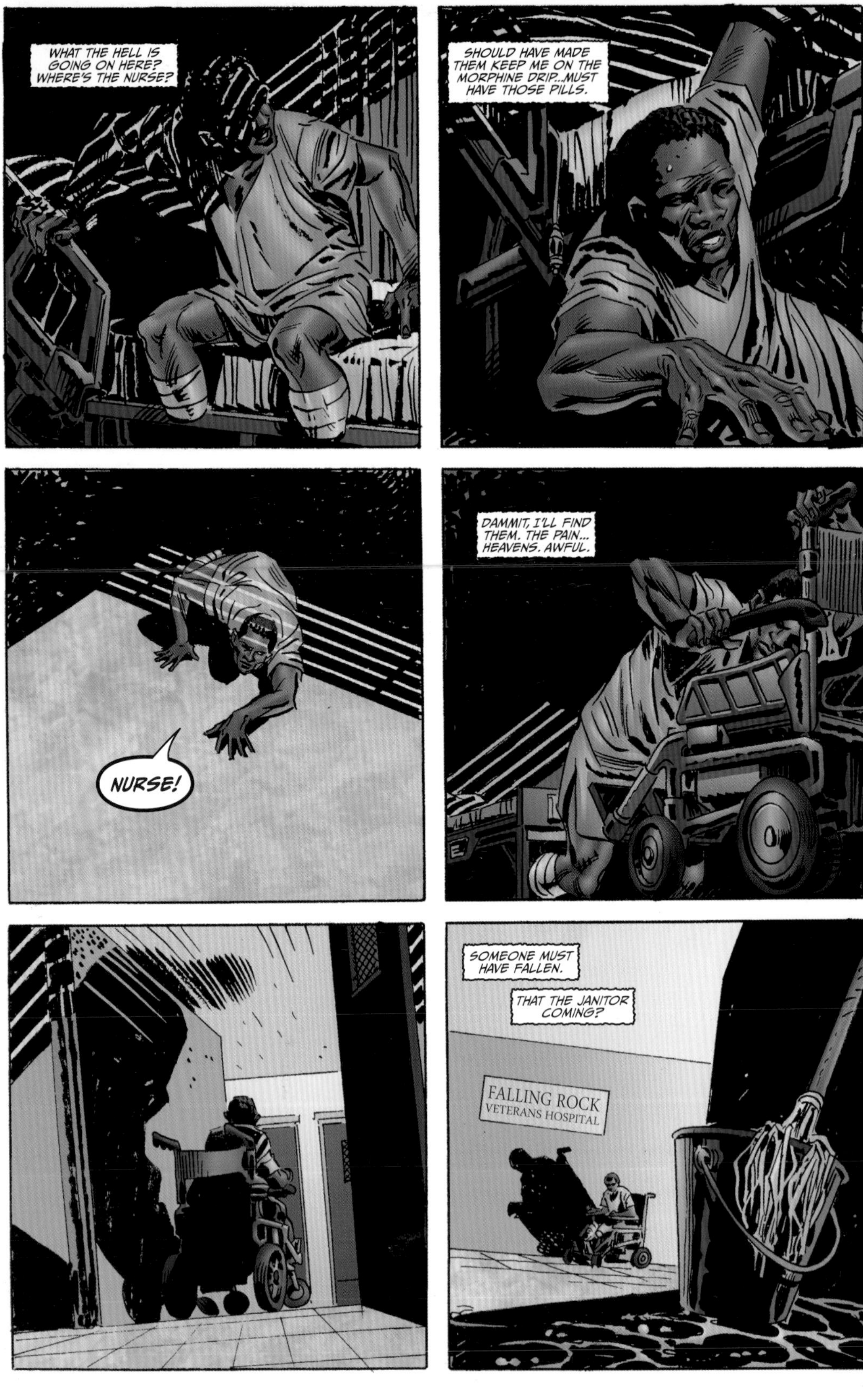
WHAT THE HELL IS GOING ON HERE? WHERE'S THE NURSE?
SHOULD HAVE MADE THEM KEEP ME ON THE MORPHINE DRIP...MUST HAVE THOSE PILLS.
NURSE!
DAMMIT, I'LL FIND THEM. THE PAIN... HEAVENS. AWFUL.
SOMEONE MUST HAVE FALLEN.
THAT THE JANITOR COMING?
FALLING ROCK
VETERANS HOSPITAL

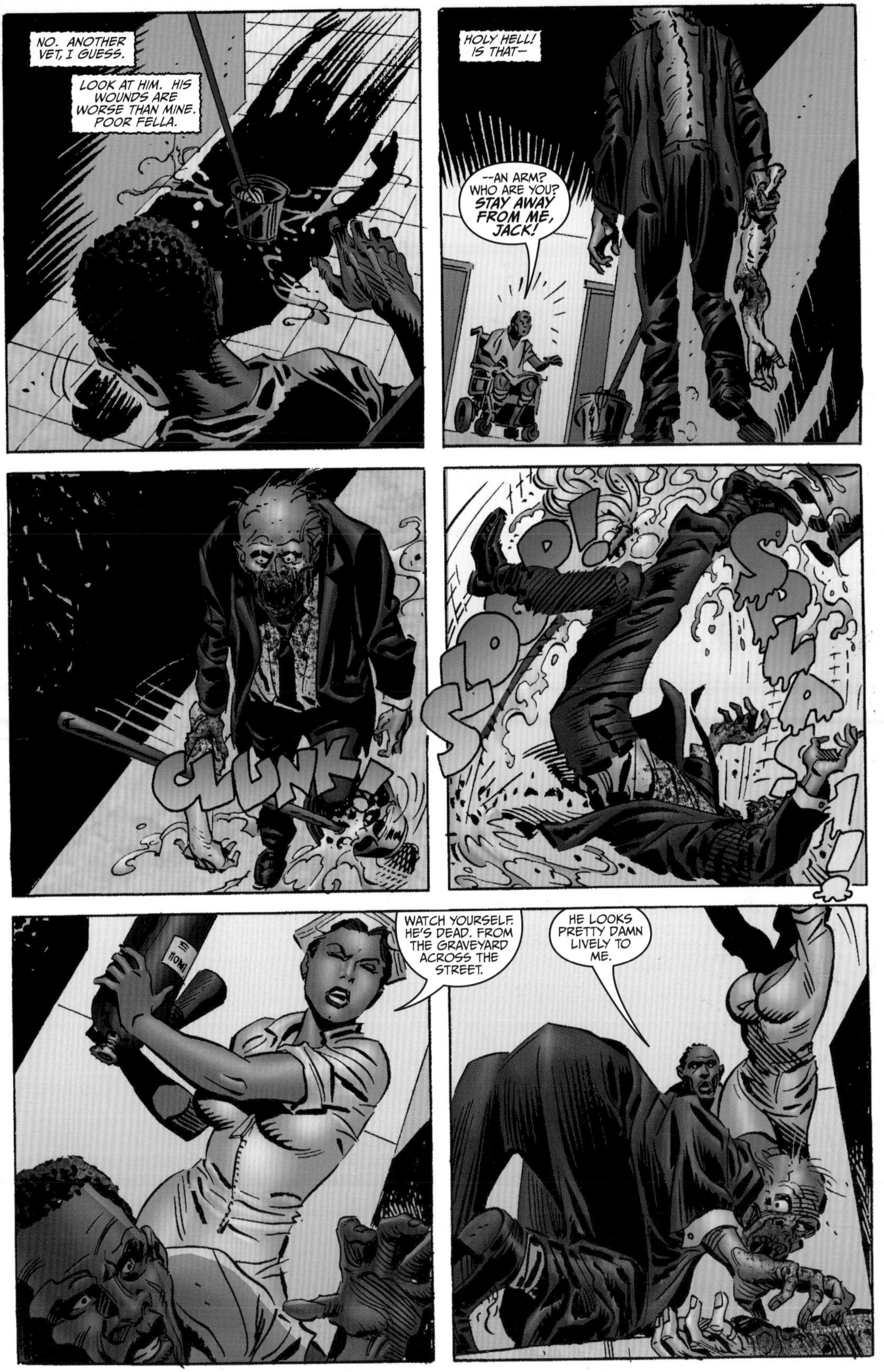
NO. ANOTHER VET, I GUESS.
LOOK AT HIM. HIS WOUNDS ARE WORSE THAN MINE. POOR FELLA.
HOLY HELL! IS THAT—
--AN ARM? WHO ARE YOU? STAY AWAY FROM ME, JACK!
CLUNK!
WATCH YOURSELF. HE'S DEAD. FROM THE GRAVEYARD ACROSS THE STREET.
HE LOOKS PRETTY DAMN LIVELY TO ME.

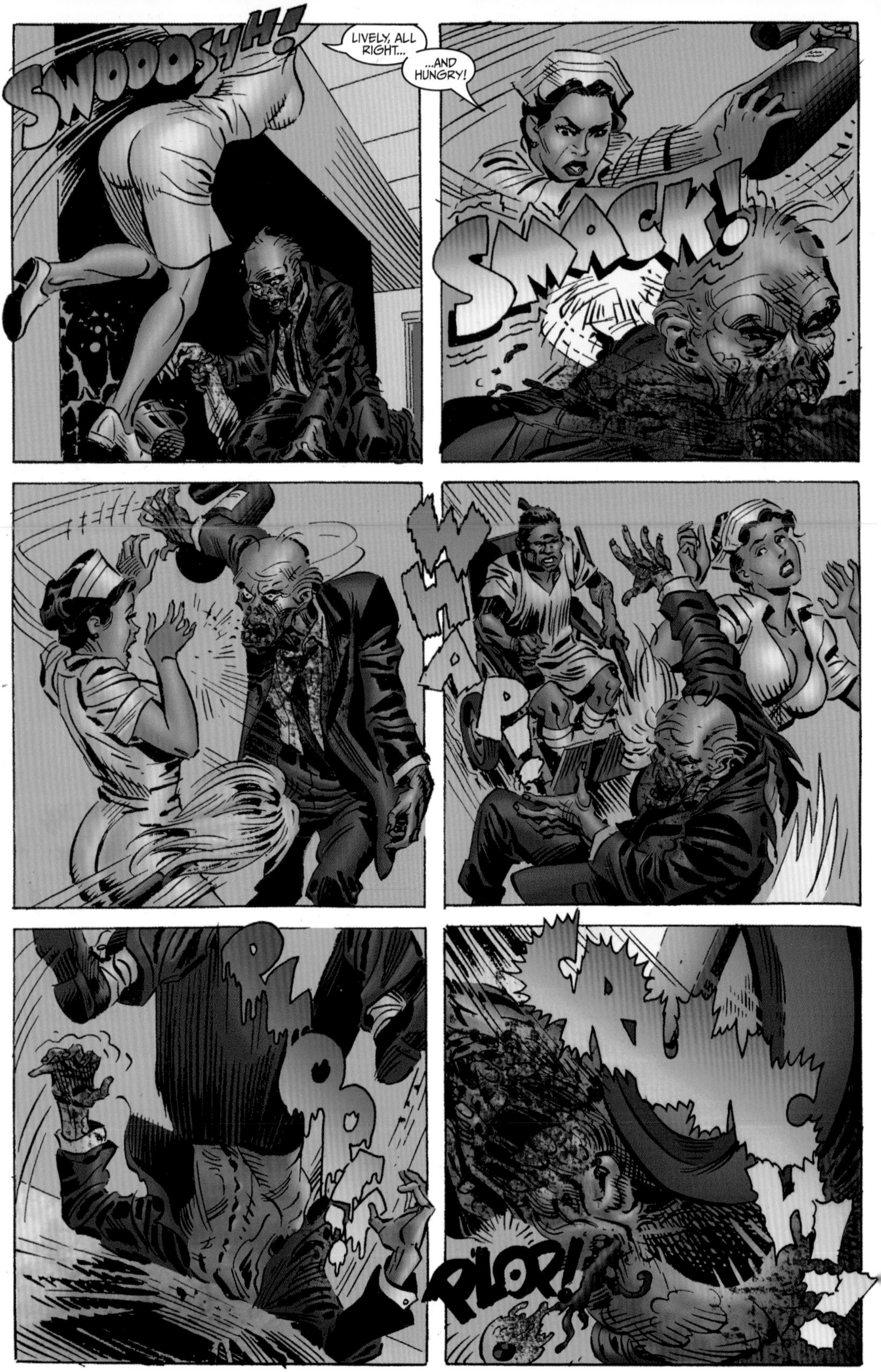
SWOOOSHH!
LIVELY, ALL RIGHT...
...AND HUNGRY!
SMACK!
WHAP
PLOR!

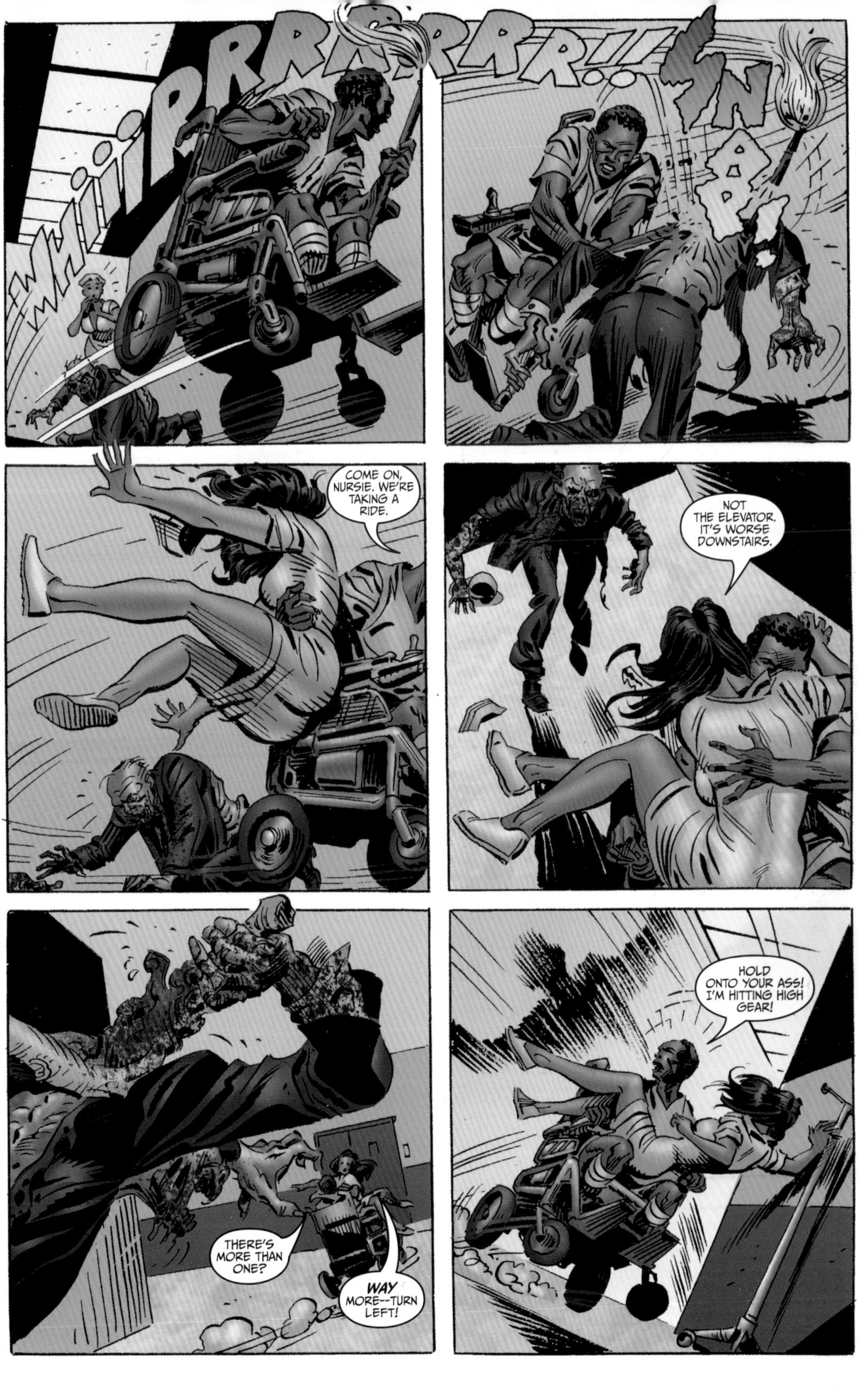
COME ON, NURSIE. WE'RE TAKING A RIDE.
NOT THE ELEVATOR. IT'S WORSE DOWNSTAIRS.
THERE'S MORE THAN ONE?
WAY MORE--TURN LEFT!
HOLD ONTO YOUR ASS! I'M HITTING HIGH GEAR!

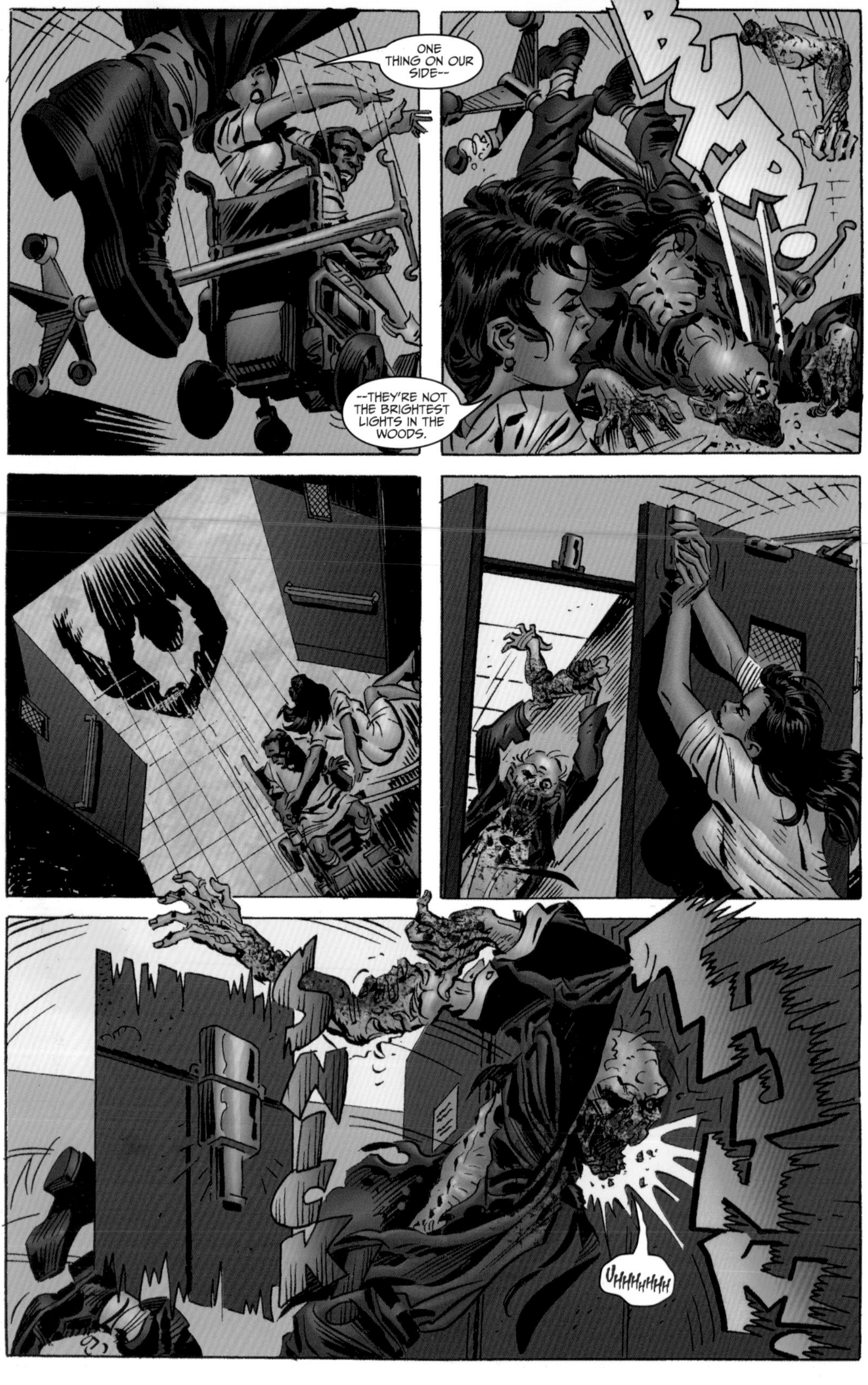

ONE THING ON OUR SIDE--
--THEY'RE NOT THE BRIGHTEST LIGHTS IN THE WOODS.
UHHHHHHH

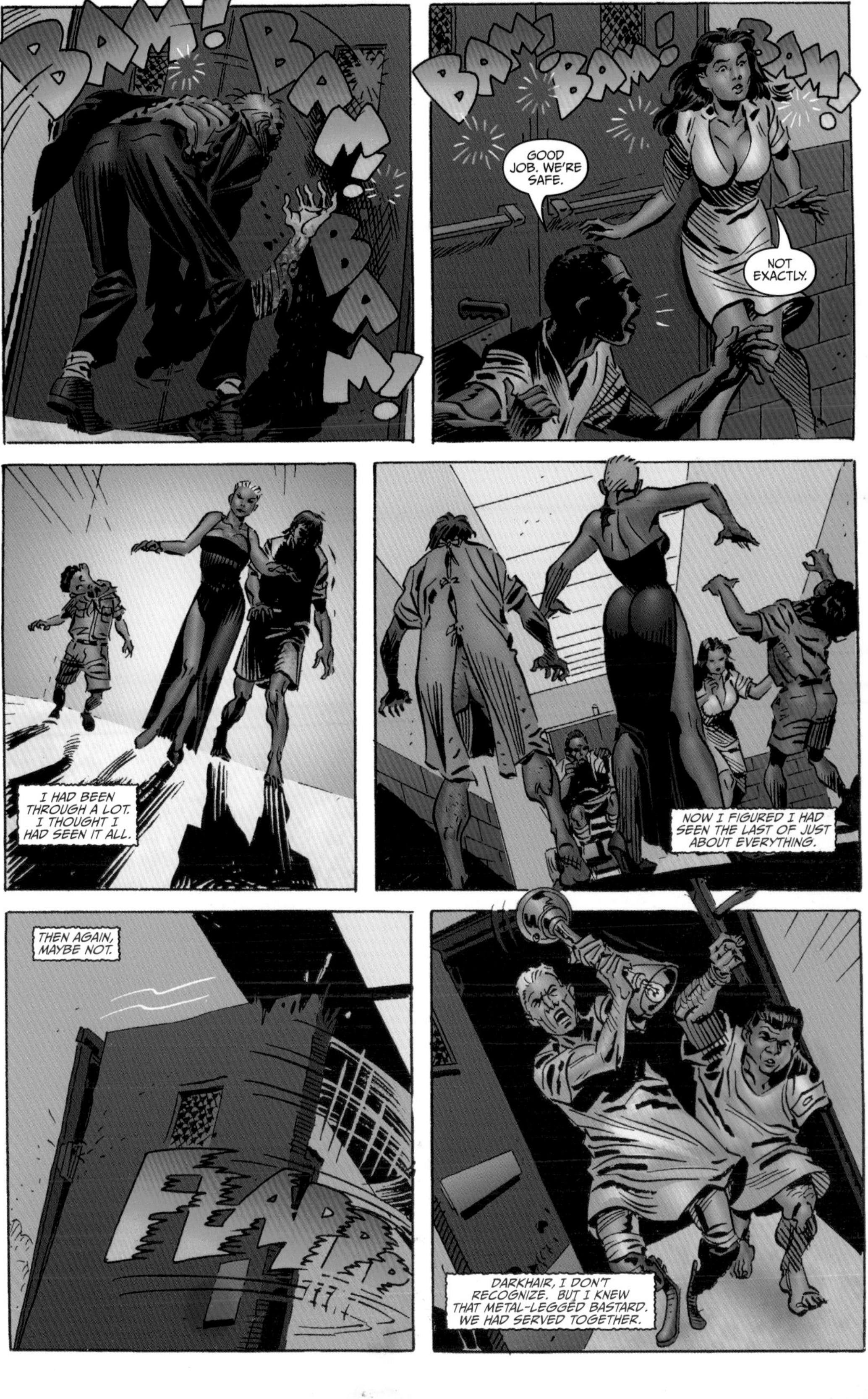
BAM! BAM! BAM! BAM!
BAM! BAM! BAM!
GOOD JOB. WE'RE SAFE.
NOT EXACTLY.
I HAD BEEN THROUGH A LOT. I THOUGHT I HAD SEEN IT ALL.
NOW I FIGURED I HAD SEEN THE LAST OF JUST ABOUT EVERYTHING.
THEN AGAIN, MAYBE NOT.
ZZAP
DARKHAIR, I DON'T RECOGNIZE. BUT I KNEW THAT METAL-LEGGED BASTARD. WE HAD SERVED TOGETHER.

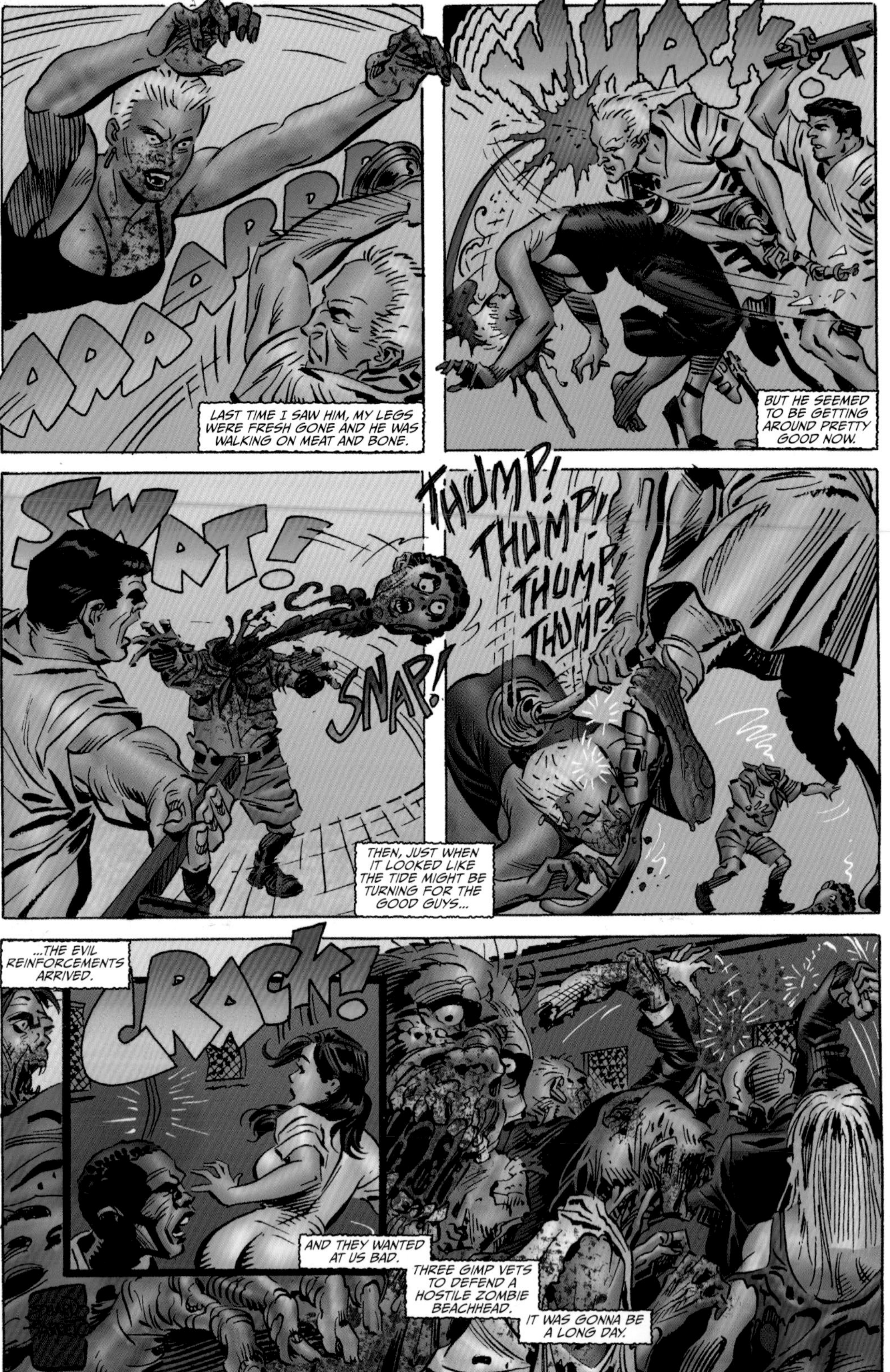
AAARRRRR
LAST TIME I SAW HIM, MY LEGS WERE FRESH GONE AND HE WAS WALKING ON MEAT AND BONE.
WHACK
BUT HE SEEMED TO BE GETTING AROUND PRETTY GOOD NOW.
SWAT!
SNAP!
THUMP! THUMP! THUMP! THUMP!
THEN, JUST WHEN IT LOOKED LIKE THE TIDE MIGHT BE TURNING FOR THE GOOD GUYS...
...THE EVIL REINFORCEMENTS ARRIVED.
CRACK!
AND THEY WANTED AT US BAD.
THREE GIMP VETS TO DEFEND A HOSTILE ZOMBIE BEACHHEAD.
IT WAS GONNA BE A LONG DAY.

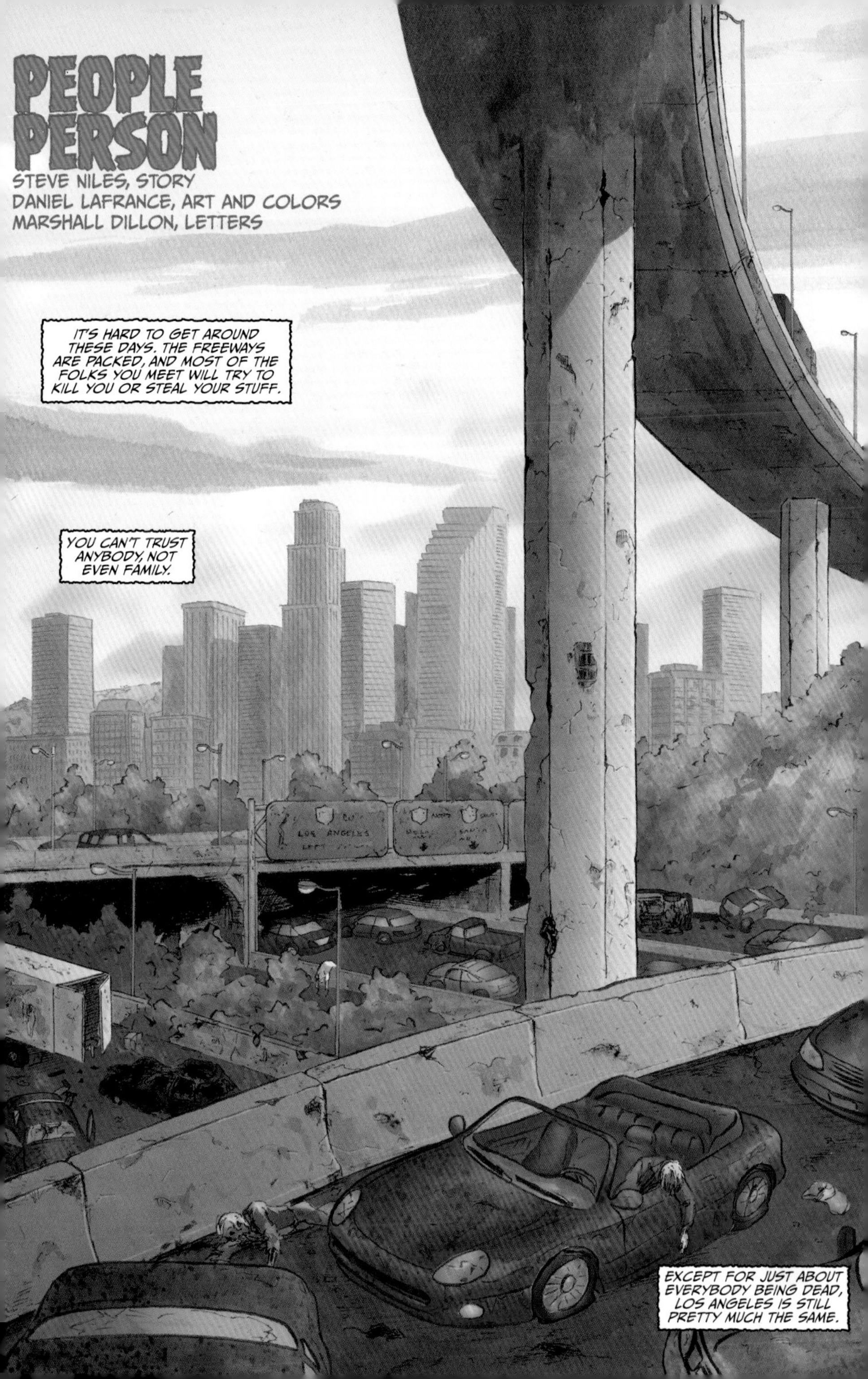
PEOPLE PERSON
STEVE NILES, STORY
DANIEL LAFRANCE, ART AND COLORS
MARSHALL DILLON, LETTERS
IT'S HARD TO GET AROUND THESE DAYS. THE FREEWAYS ARE PACKED, AND MOST OF THE FOLKS YOU MEET WILL TRY TO KILL YOU OR STEAL YOUR STUFF.
YOU CAN'T TRUST ANYBODY, NOT EVEN FAMILY.
EXCEPT FOR JUST ABOUT EVERYBODY BEING DEAD, LOS ANGELES IS STILL PRETTY MUCH THE SAME.

MY NAME IS SCOTT BALL.

I USED TO OWN AND RUN A USED BOOKSTORE IN BURBANK BEFORE ALL THIS CRAP HAPPENED.

IT WAS A PRETTY BORING LIFE I HAD GOING.

NOW, EVERY DAY IS AN ADVENTURE.

SCOTT! I KNOW YOU'RE HERE, SCOTT!

I CAN SMEEEEELL YOU, SCOTT!

THAT'S THE WIFE.

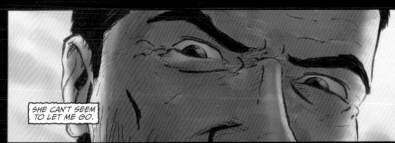

SHE CAN'T SEEM TO LET ME GO.

TODAY, I'M GONNA HELP HER.

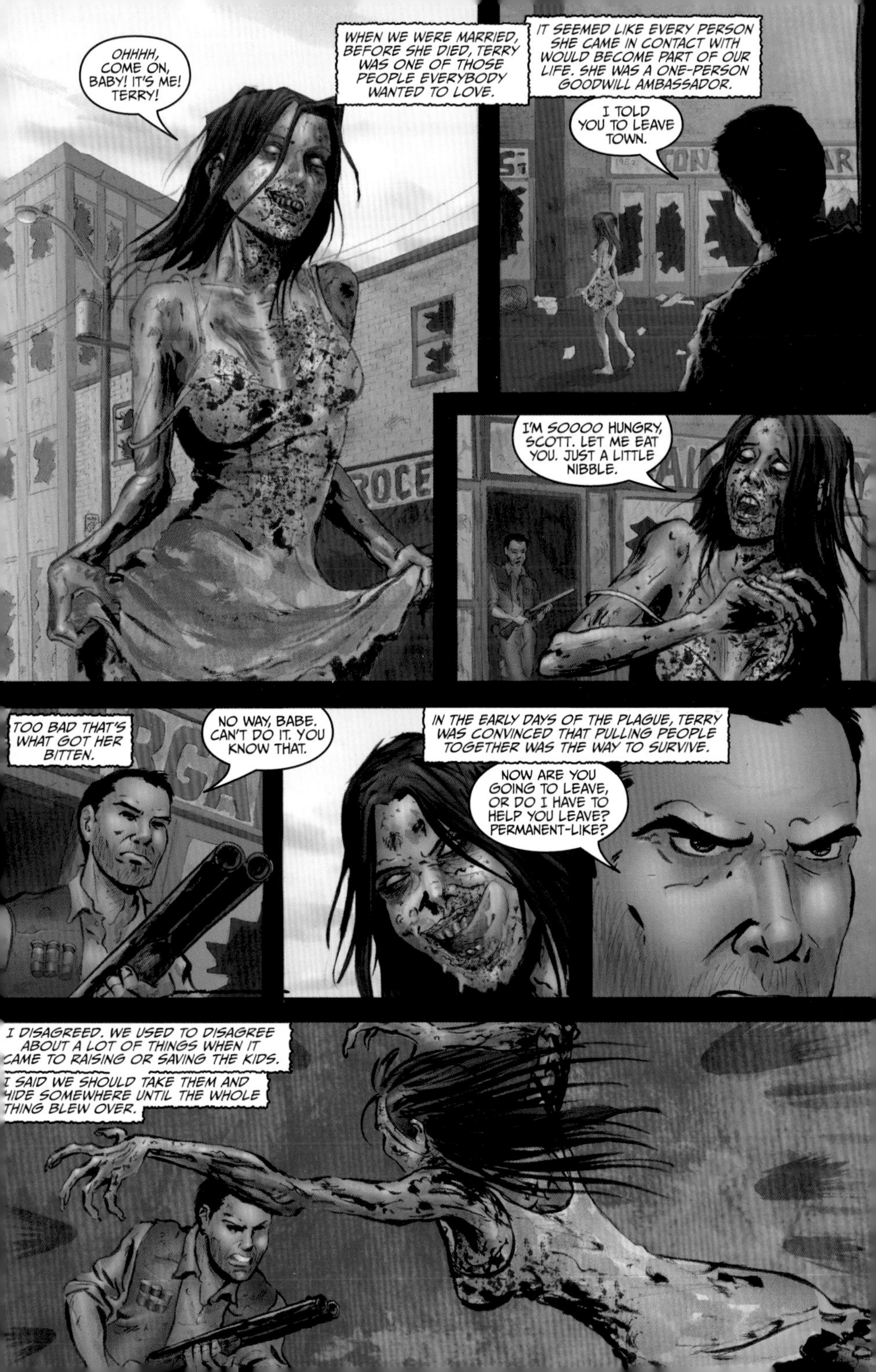
OHHHH, COME ON, BABY! IT'S ME! TERRY!
WHEN WE WERE MARRIED, BEFORE SHE DIED, TERRY WAS ONE OF THOSE PEOPLE EVERYBODY WANTED TO LOVE.
IT SEEMED LIKE EVERY PERSON SHE CAME IN CONTACT WITH WOULD BECOME PART OF OUR LIFE. SHE WAS A ONE-PERSON GOODWILL AMBASSADOR.
I TOLD YOU TO LEAVE TOWN.
I'M SOOOO HUNGRY, SCOTT. LET ME EAT YOU. JUST A LITTLE NIBBLE.
TOO BAD THAT'S WHAT GOT HER BITTEN.
NO WAY, BABE. CAN'T DO IT. YOU KNOW THAT.
IN THE EARLY DAYS OF THE PLAGUE, TERRY WAS CONVINCED THAT PULLING PEOPLE TOGETHER WAS THE WAY TO SURVIVE.
NOW ARE YOU GOING TO LEAVE, OR DO I HAVE TO HELP YOU LEAVE? PERMANENT-LIKE?
I DISAGREED. WE USED TO DISAGREE ABOUT A LOT OF THINGS WHEN IT CAME TO RAISING OR SAVING THE KIDS.
I SAID WE SHOULD TAKE THEM AND HIDE SOMEWHERE UNTIL THE WHOLE THING BLEW OVER.

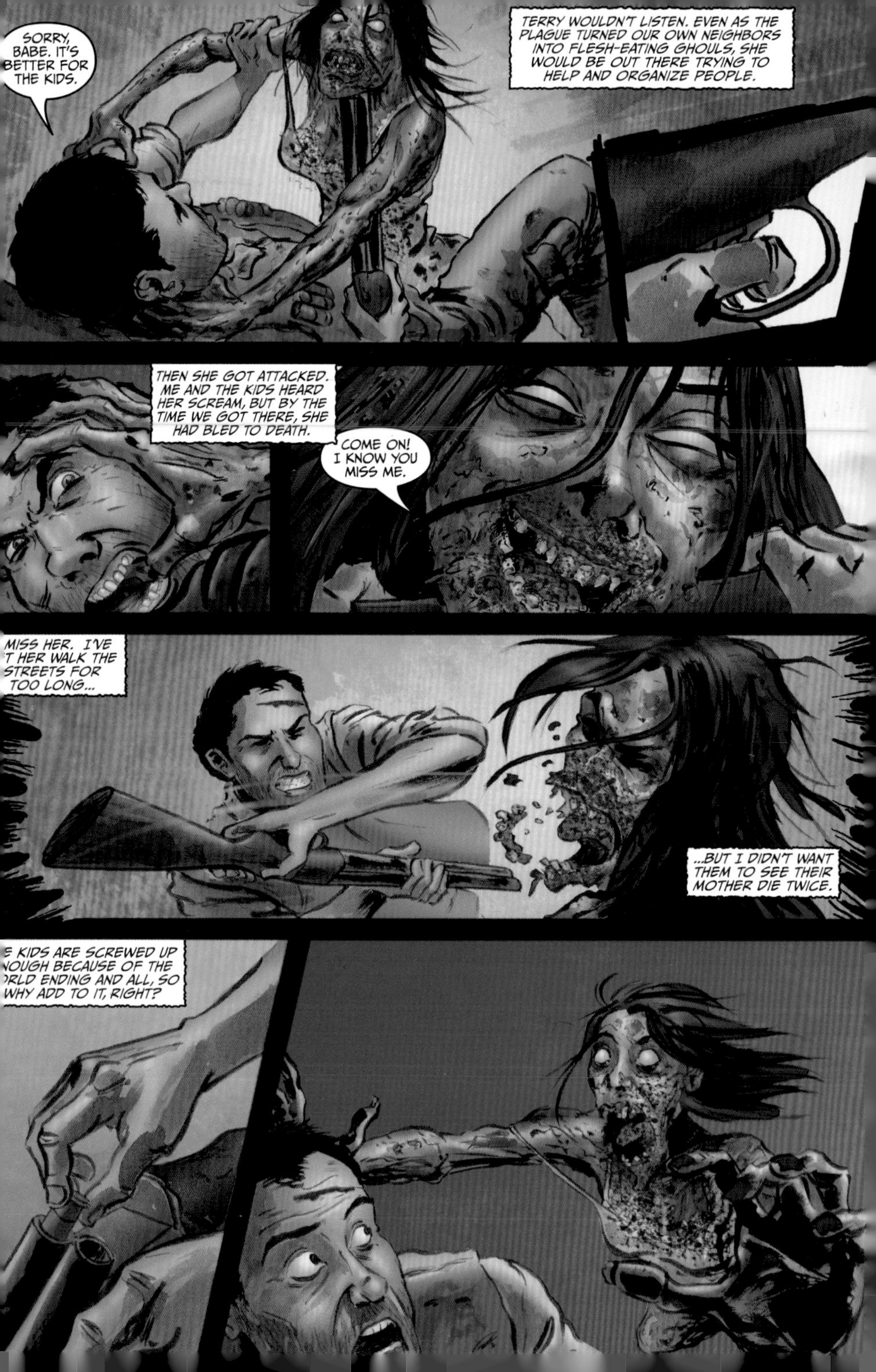

SORRY, BABE. IT'S BETTER FOR THE KIDS.
TERRY WOULDN'T LISTEN. EVEN AS THE PLAGUE TURNED OUR OWN NEIGHBORS INTO FLESH-EATING GHOULS, SHE WOULD BE OUT THERE TRYING TO HELP AND ORGANIZE PEOPLE.
THEN SHE GOT ATTACKED. ME AND THE KIDS HEARD HER SCREAM, BUT BY THE TIME WE GOT THERE, SHE HAD BLED TO DEATH.
COME ON! I KNOW YOU MISS ME.
MISS HER. I'VE T HER WALK THE STREETS FOR TOO LONG...
...BUT I DIDN'T WANT THEM TO SEE THEIR MOTHER DIE TWICE.
E KIDS ARE SCREWED UP NOUGH BECAUSE OF THE ORLD ENDING AND ALL, SO WHY ADD TO IT, RIGHT?

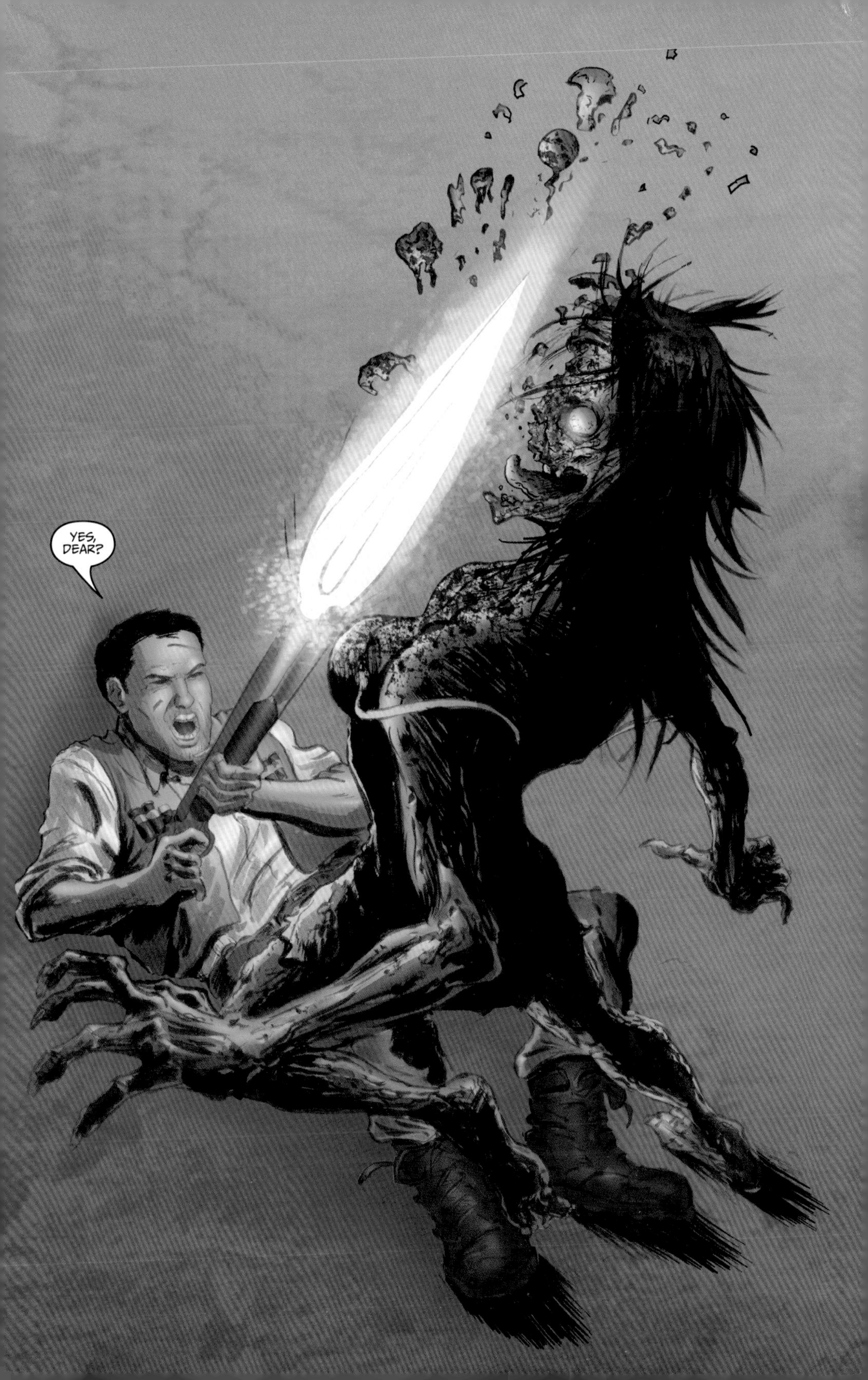
YES, DEAR?

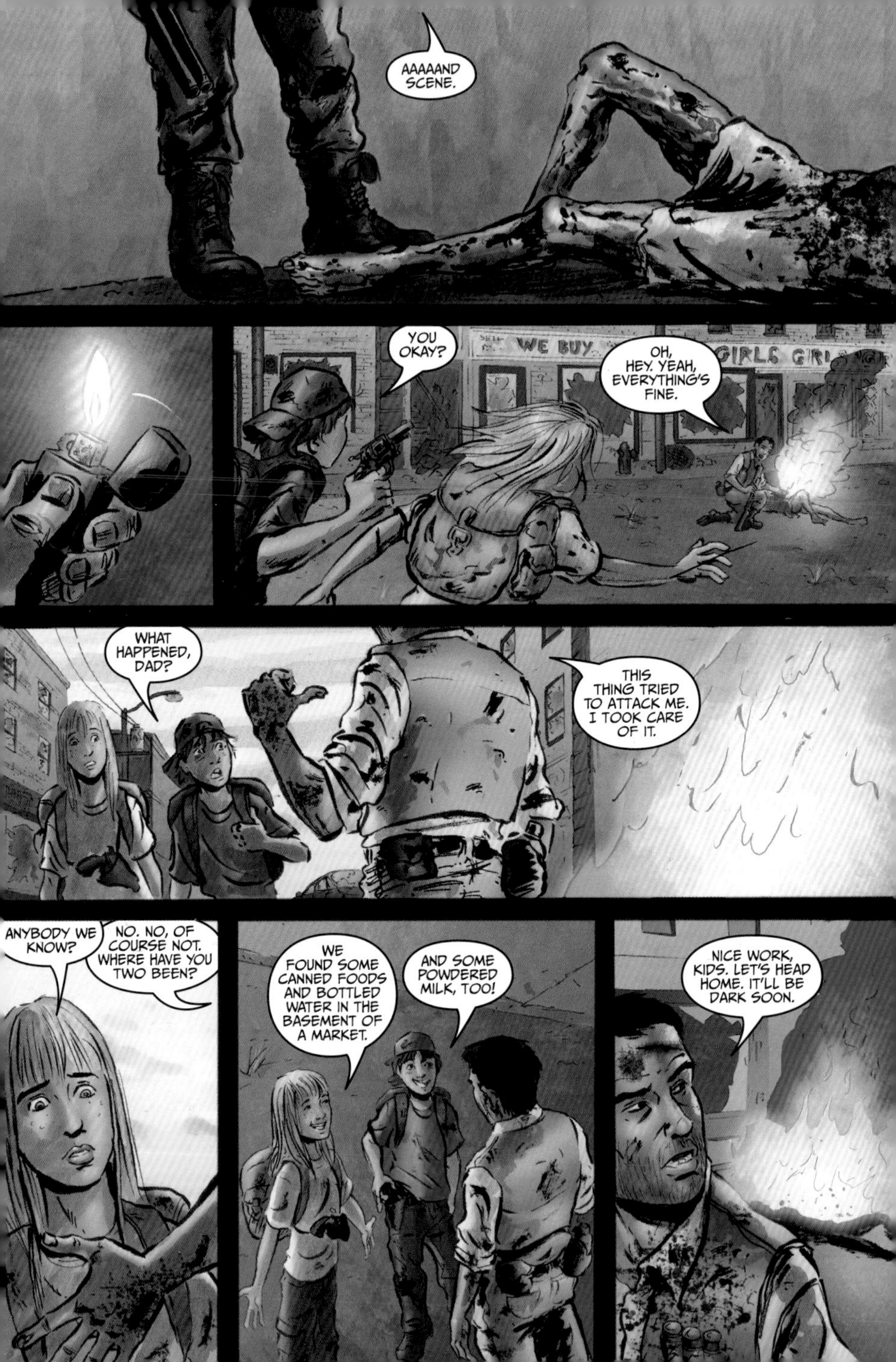
AAAAAND SCENE.
YOU OKAY?
OH, HEY. YEAH, EVERYTHING'S FINE.
WE BUY
GIRLS
WHAT HAPPENED, DAD?
THIS THING TRIED TO ATTACK ME. I TOOK CARE OF IT.
ANYBODY WE KNOW?
NO. NO, OF COURSE NOT. WHERE HAVE YOU TWO BEEN?
WE FOUND SOME CANNED FOODS AND BOTTLED WATER IN THE BASEMENT OF A MARKET.
AND SOME POWDERED MILK, TOO!
NICE WORK, KIDS. LET'S HEAD HOME. IT'LL BE DARK SOON.

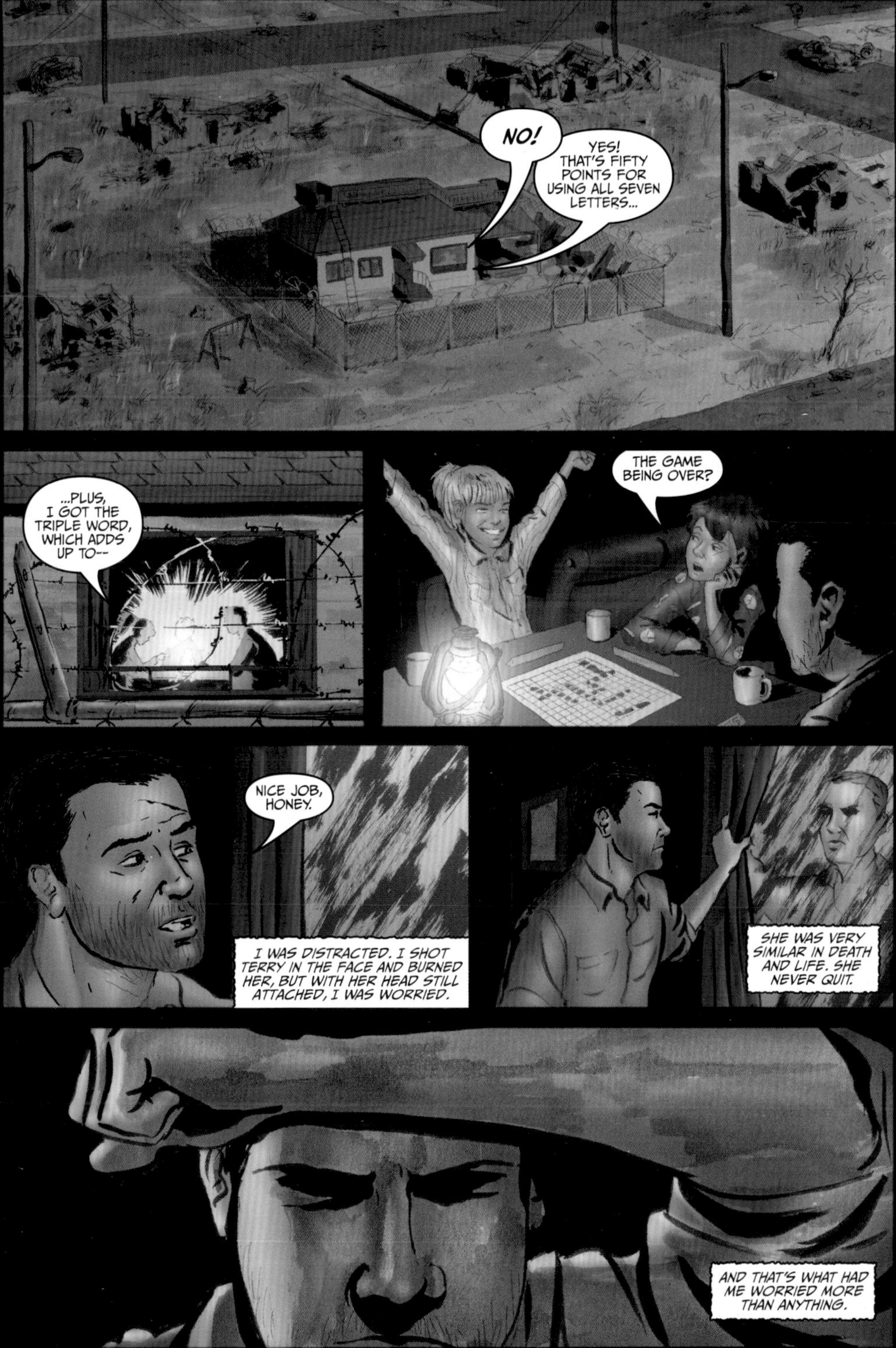
NO!
YES! THAT'S FIFTY POINTS FOR USING ALL SEVEN LETTERS...
...PLUS, I GOT THE TRIPLE WORD, WHICH ADDS UP TO--
THE GAME BEING OVER?
NICE JOB, HONEY.
I WAS DISTRACTED. I SHOT TERRY IN THE FACE AND BURNED HER, BUT WITH HER HEAD STILL ATTACHED, I WAS WORRIED.
SHE WAS VERY SIMILAR IN DEATH AND LIFE. SHE NEVER QUIT.
AND THAT'S WHAT HAD ME WORRIED MORE THAN ANYTHING.

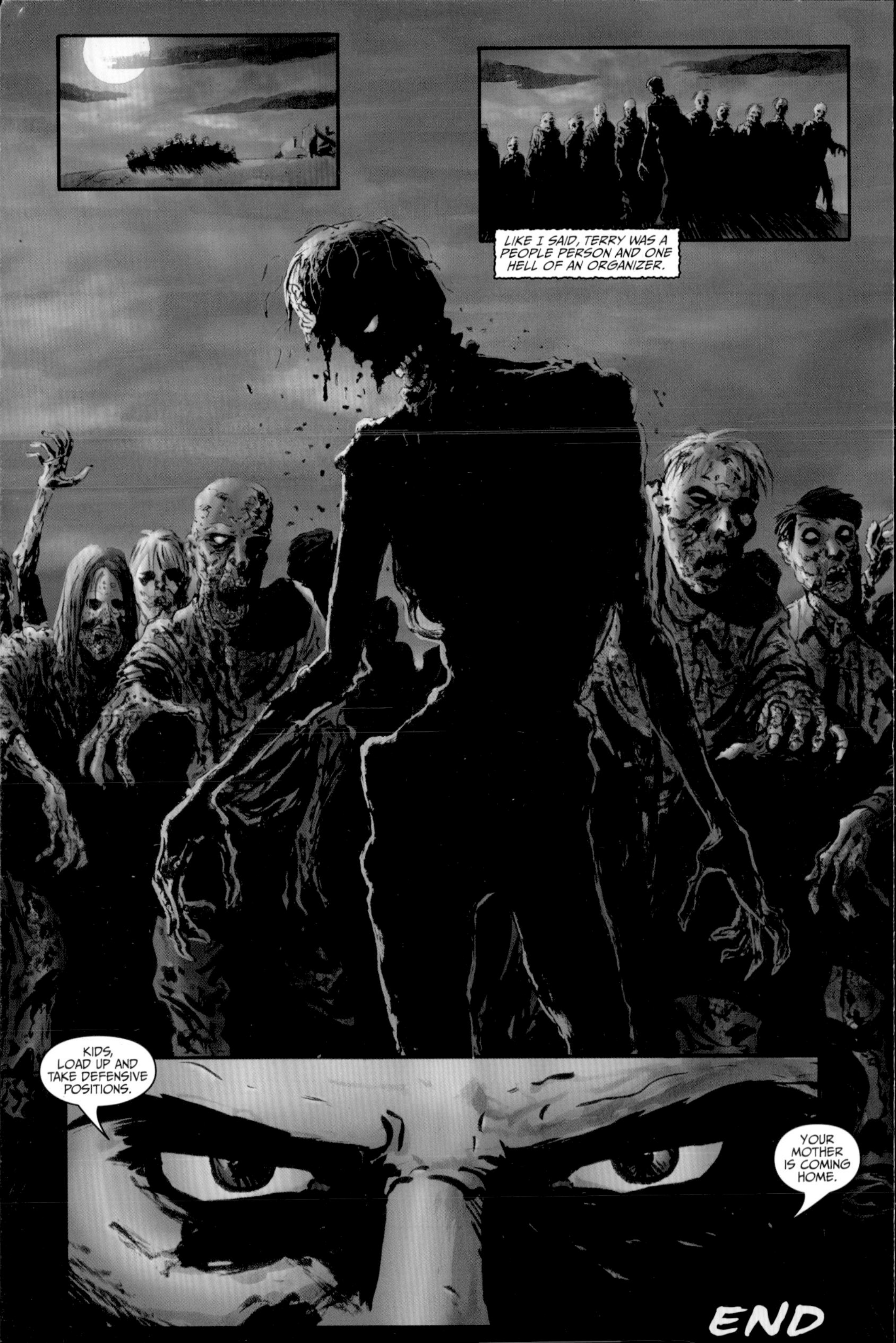
LIKE I SAID, TERRY WAS A PEOPLE PERSON AND ONE HELL OF AN ORGANIZER.
KIDS, LOAD UP AND TAKE DEFENSIVE POSITIONS.
YOUR MOTHER IS COMING HOME.
END

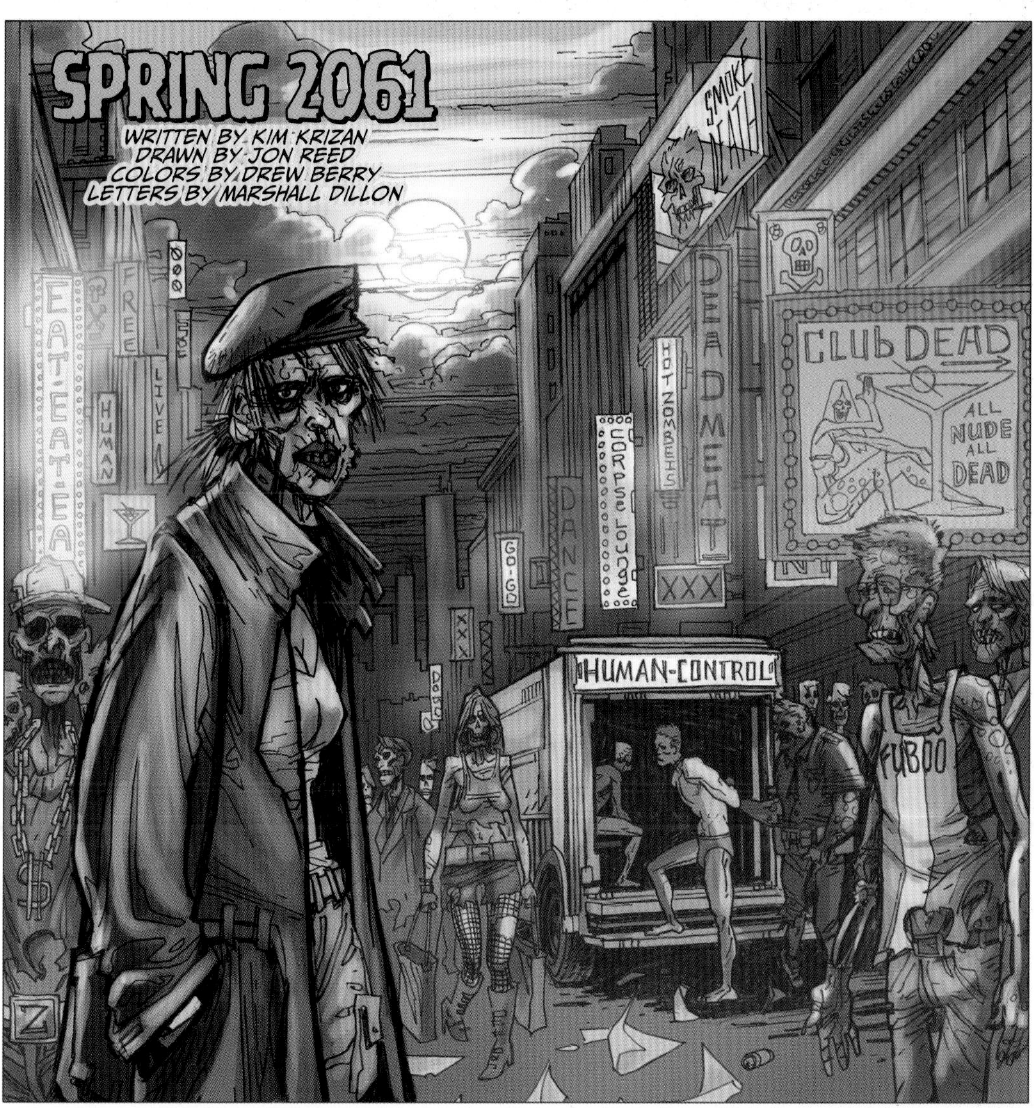
SPRING 2061
WRITTEN BY KIM KRIZAN
DRAWN BY JON REED
COLORS BY DREW BERRY
LETTERS BY MARSHALL DILLON
SMOKE DEATH
EAT-EAT-EAT-EA
FREE
HUMAN
LIVE
DEAD MEAT
HOT ZOMBIES
CORPSE LOUNGE
DANCE
GO-GO
XXX
CLUB DEAD
ALL NUDE ALL DEAD
HUMAN-CONTROL
FUBOO

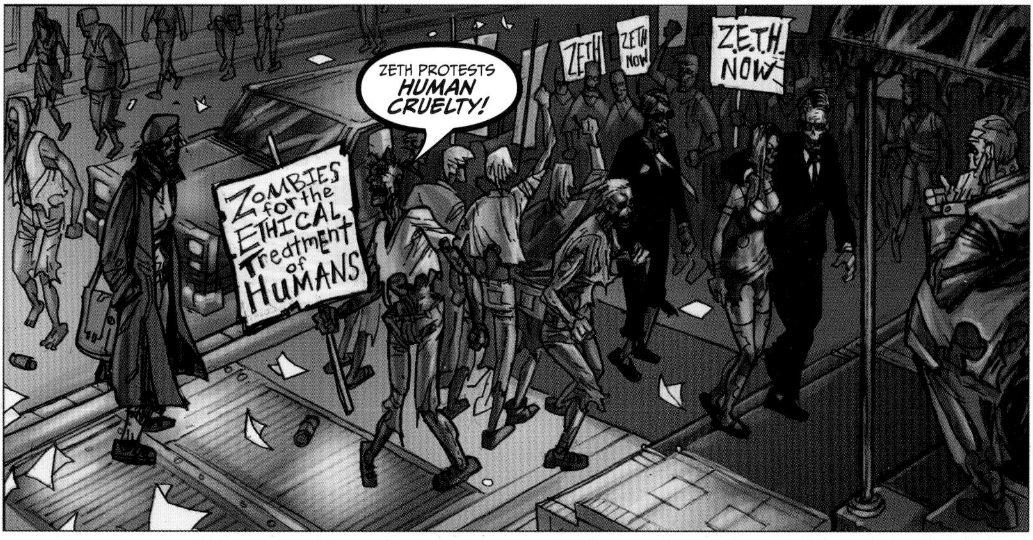
ZETH PROTESTS HUMAN CRUELTY!
ZETH
ZETH NOW
Z.E.T.H. NOW
ZOMBIES for the ETHICAL Treatment of HUMANS

THE *SHOW* IS READY TO BEGIN! PLEASE TAKE YOUR SEATS!

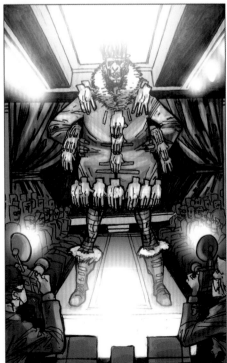

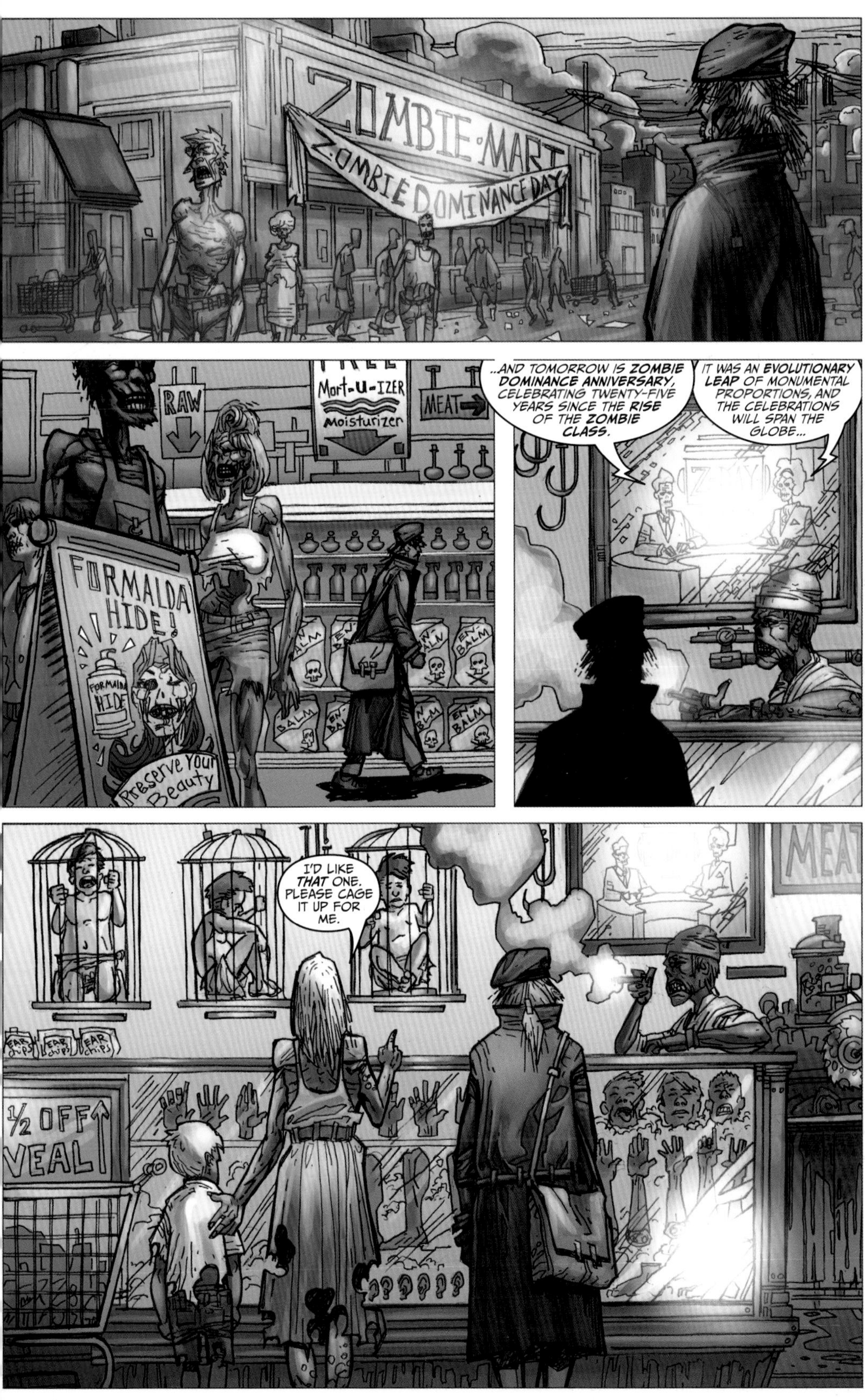
ZOMBIE-MART
ZOMBIE DOMINANCE DAY
RAW
FREE
Mort-U-IZER
Moisturizer
MEAT
FORMALDAHIDE!
FORMALDAHIDE
Preserve Your Beauty
EN-BALM
...AND TOMORROW IS ZOMBIE DOMINANCE ANNIVERSARY, CELEBRATING TWENTY-FIVE YEARS SINCE THE RISE OF THE ZOMBIE CLASS.
IT WAS AN EVOLUTIONARY LEAP OF MONUMENTAL PROPORTIONS, AND THE CELEBRATIONS WILL SPAN THE GLOBE...
I'D LIKE THAT ONE. PLEASE CAGE IT UP FOR ME.
MEAT
EAR chips
1/2 OFF VEAL

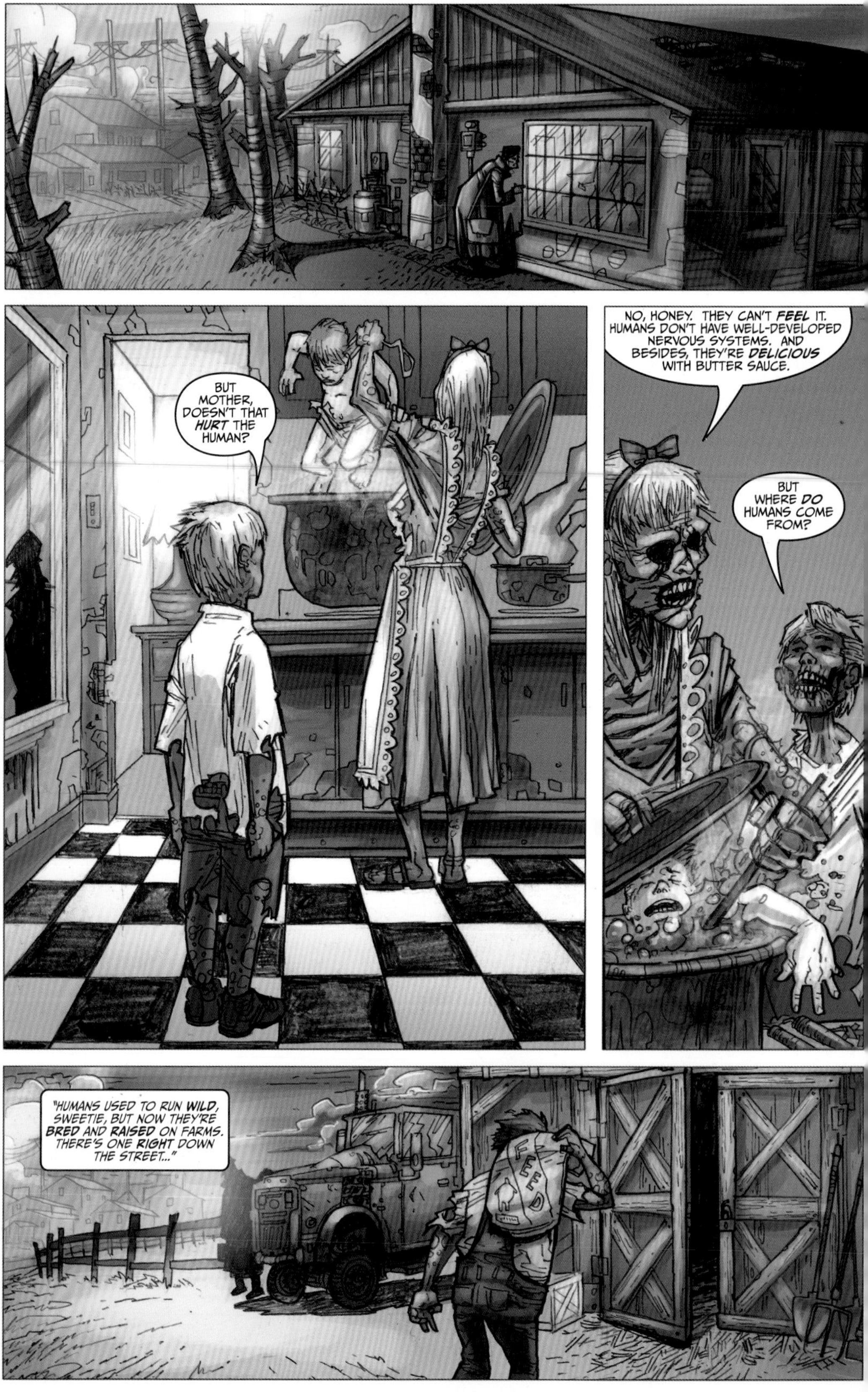
BUT MOTHER, DOESN'T THAT HURT THE HUMAN?
NO, HONEY. THEY CAN'T FEEL IT. HUMANS DON'T HAVE WELL-DEVELOPED NERVOUS SYSTEMS. AND BESIDES, THEY'RE DELICIOUS WITH BUTTER SAUCE.
BUT WHERE DO HUMANS COME FROM?
"HUMANS USED TO RUN WILD, SWEETIE, BUT NOW THEY'RE BRED AND RAISED ON FARMS. THERE'S ONE RIGHT DOWN THE STREET..."
FEED

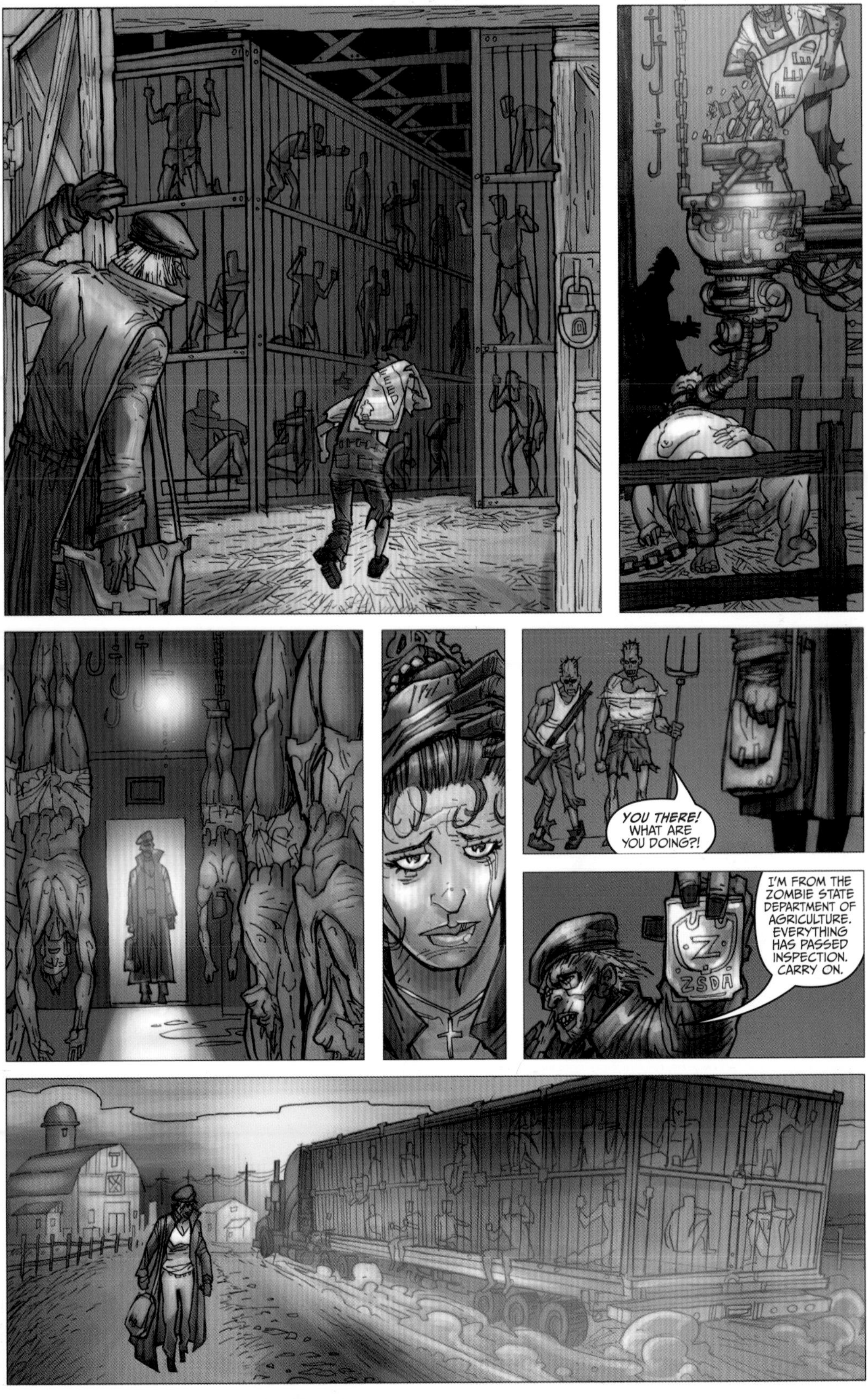
YOU THERE! WHAT ARE YOU DOING?!
I'M FROM THE ZOMBIE STATE DEPARTMENT OF AGRICULTURE. EVERYTHING HAS PASSED INSPECTION. CARRY ON.
ZSDA

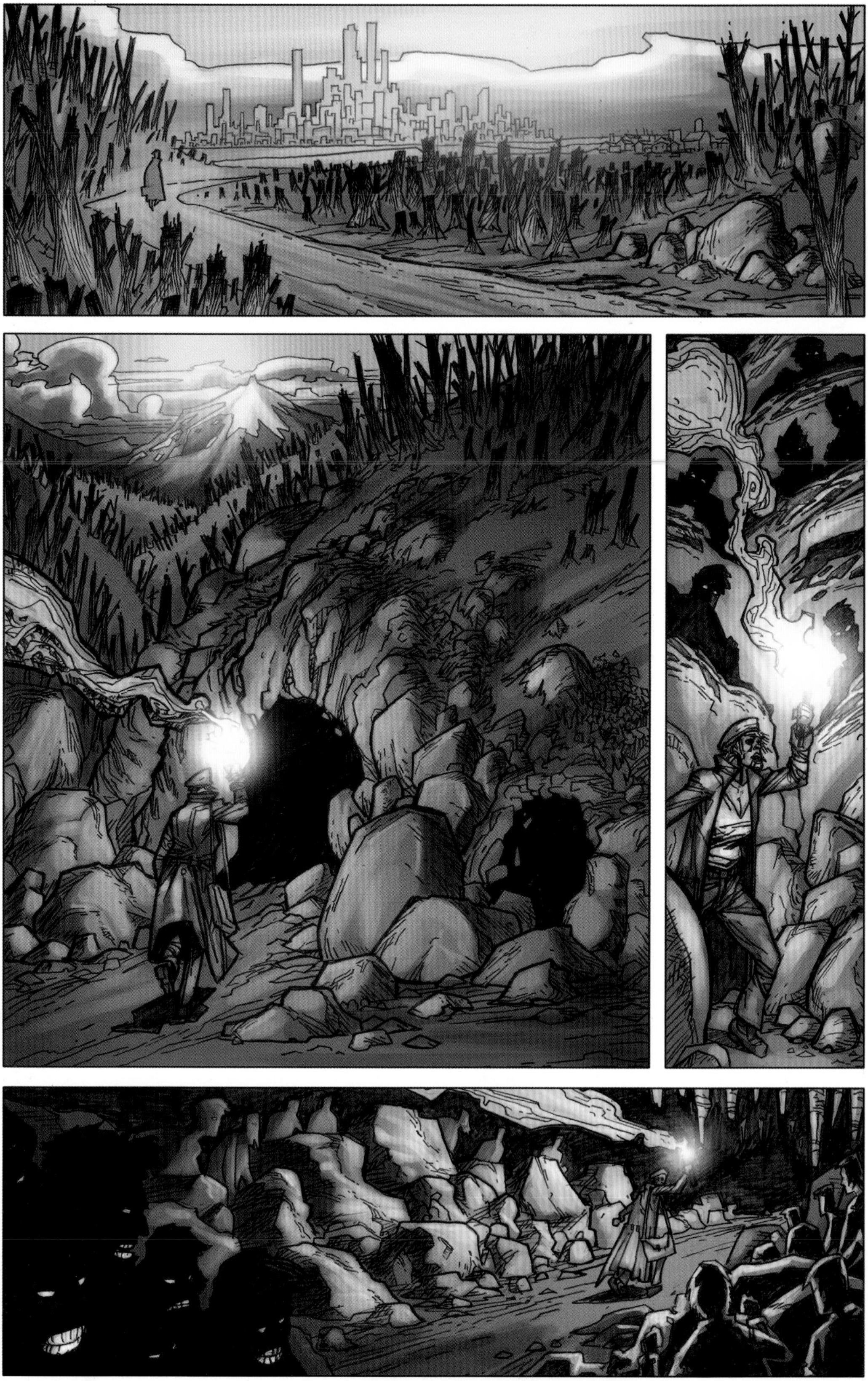

SISTERS. BROTHERS. IT IS ME.

IT IS OUR EMISSARY!

WHAT IS IT LIKE ON THE OUTSIDE?

THE WORLD OUR PARENTS SPEAK OF NO LONGER EXISTS. THERE ARE NO TREES. THERE IS NO BLUE SKY. OUR KIND HAS BEEN MADE SLAVES.

THE WORLD OF OUR PARENTS WAS A FAIRY TALE! WE HAVE ALWAYS BEEN OPPRESSED AND ALWAYS WILL BE!

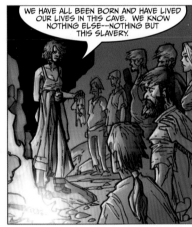

WE HAVE ALL BEEN BORN AND HAVE LIVED OUR LIVES IN THIS CAVE. WE KNOW NOTHING ELSE--NOTHING BUT THIS SLAVERY.

BUT IF WE HAVE THE COURAGE TO BELIEVE SOMETHING BETTER IS POSSIBLE FOR OUR KIND AND FOR THE WORLD...AND IF WE HAVE THE COURAGE TO FIGHT FOR IT, WE MAY BE ABLE TO CREATE IT. WE MUST ACT NOW.

BUT IF WE FIGHT, WE RISK OUR LIVES!

WE MAY FAIL!

THE ENEMY IS STRONG!

YES, IT IS TRUE. WE DO NOT KNOW THE OUTCOME. BUT I HAVE MADE MY DECISION. I WILL FIGHT.

I WILL NEVER STOP FIGHTING THOSE WHO WOULD RUIN THIS WORLD AND ENSLAVE MY PEOPLE.

WHO WILL TAKE UP ARMS AND JOIN ME?

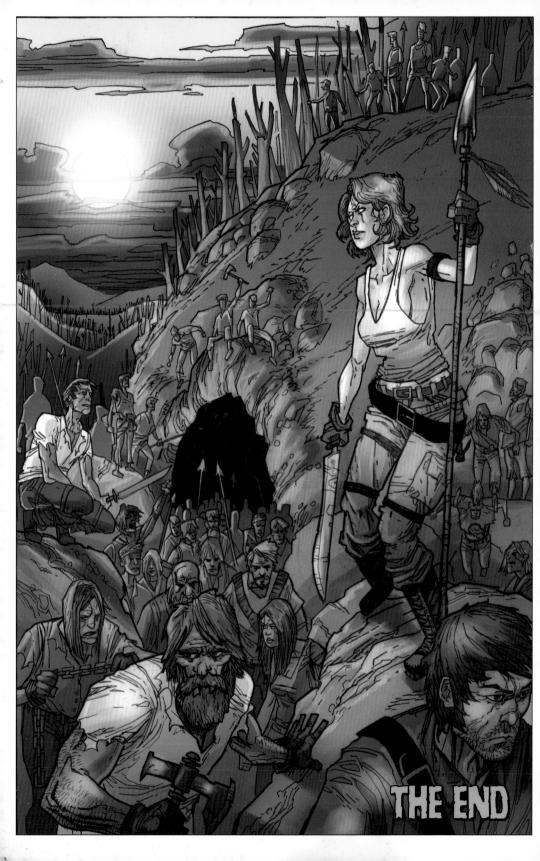

THE END

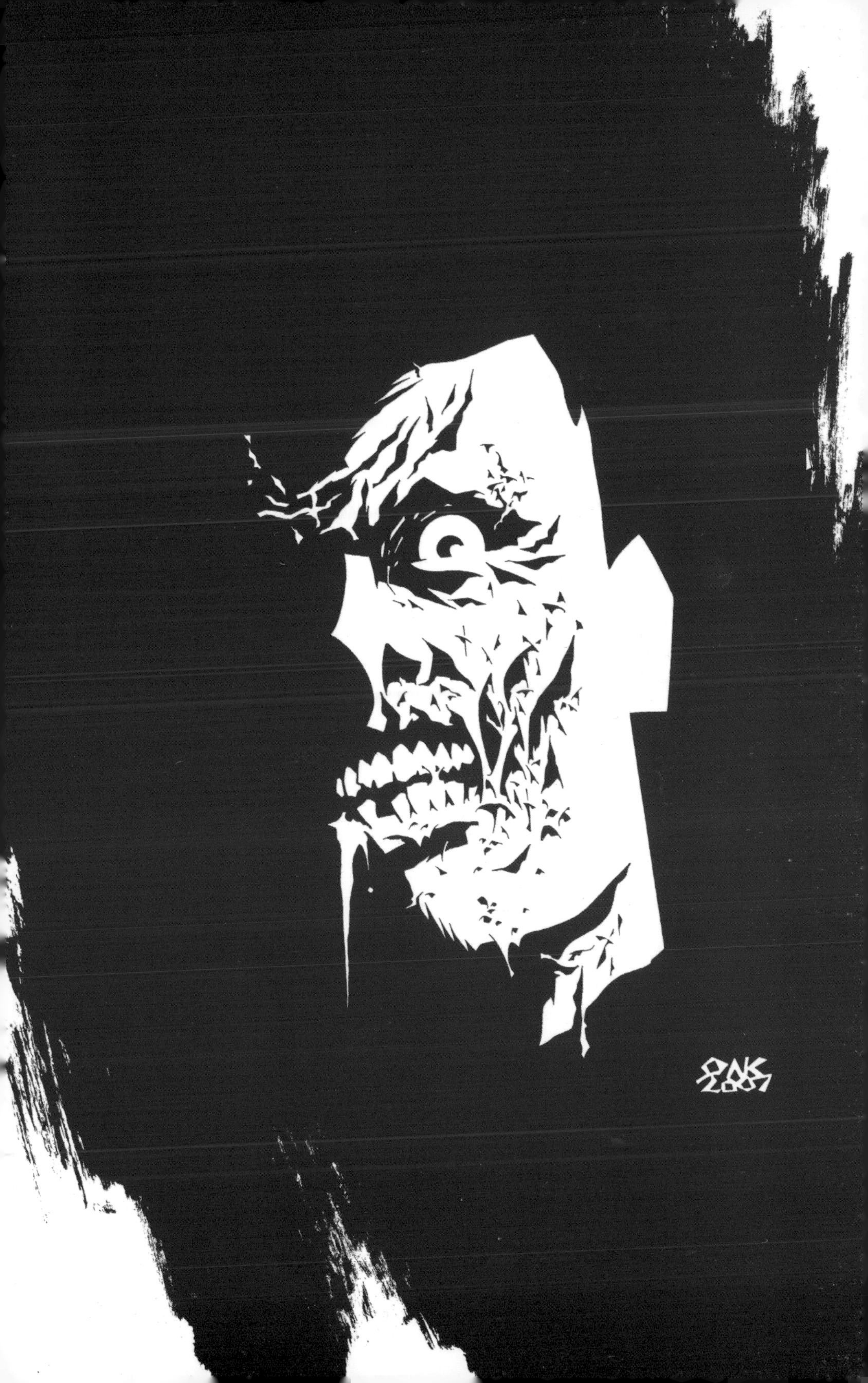

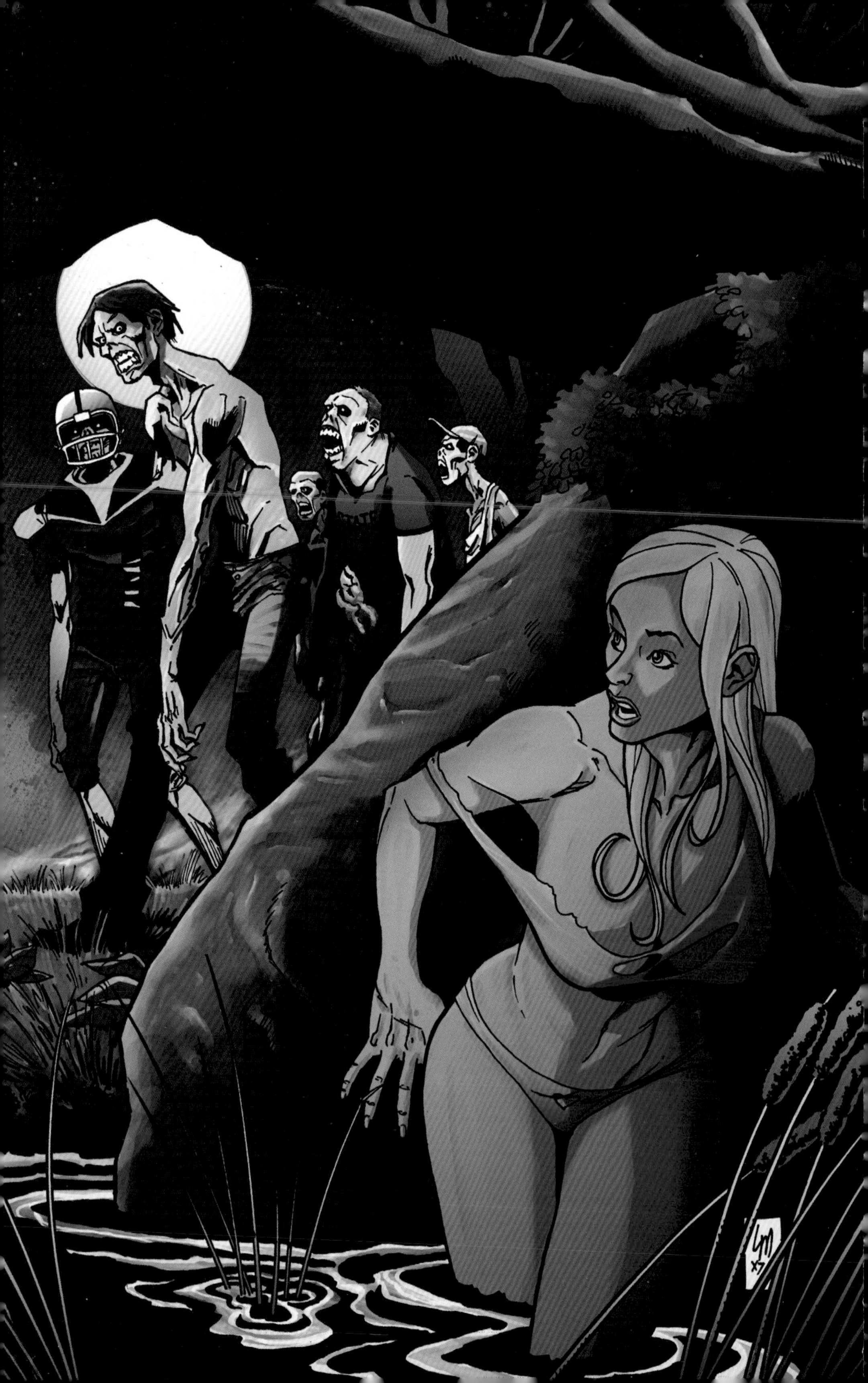

THE WAR AT HOME
Part Two:
BLOOD AND ICE CREAM, A VIEW OF THE ZOO

Story: JOE R. LANSDALE

Art: EDUARDO BARRETO

DOUBLE PORTRAIT

Story: CHRISTINE BOYLAN

Art: HANZO STEINBACH

ZOUNDS!

Story: TODD LEPRE

Art: CHEE

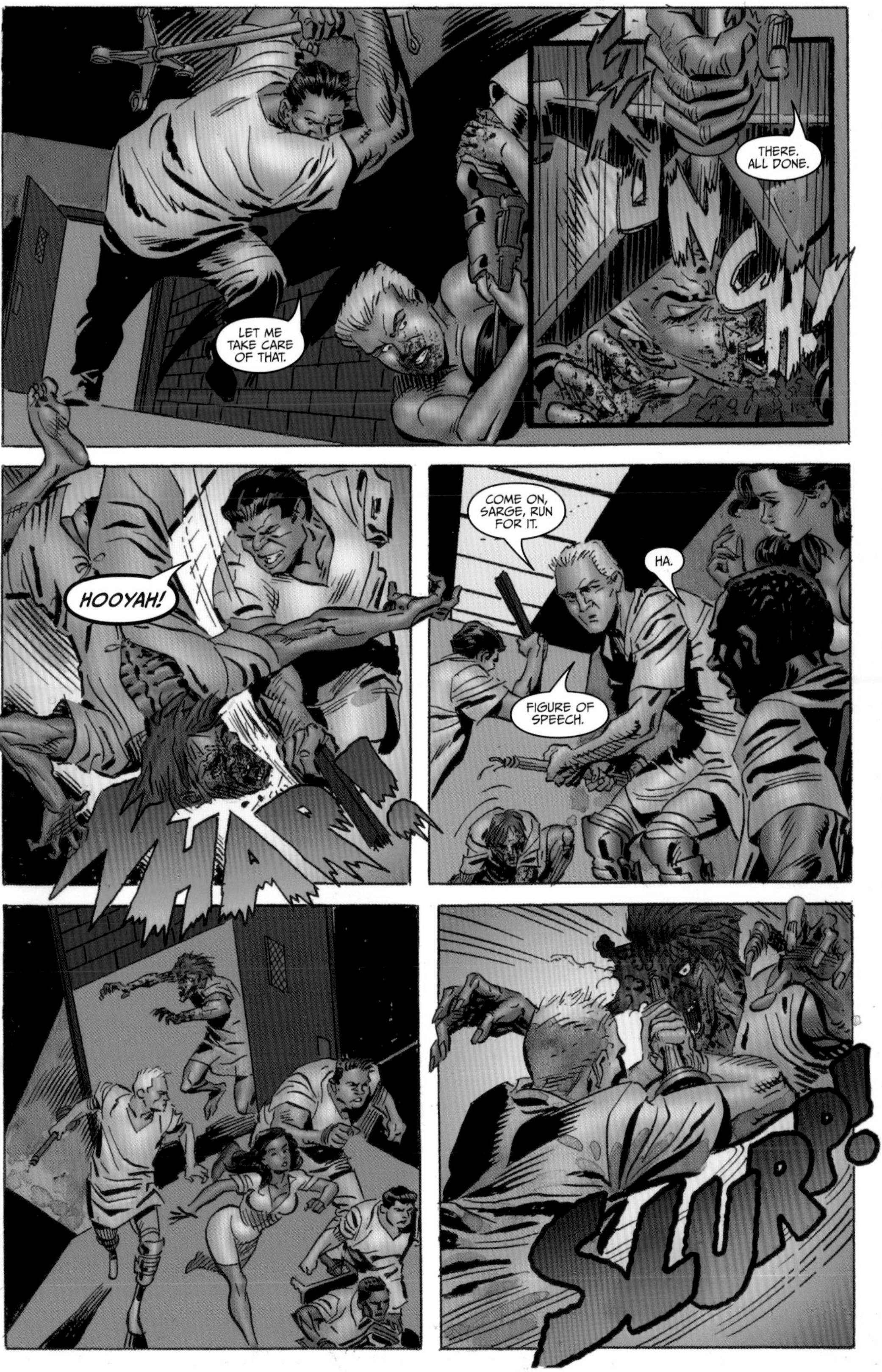
LET ME TAKE CARE OF THAT.
THERE. ALL DONE.
HOOYAH!
COME ON, SARGE, RUN FOR IT.
HA.
FIGURE OF SPEECH.
SLURP!

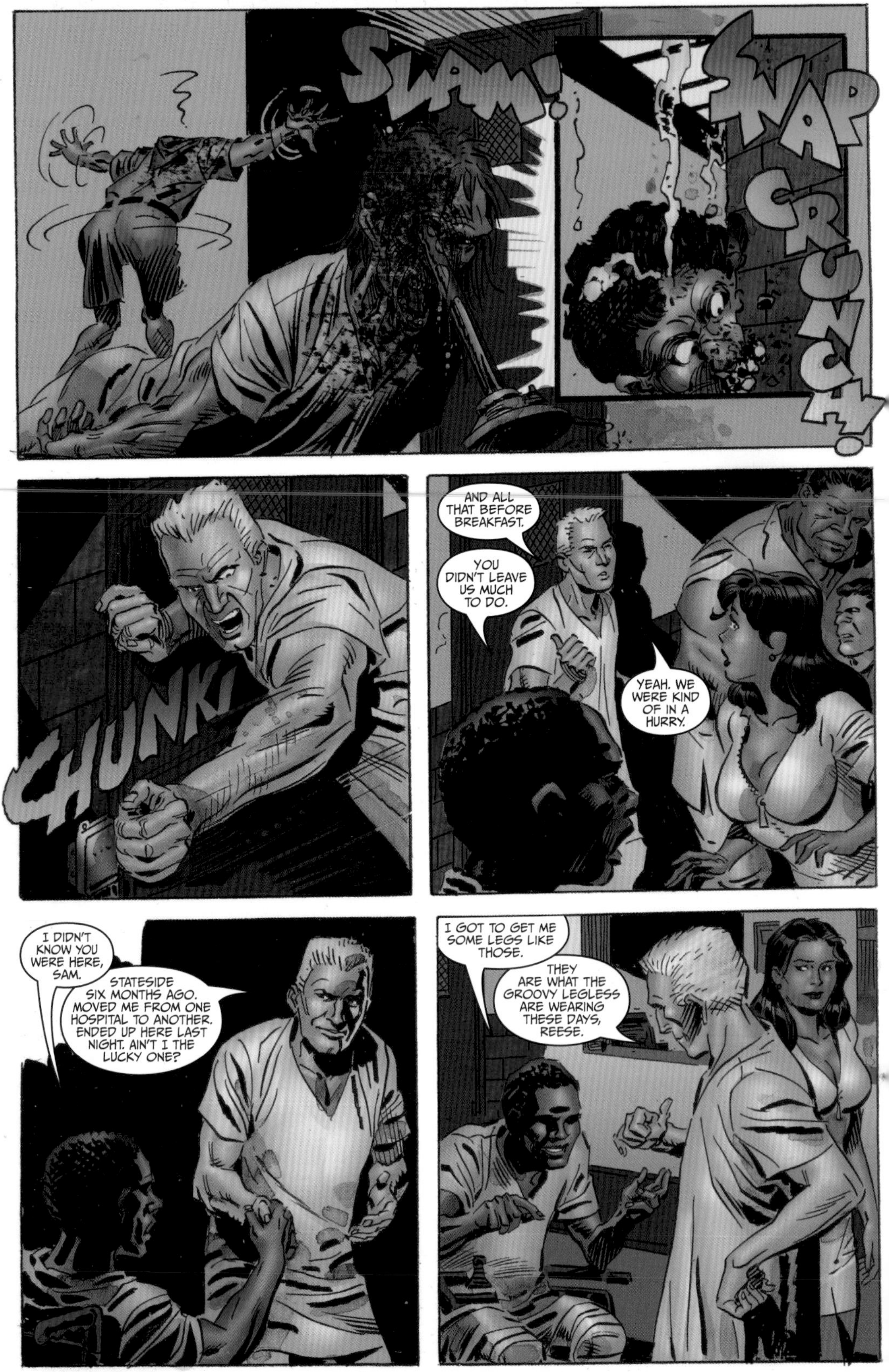
SLAM!
SNAP
CRUNCH!
CHUNK!
AND ALL THAT BEFORE BREAKFAST.
YOU DIDN'T LEAVE US MUCH TO DO.
YEAH. WE WERE KIND OF IN A HURRY.
I DIDN'T KNOW YOU WERE HERE, SAM.
STATESIDE SIX MONTHS AGO. MOVED ME FROM ONE HOSPITAL TO ANOTHER. ENDED UP HERE LAST NIGHT. AIN'T I THE LUCKY ONE?
I GOT TO GET ME SOME LEGS LIKE THOSE.
THEY ARE WHAT THE GROOVY LEGLESS ARE WEARING THESE DAYS, REESE.

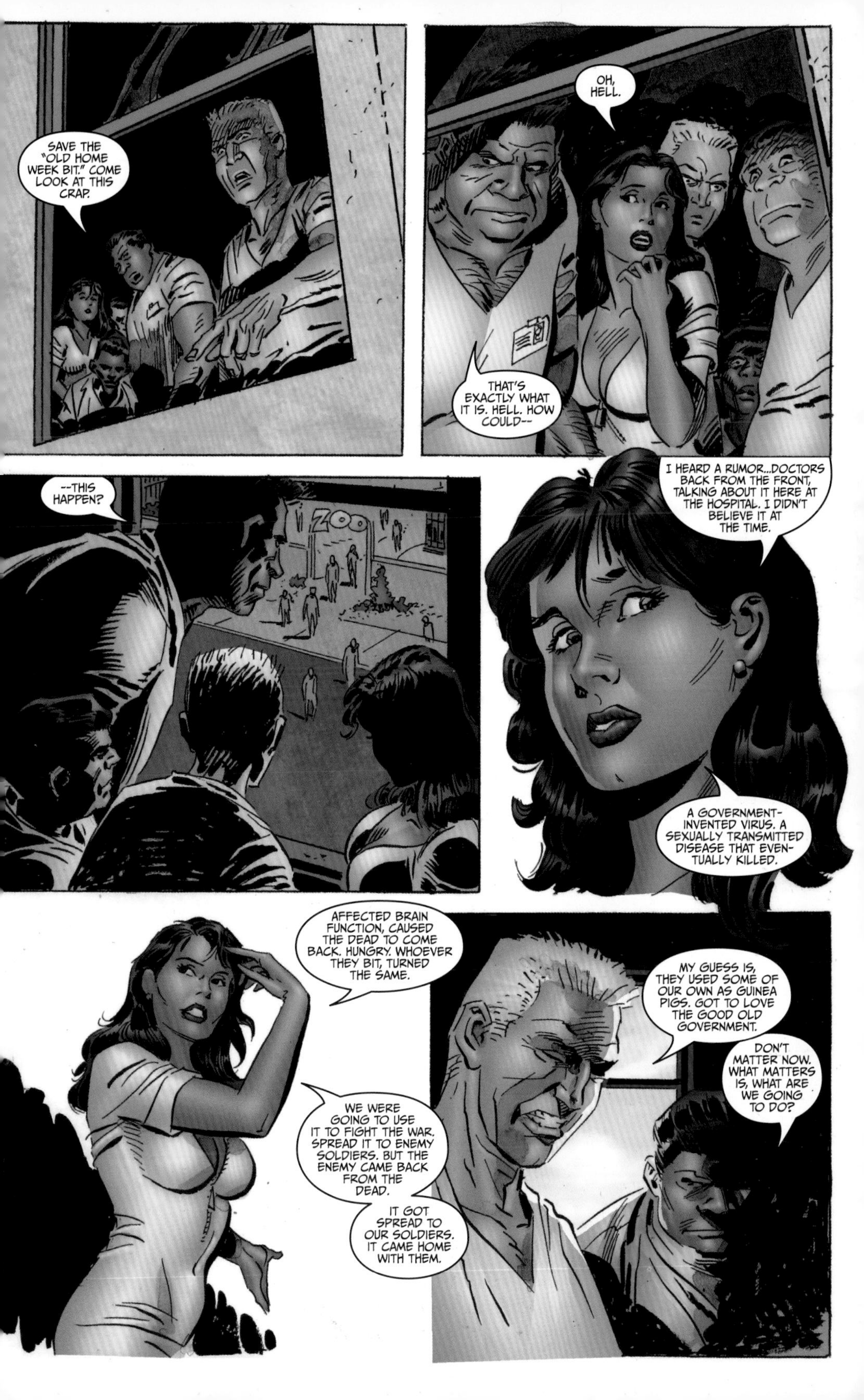
SAVE THE "OLD HOME WEEK BIT." COME LOOK AT THIS CRAP.
OH, HELL.
THAT'S EXACTLY WHAT IT IS. HELL. HOW COULD--
--THIS HAPPEN?
I HEARD A RUMOR...DOCTORS BACK FROM THE FRONT, TALKING ABOUT IT HERE AT THE HOSPITAL. I DIDN'T BELIEVE IT AT THE TIME.
A GOVERNMENT-INVENTED VIRUS. A SEXUALLY TRANSMITTED DISEASE THAT EVEN-TUALLY KILLED.
AFFECTED BRAIN FUNCTION, CAUSED THE DEAD TO COME BACK. HUNGRY. WHOEVER THEY BIT, TURNED THE SAME.
WE WERE GOING TO USE IT TO FIGHT THE WAR. SPREAD IT TO ENEMY SOLDIERS. BUT THE ENEMY CAME BACK FROM THE DEAD.
IT GOT SPREAD TO OUR SOLDIERS. IT CAME HOME WITH THEM.
MY GUESS IS, THEY USED SOME OF OUR OWN AS GUINEA PIGS. GOT TO LOVE THE GOOD OLD GOVERNMENT.
DON'T MATTER NOW. WHAT MATTERS IS, WHAT ARE WE GOING TO DO?

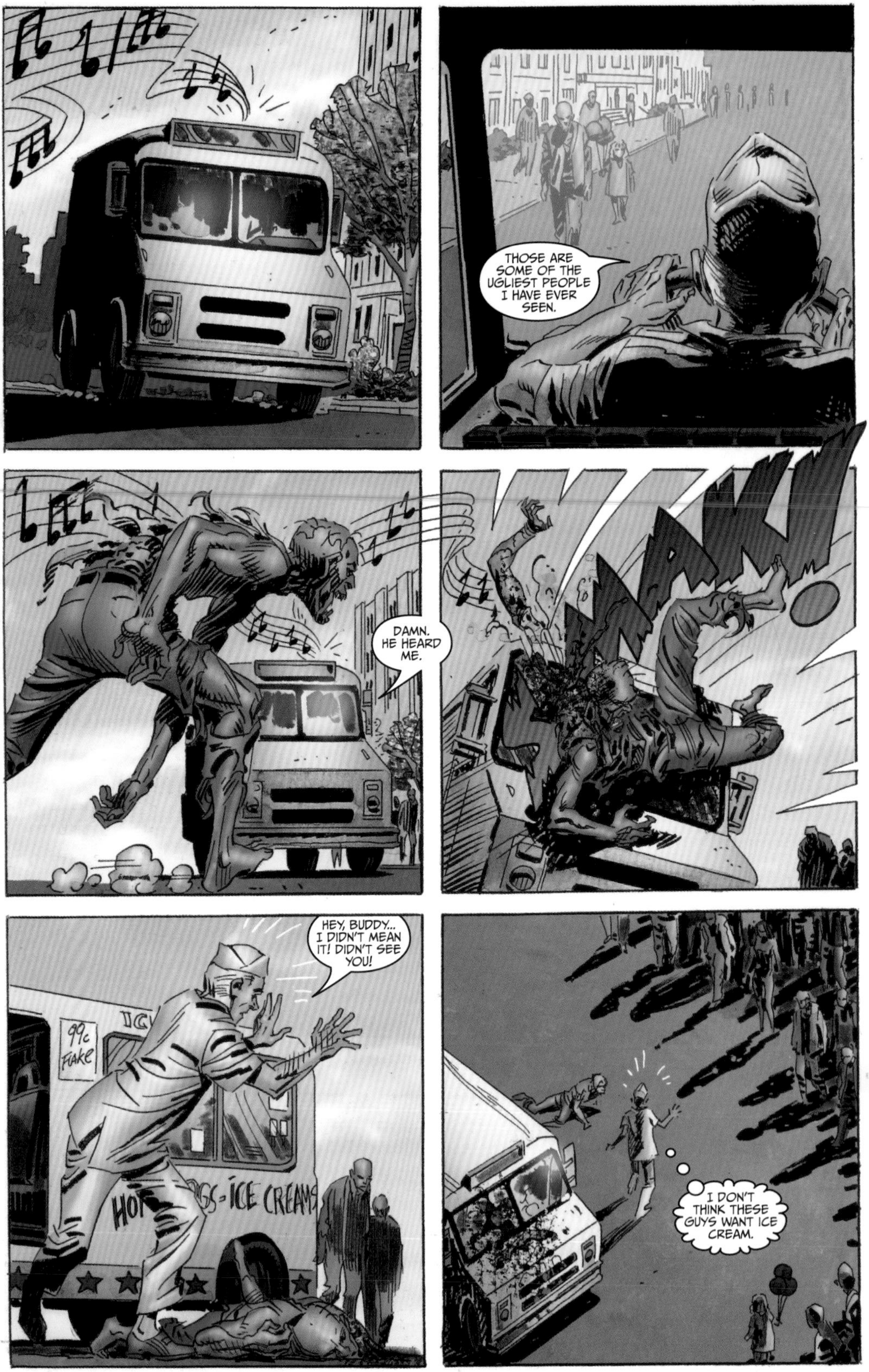
THOSE ARE SOME OF THE UGLIEST PEOPLE I HAVE EVER SEEN.
DAMN. HE HEARD ME.
HEY, BUDDY... I DIDN'T MEAN IT! DIDN'T SEE YOU!
99c Flake
I DON'T THINK THESE GUYS WANT ICE CREAM.

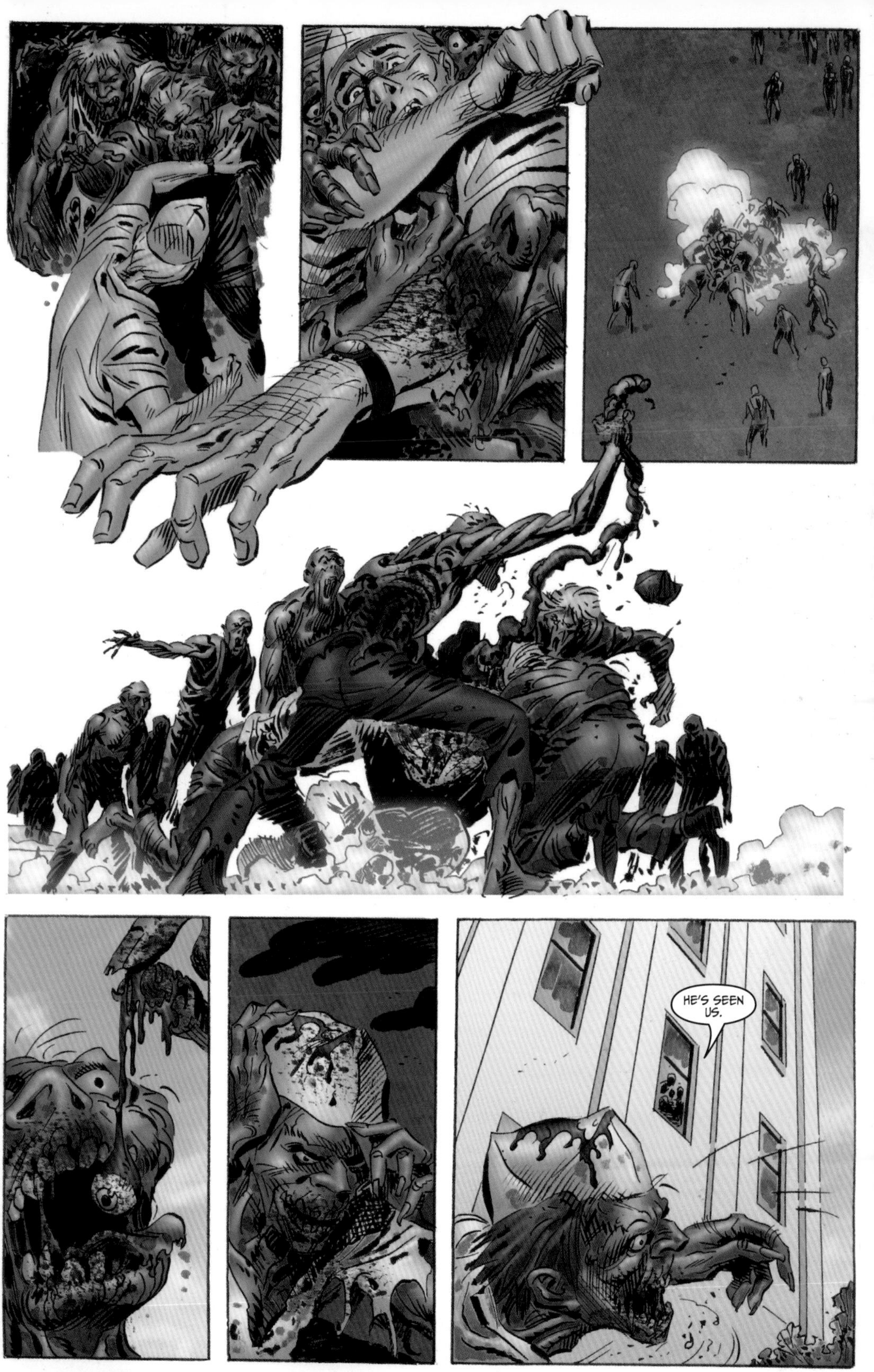
HE'S SEEN US.

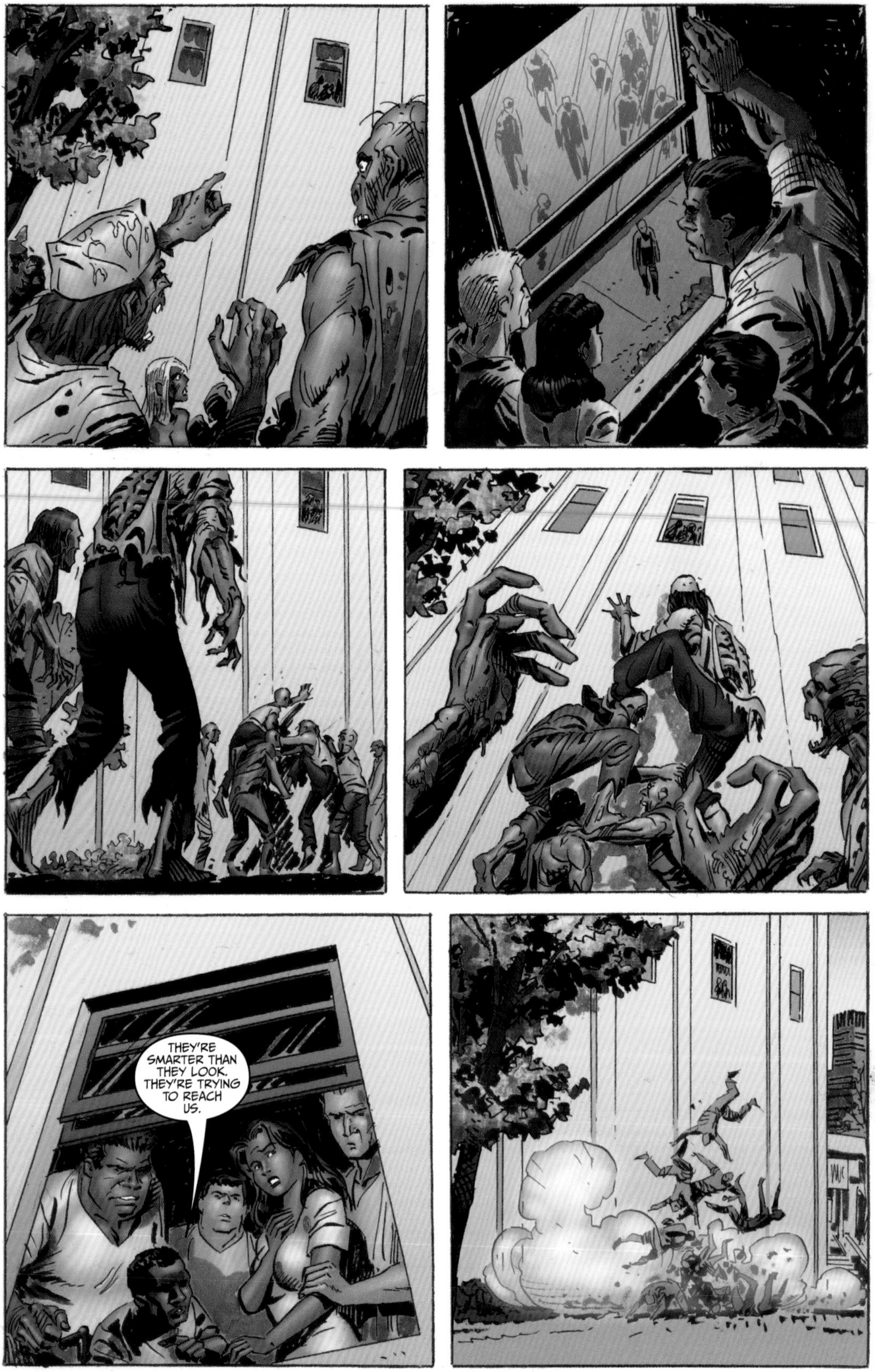
THEY'RE SMARTER THAN THEY LOOK. THEY'RE TRYING TO REACH US.

FORTUNATELY, THEY AREN'T ACROBATS. ARE ALL THE WAYS INTO THIS PART OF THE HOSPITAL LOCKED?

OH, YEAH. WE HEARD YOU TWO TALKING OUT IN THE HALL, OR WE'D NEVER HAVE OPENED THAT DOOR.

WE HAVE A LARGE SECTION BLOCKED OFF. THE KITCHEN. THE PHARMACY.

AT LEAST WE WON'T STARVE.

BUT I'VE BEEN NEEDING PAIN PILLS SINCE I WOKE UP.

I CAN FIX YOU UP HERE.

WHAT HAPPENS WHEN THE FOOD RUNS OUT?

YEAH. WE GOT TO FIND A WAY OUT OF HERE.

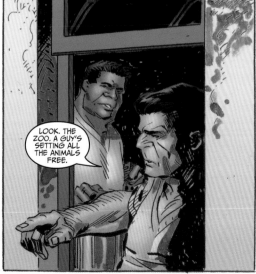

LOOK. THE ZOO. A GUY'S SETTING ALL THE ANIMALS FREE.

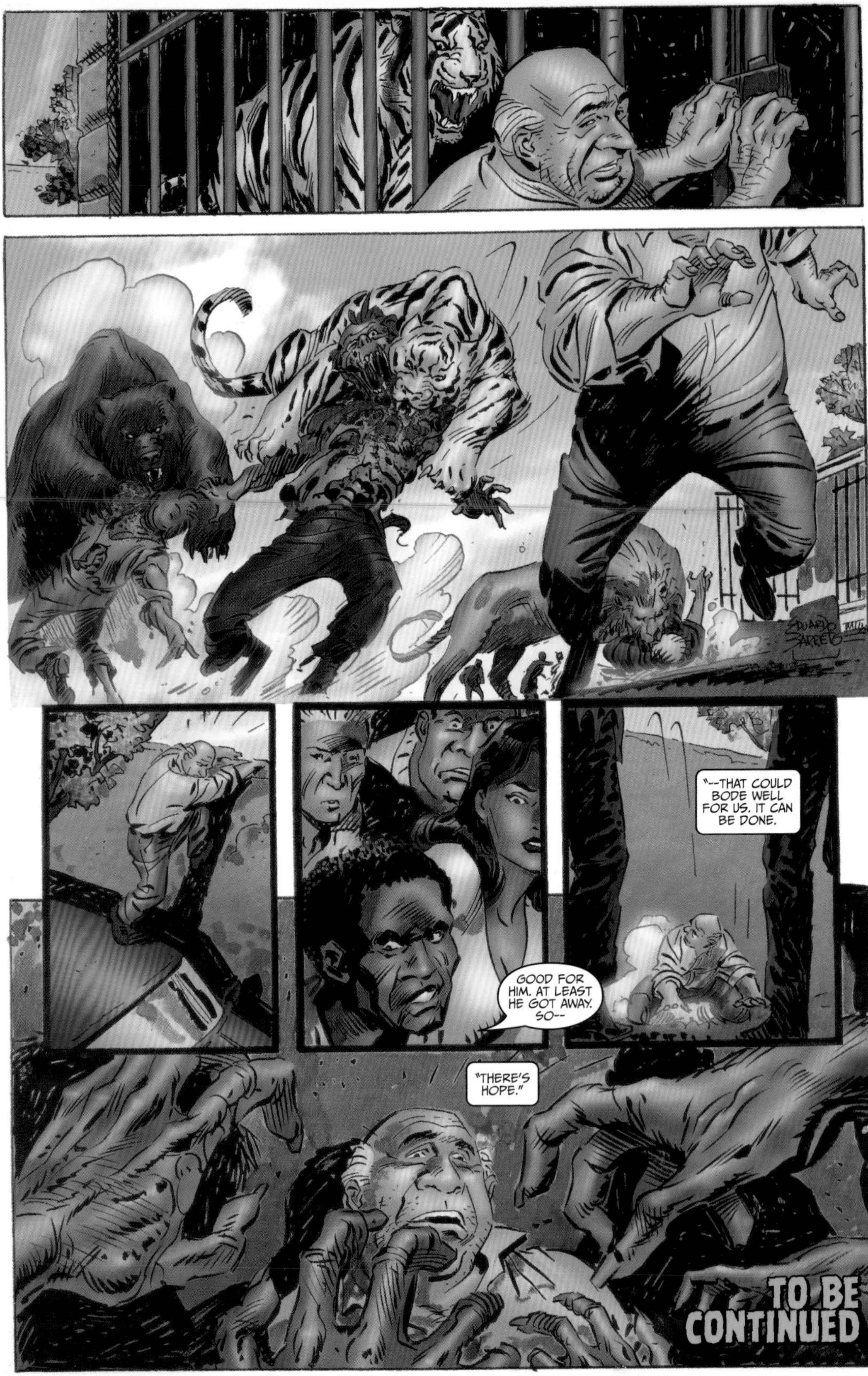

EDUARDO BARRETO
"--THAT COULD BODE WELL FOR US. IT CAN BE DONE.
GOOD FOR HIM. AT LEAST HE GOT AWAY. SO--
"THERE'S HOPE."
TO BE CONTINUED

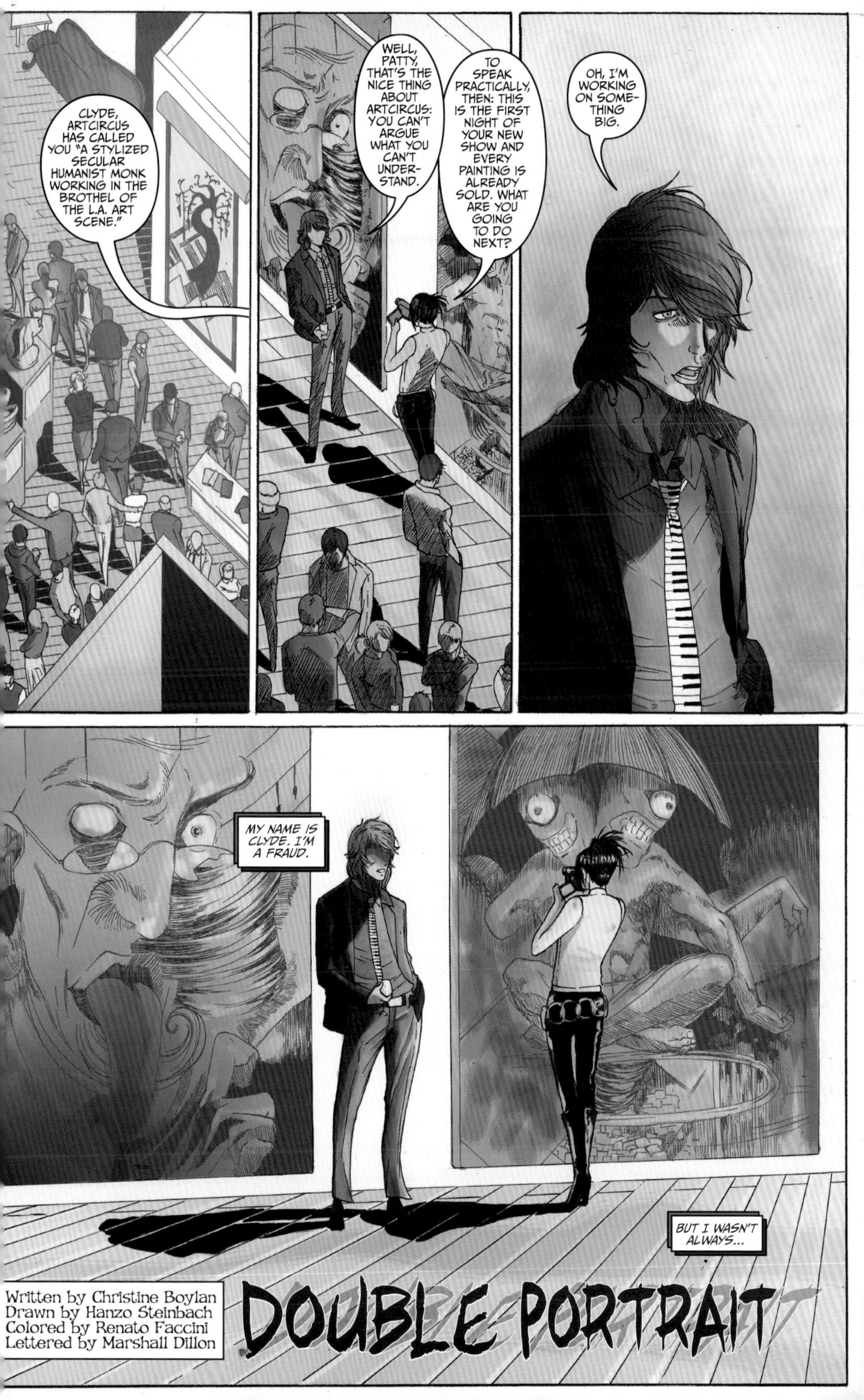
CLYDE, ARTCIRCUS HAS CALLED YOU "A STYLIZED SECULAR HUMANIST MONK WORKING IN THE BROTHEL OF THE L.A. ART SCENE."
WELL, PATTY, THAT'S THE NICE THING ABOUT ARTCIRCUS: YOU CAN'T ARGUE WHAT YOU CAN'T UNDER-STAND.
TO SPEAK PRACTICALLY, THEN: THIS IS THE FIRST NIGHT OF YOUR NEW SHOW AND EVERY PAINTING IS ALREADY SOLD. WHAT ARE YOU GOING TO DO NEXT?
OH, I'M WORKING ON SOME-THING BIG.
MY NAME IS CLYDE. I'M A FRAUD.
BUT I WASN'T ALWAYS...
Written by Christine Boylan
Drawn by Hanzo Steinbach
Colored by Renato Faccini
Lettered by Marshall Dillon
DOUBLE PORTRAIT

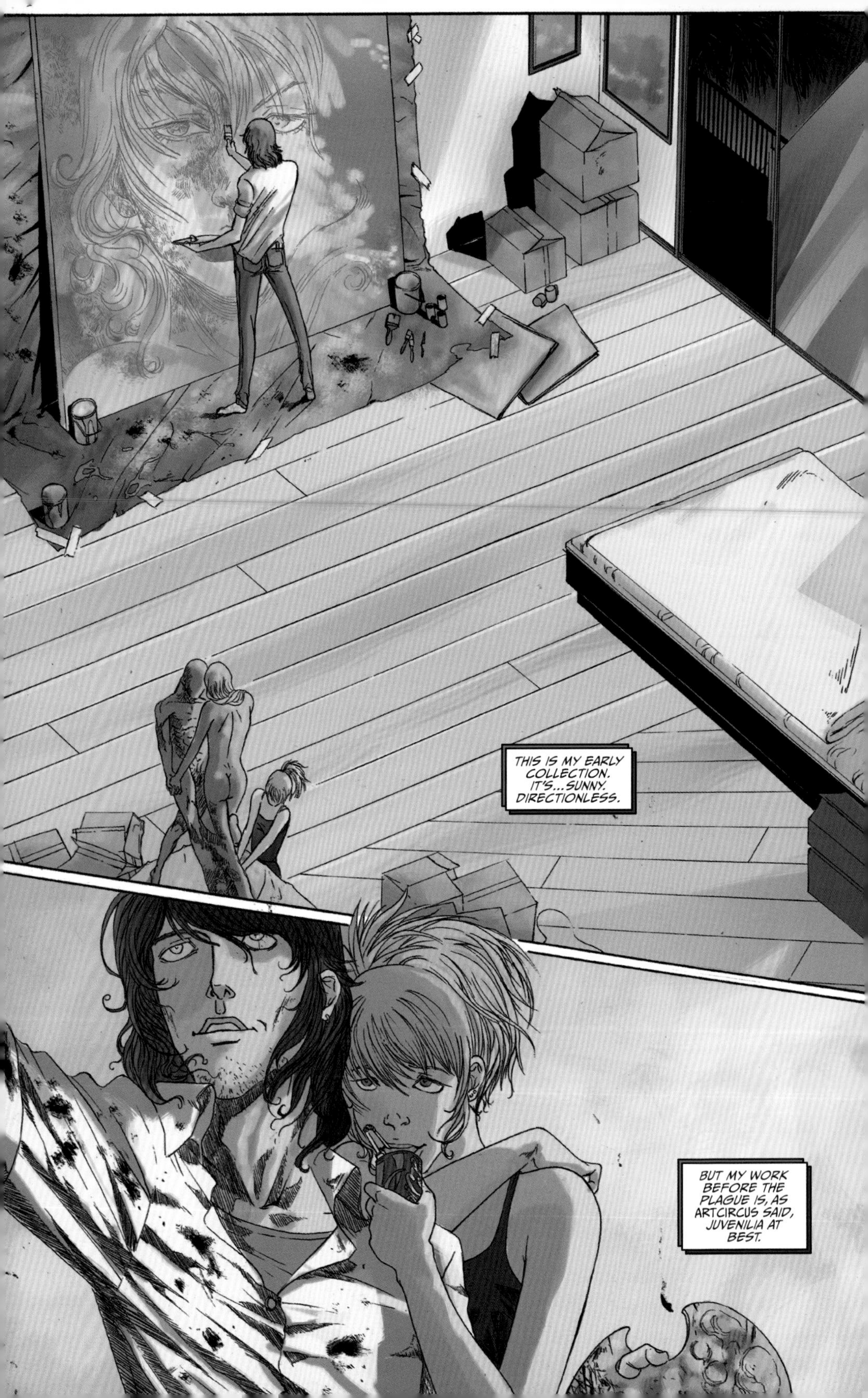
THIS IS MY EARLY COLLECTION. IT'S...SUNNY. DIRECTIONLESS.
BUT MY WORK BEFORE THE PLAGUE IS, AS ARTCIRCUS SAID, JUVENILIA AT BEST.

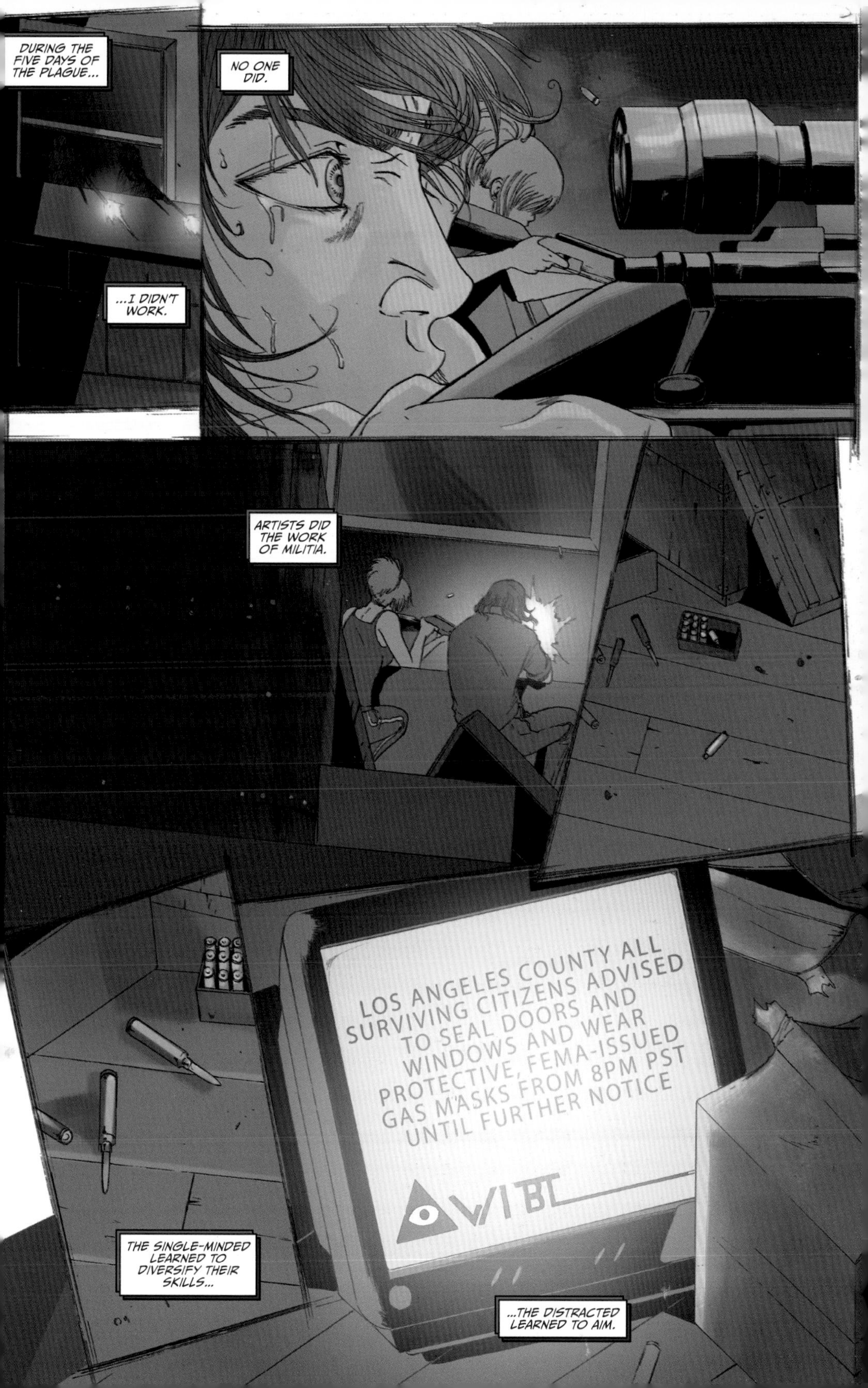
DURING THE FIVE DAYS OF THE PLAGUE...
NO ONE DID.
...I DIDN'T WORK.
ARTISTS DID THE WORK OF MILITIA.
LOS ANGELES COUNTY ALL SURVIVING CITIZENS ADVISED TO SEAL DOORS AND WINDOWS AND WEAR PROTECTIVE, FEMA-ISSUED GAS MASKS FROM 8PM PST UNTIL FURTHER NOTICE
THE SINGLE-MINDED LEARNED TO DIVERSIFY THEIR SKILLS...
...THE DISTRACTED LEARNED TO AIM.

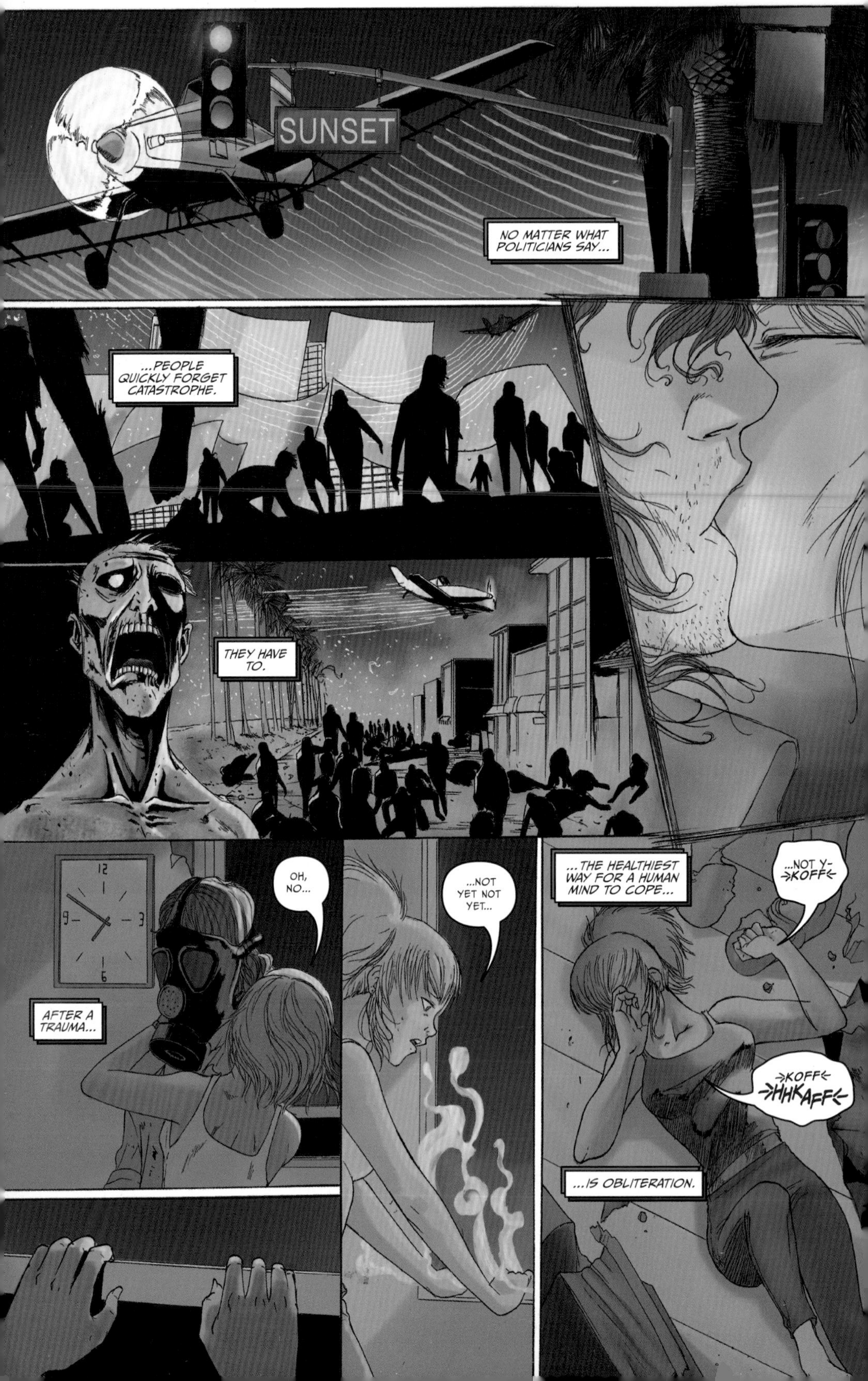
SUNSET
NO MATTER WHAT POLITICIANS SAY...
...PEOPLE QUICKLY FORGET CATASTROPHE.
THEY HAVE TO.
AFTER A TRAUMA...
OH, NO...
...NOT YET NOT YET...
...THE HEALTHIEST WAY FOR A HUMAN MIND TO COPE...
...NOT Y- KOFF
KOFF HHKAFF
...IS OBLITERATION.

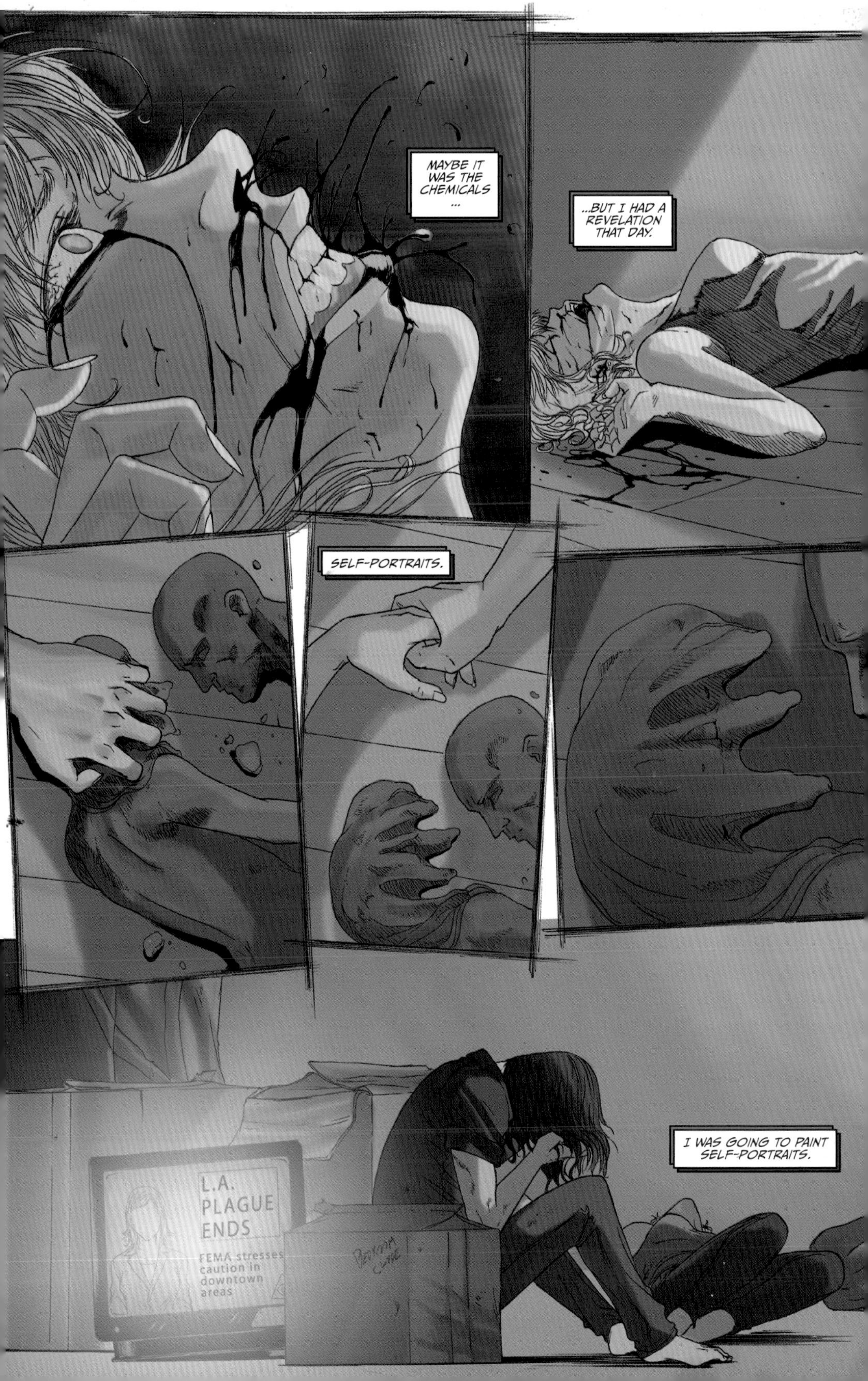
MAYBE IT WAS THE CHEMICALS ...
...BUT I HAD A REVELATION THAT DAY.
SELF-PORTRAITS.
L.A. PLAGUE ENDS
FEMA stresses caution in downtown areas
I WAS GOING TO PAINT SELF-PORTRAITS.

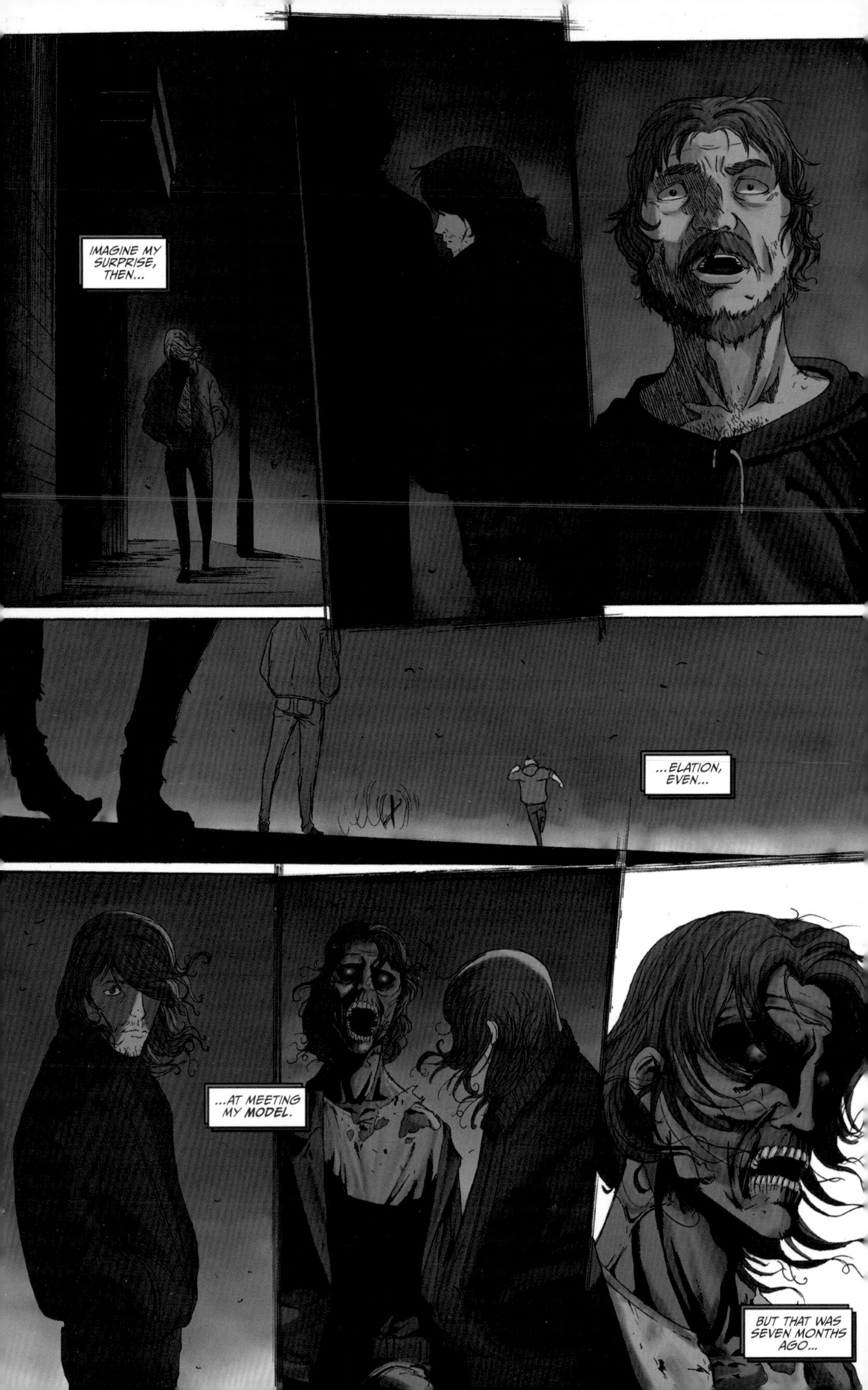
IMAGINE MY SURPRISE, THEN...
...ELATION, EVEN...
...AT MEETING MY MODEL.
BUT THAT WAS SEVEN MONTHS AGO...

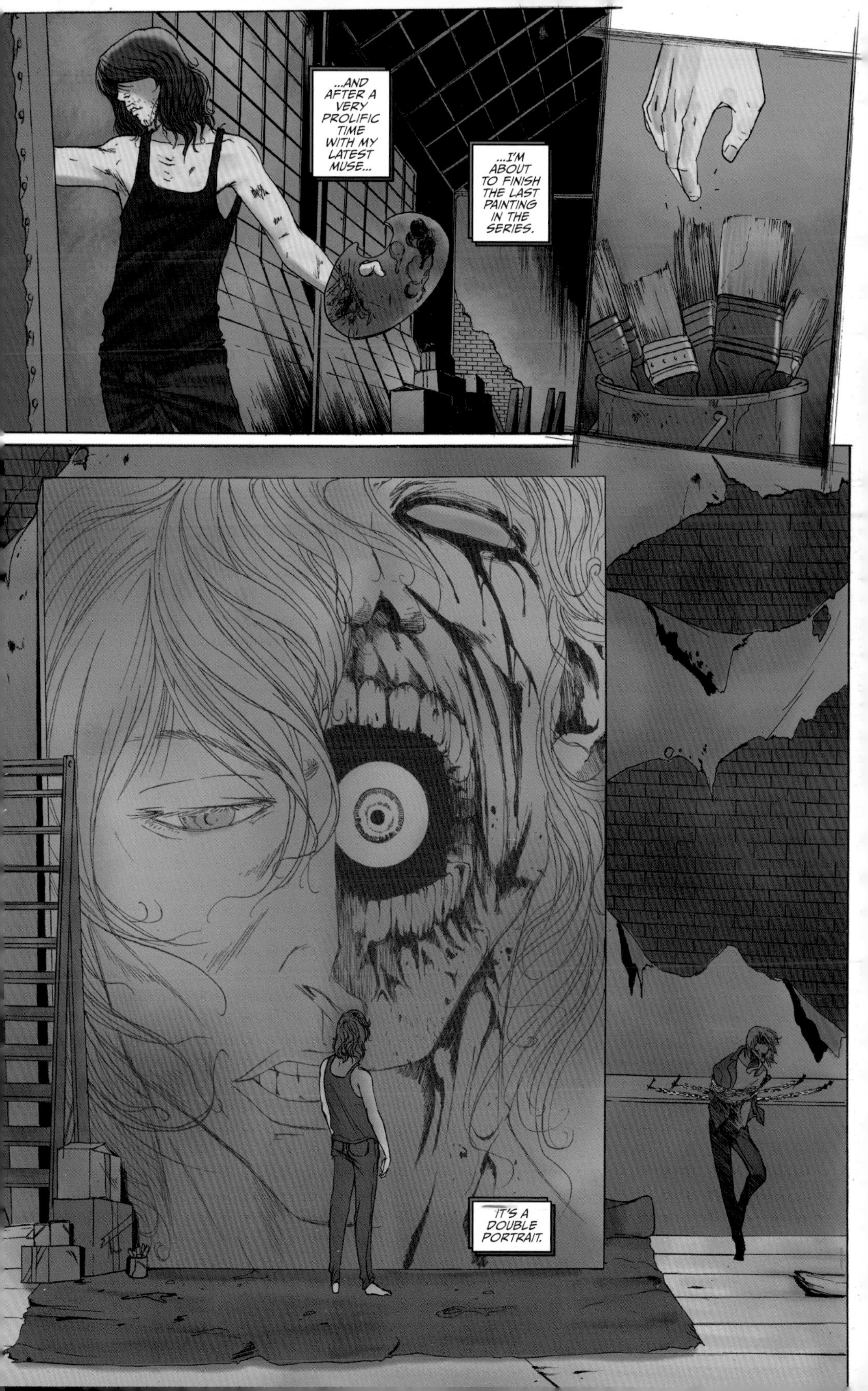
...AND AFTER A VERY PROLIFIC TIME WITH MY LATEST MUSE...
...I'M ABOUT TO FINISH THE LAST PAINTING IN THE SERIES.
IT'S A DOUBLE PORTRAIT.

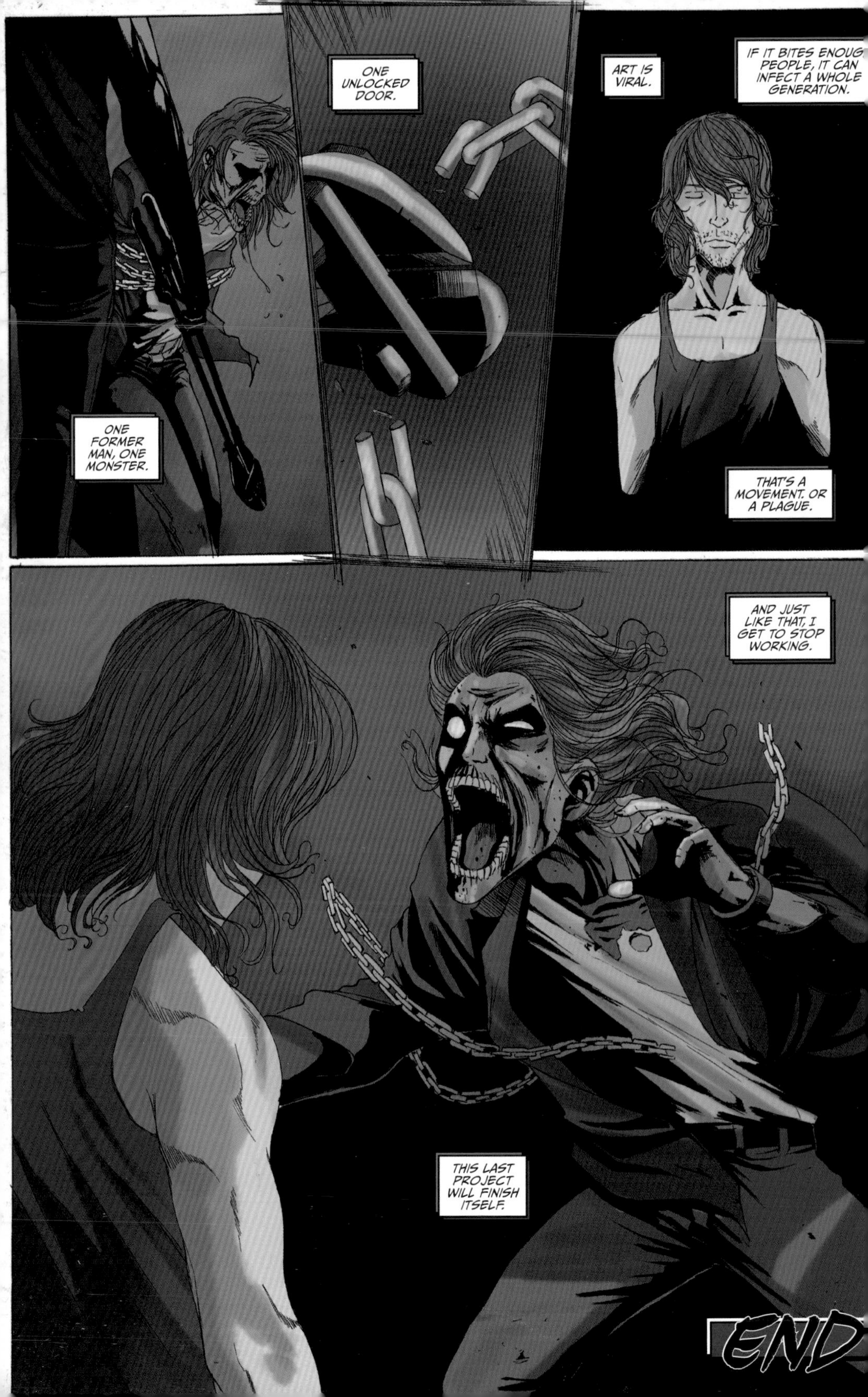
ONE UNLOCKED DOOR.
ONE FORMER MAN, ONE MONSTER.
ART IS VIRAL.
IF IT BITES ENOUG PEOPLE, IT CAN INFECT A WHOLE GENERATION.
THAT'S A MOVEMENT. OR A PLAGUE.
AND JUST LIKE THAT, I GET TO STOP WORKING.
THIS LAST PROJECT WILL FINISH ITSELF.
END

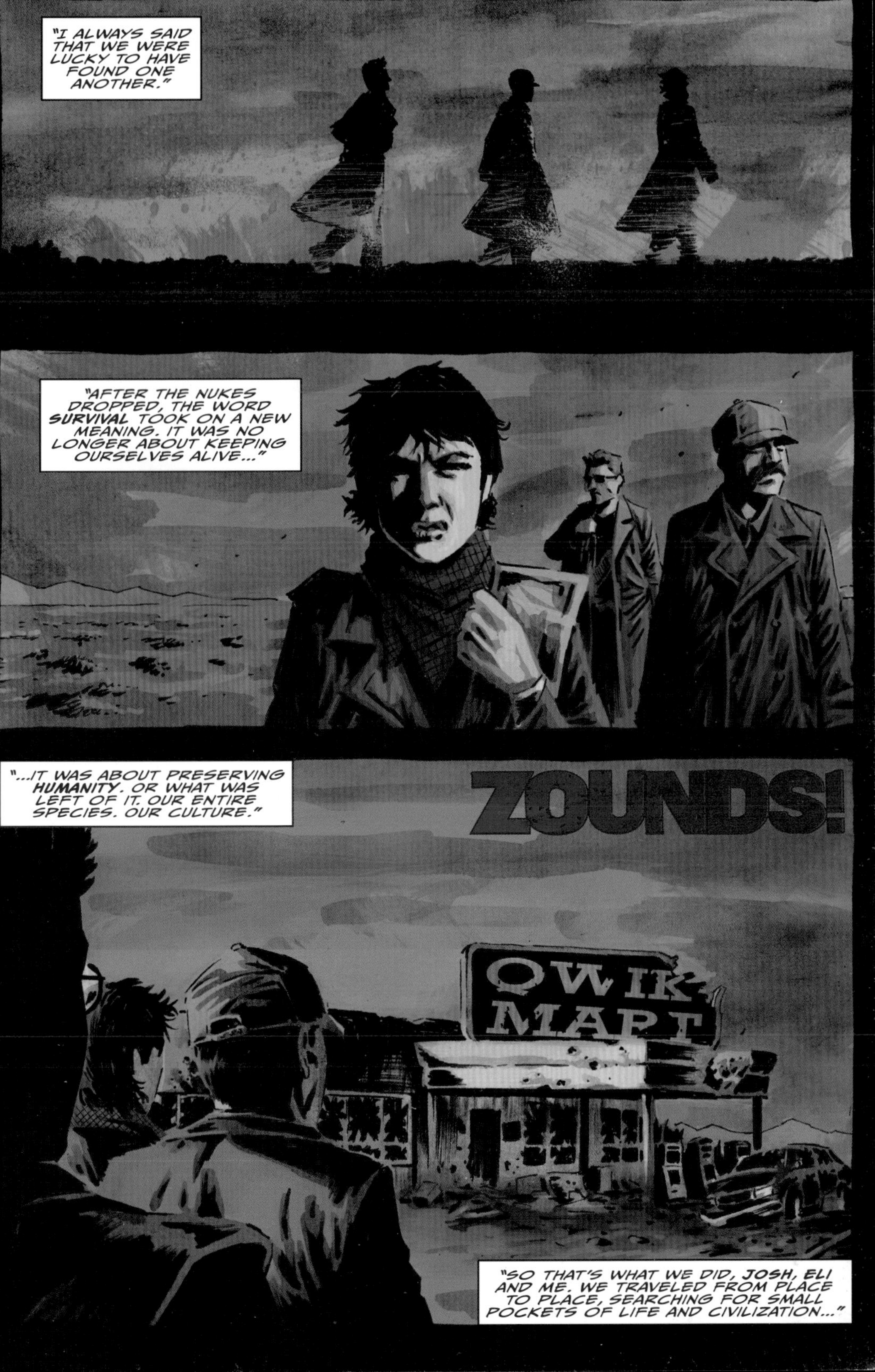
"I ALWAYS SAID THAT WE WERE LUCKY TO HAVE FOUND ONE ANOTHER."
"AFTER THE NUKES DROPPED, THE WORD **SURVIVAL** TOOK ON A NEW MEANING. IT WAS NO LONGER ABOUT KEEPING OURSELVES ALIVE..."
"...IT WAS ABOUT PRESERVING **HUMANITY**. OR WHAT WAS LEFT OF IT. OUR ENTIRE SPECIES. OUR CULTURE."
ZOUNDS!
QWIK MART
"SO THAT'S WHAT WE DID, **JOSH**, **ELI** AND ME. WE TRAVELED FROM PLACE TO PLACE, SEARCHING FOR SMALL POCKETS OF LIFE AND CIVILIZATION..."

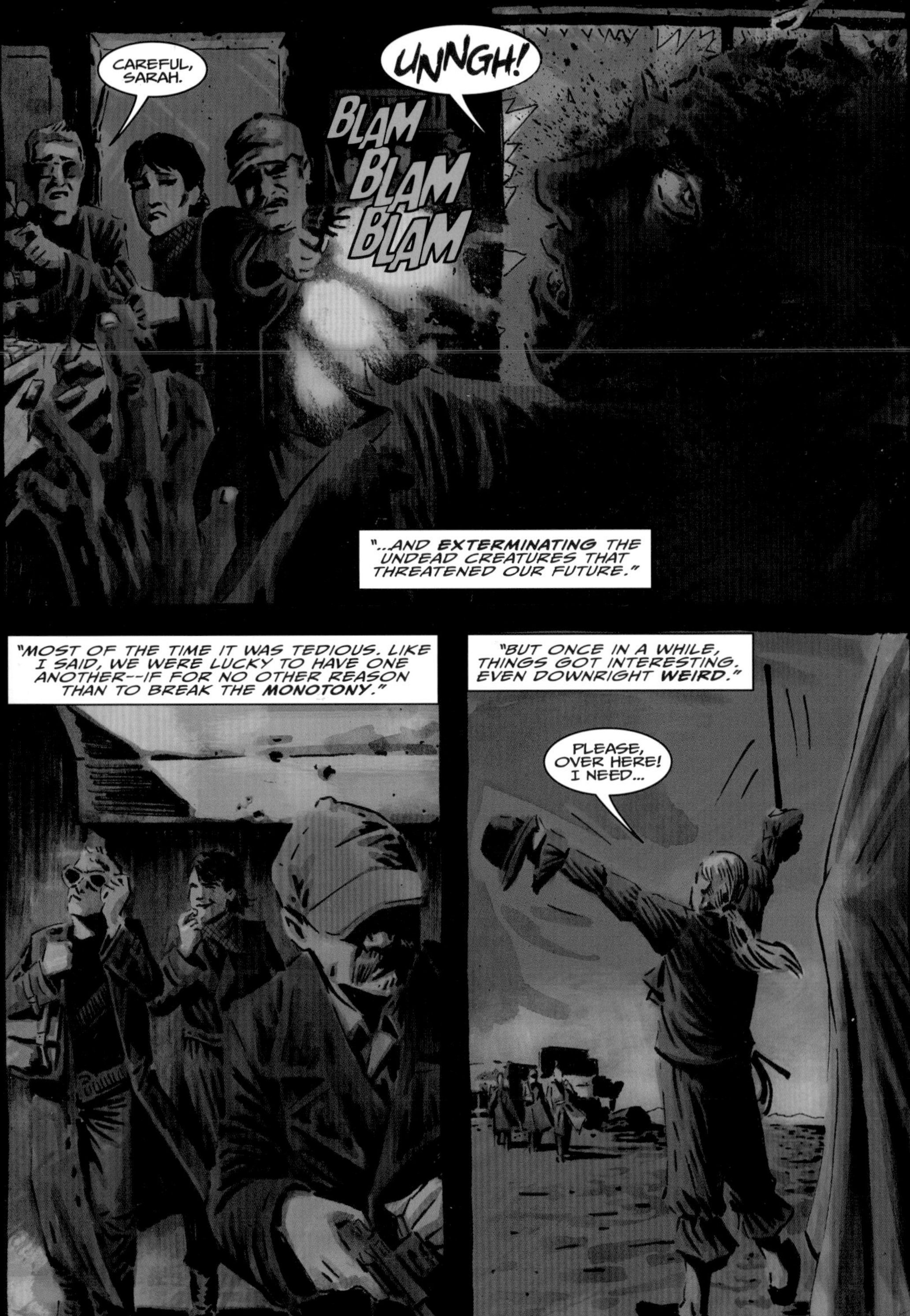
CAREFUL, SARAH.
UNNGH!
BLAM BLAM BLAM
"...AND EXTERMINATING THE UNDEAD CREATURES THAT THREATENED OUR FUTURE."
"MOST OF THE TIME IT WAS TEDIOUS. LIKE I SAID, WE WERE LUCKY TO HAVE ONE ANOTHER--IF FOR NO OTHER REASON THAN TO BREAK THE MONOTONY."
"BUT ONCE IN A WHILE, THINGS GOT INTERESTING. EVEN DOWNRIGHT WEIRD."
PLEASE, OVER HERE! I NEED...

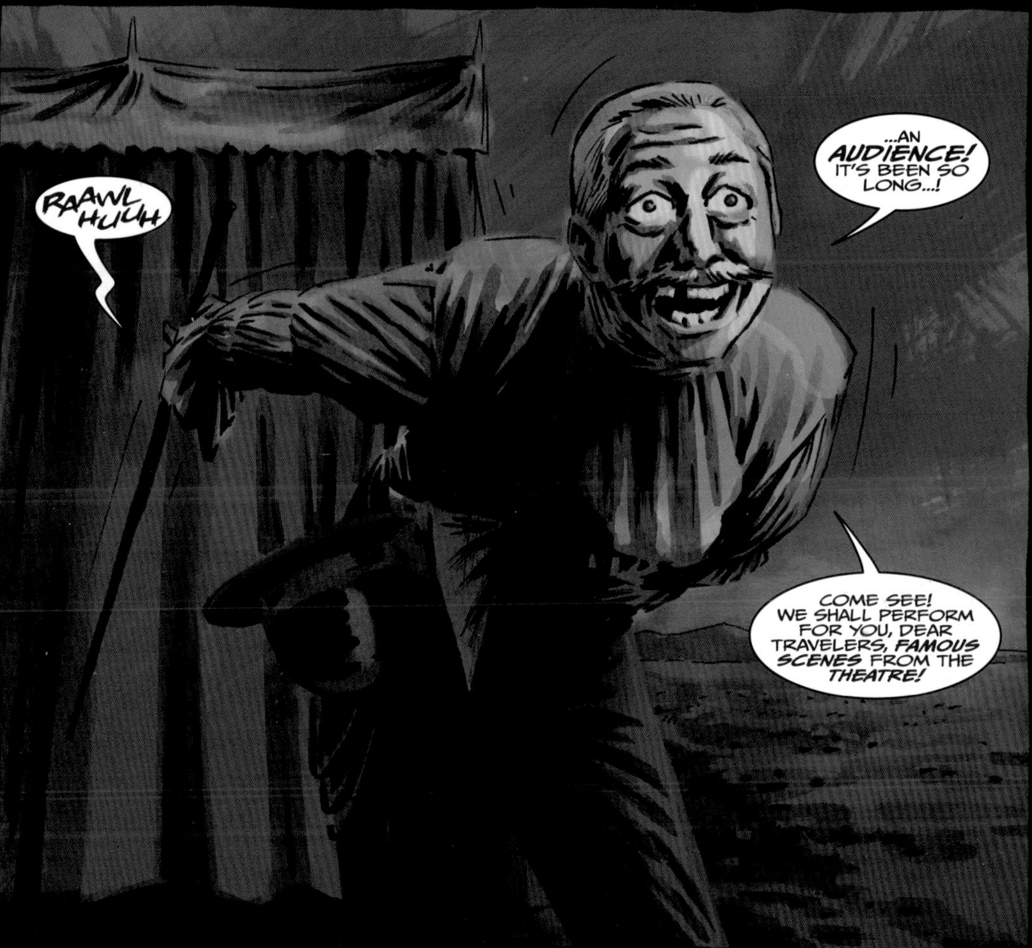
RAAWL HUUH
...AN AUDIENCE! IT'S BEEN SO LONG...!
COME SEE! WE SHALL PERFORM FOR YOU, DEAR TRAVELERS, FAMOUS SCENES FROM THE THEATRE!

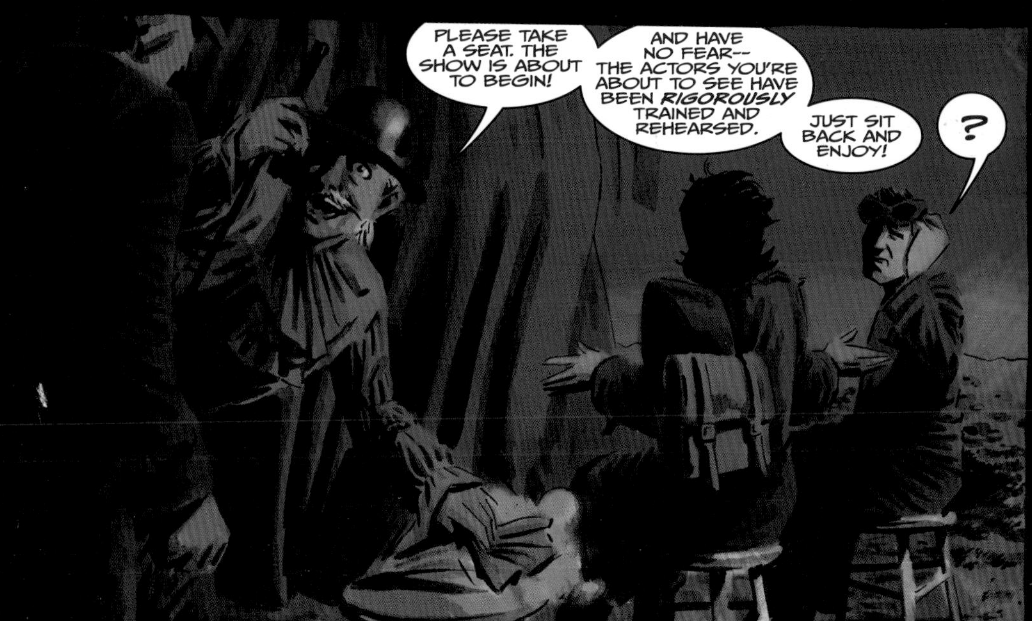
PLEASE TAKE A SEAT. THE SHOW IS ABOUT TO BEGIN!
AND HAVE NO FEAR-- THE ACTORS YOU'RE ABOUT TO SEE HAVE BEEN RIGOROUSLY TRAINED AND REHEARSED.
JUST SIT BACK AND ENJOY!
?

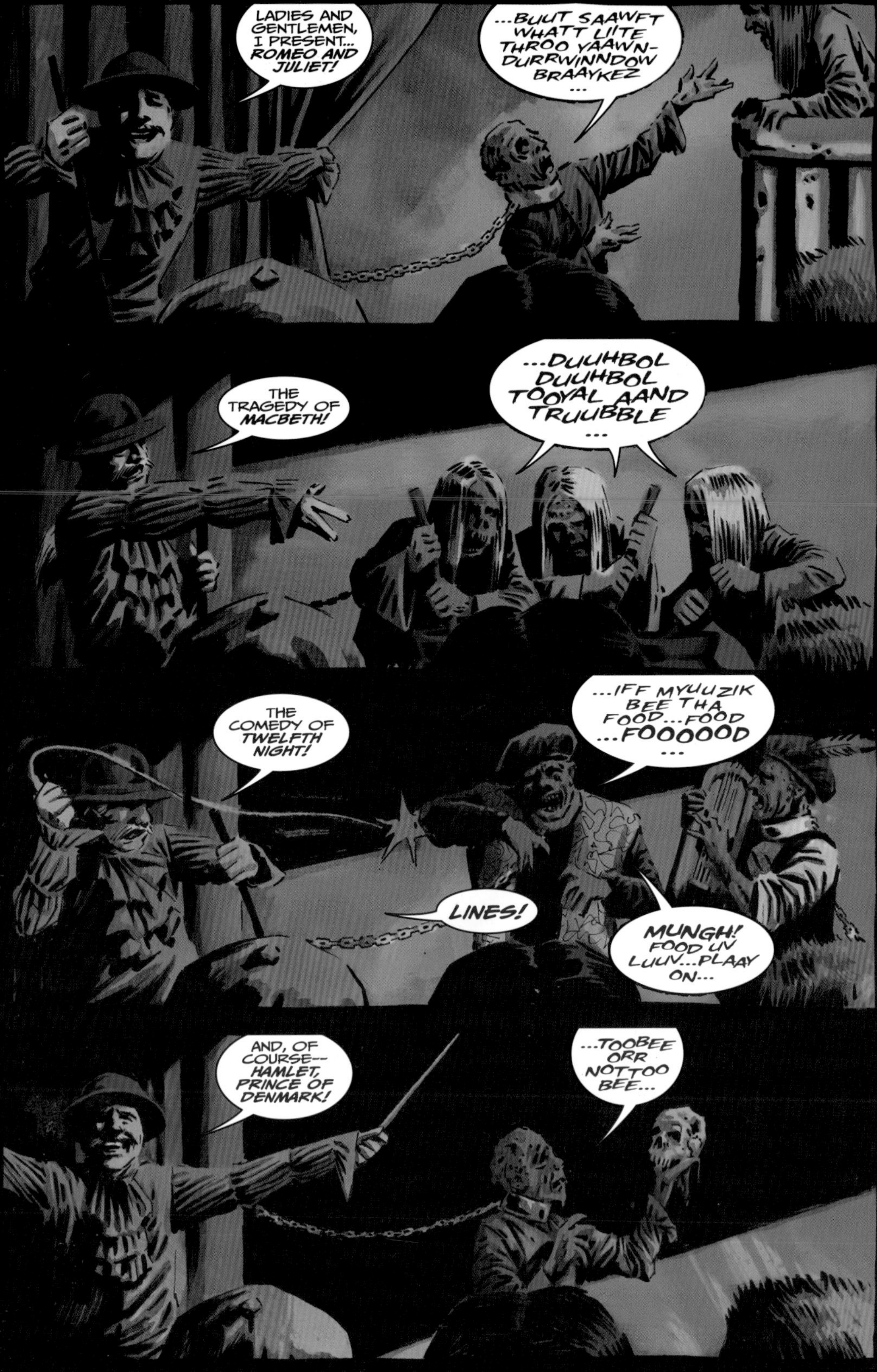

LADIES AND GENTLEMEN, I PRESENT... ROMEO AND JULIET!
...BUUT SAAWFT WHATT LIITE THROO YAAWN-DURRWINNDOW BRAAYKEZ ...
THE TRAGEDY OF MACBETH!
...DUUHBOL DUUHBOL TOOYAL AAND TRUUBBLE ...
THE COMEDY OF TWELFTH NIGHT!
...IFF MYUUZIK BEE THA FOOD...FOOD ...FOOOOOD ...
LINES!
MUNGH! FOOD UV LUUV...PLAAY ON...
AND, OF COURSE-- HAMLET, PRINCE OF DENMARK!
...TOOBEE ORR NOTTOO BEE...

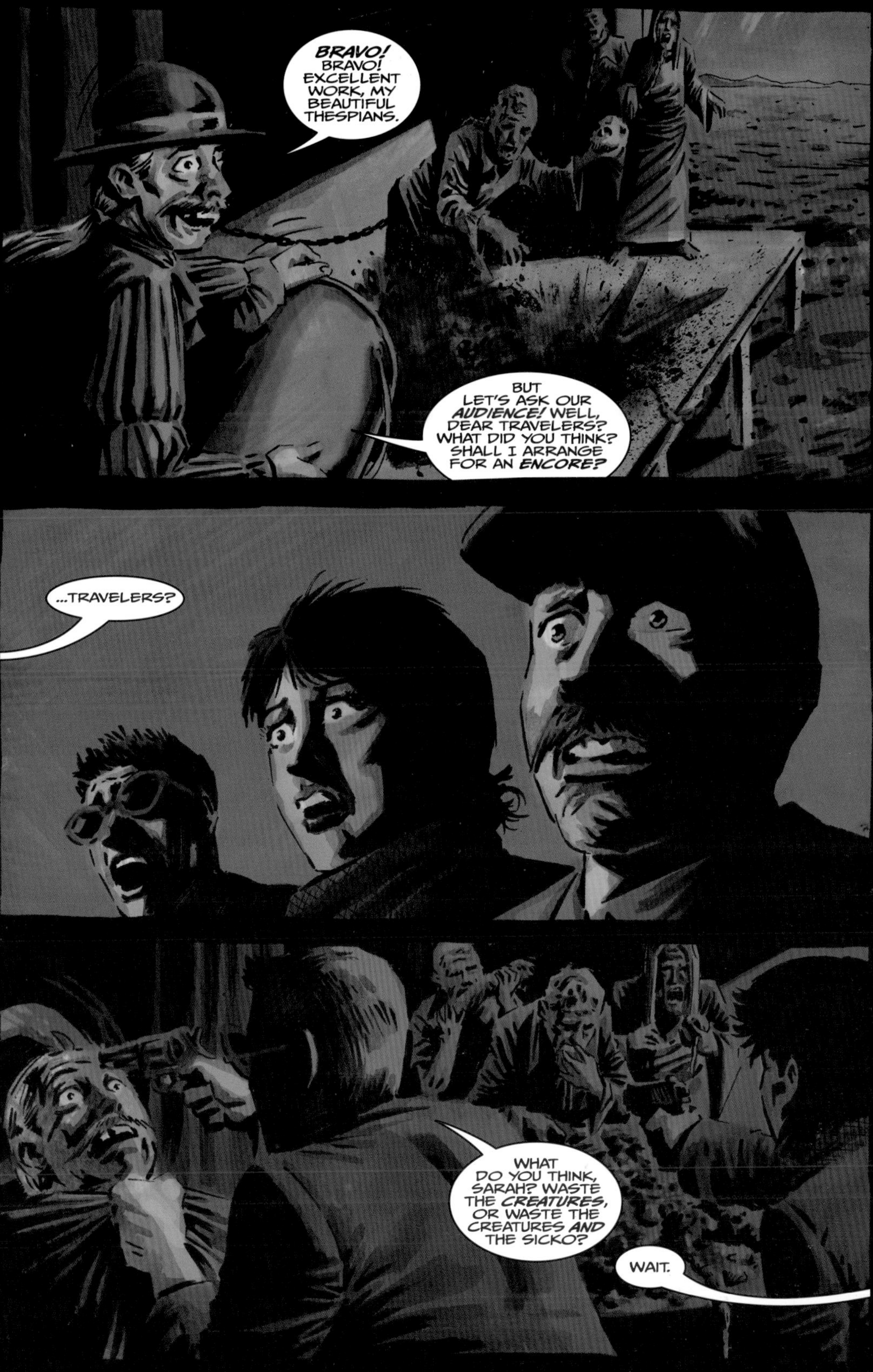
BRAVO! BRAVO! EXCELLENT WORK, MY BEAUTIFUL THESPIANS.
BUT LET'S ASK OUR AUDIENCE! WELL, DEAR TRAVELERS? WHAT DID YOU THINK? SHALL I ARRANGE FOR AN ENCORE?
...TRAVELERS?
WHAT DO YOU THINK, SARAH? WASTE THE CREATURES, OR WASTE THE CREATURES AND THE SICKO?
WAIT.

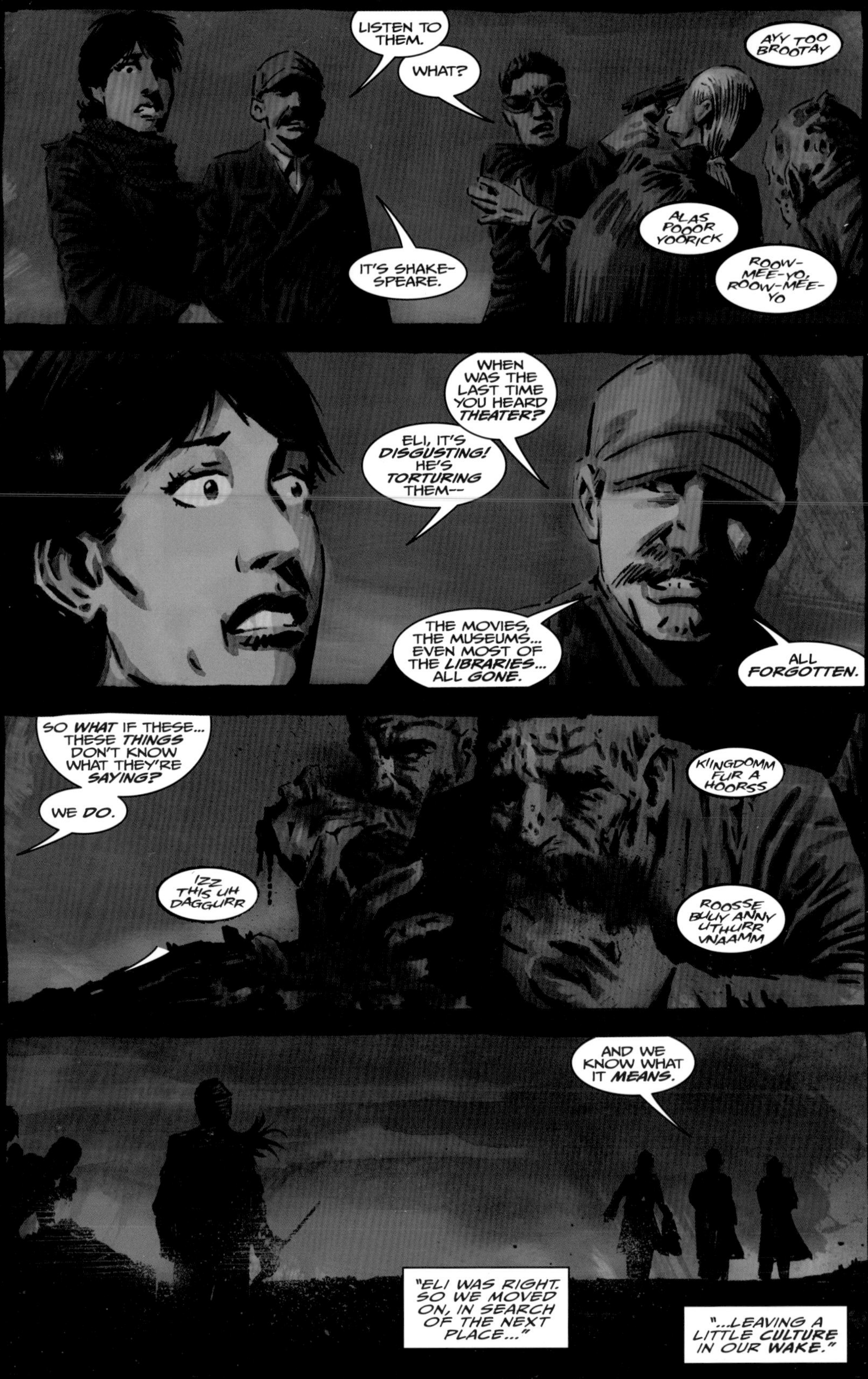
LISTEN TO THEM.
WHAT?
IT'S SHAKE-SPEARE.
AYY TOO BROOTAY
ALAS POOOR YOORICK
ROOW-MEE-YO, ROOW-MEE-YO
WHEN WAS THE LAST TIME YOU HEARD THEATER?
ELI, IT'S DISGUSTING! HE'S TORTURING THEM--
THE MOVIES, THE MUSEUMS... EVEN MOST OF THE LIBRARIES... ALL GONE.
ALL FORGOTTEN.
SO WHAT IF THESE... THESE THINGS DON'T KNOW WHAT THEY'RE SAYING?
WE DO.
KIINGDOMM FUR A HOORSS
IZZ THIS UH DAGGURR
ROOSSE BUUY ANNY UTHURR VNAAMM
AND WE KNOW WHAT IT MEANS.
"ELI WAS RIGHT. SO WE MOVED ON, IN SEARCH OF THE NEXT PLACE..."
"...LEAVING A LITTLE CULTURE IN OUR WAKE."

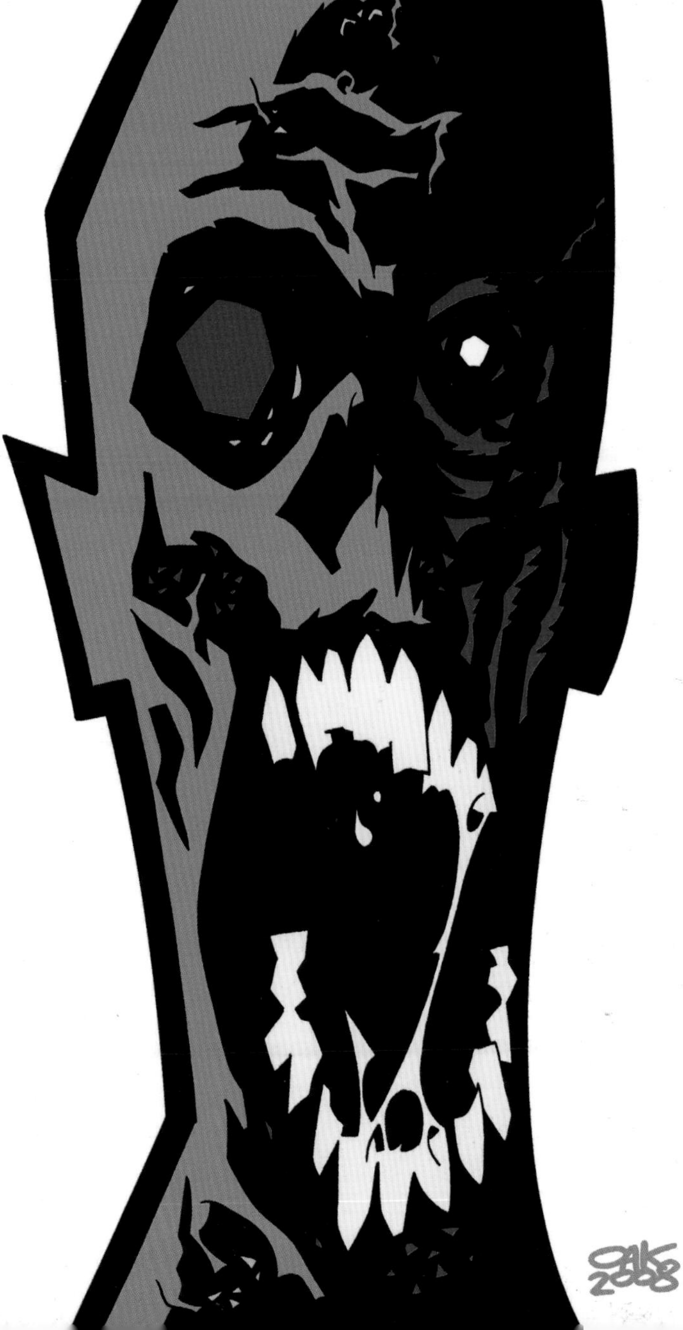
OAKS
2008

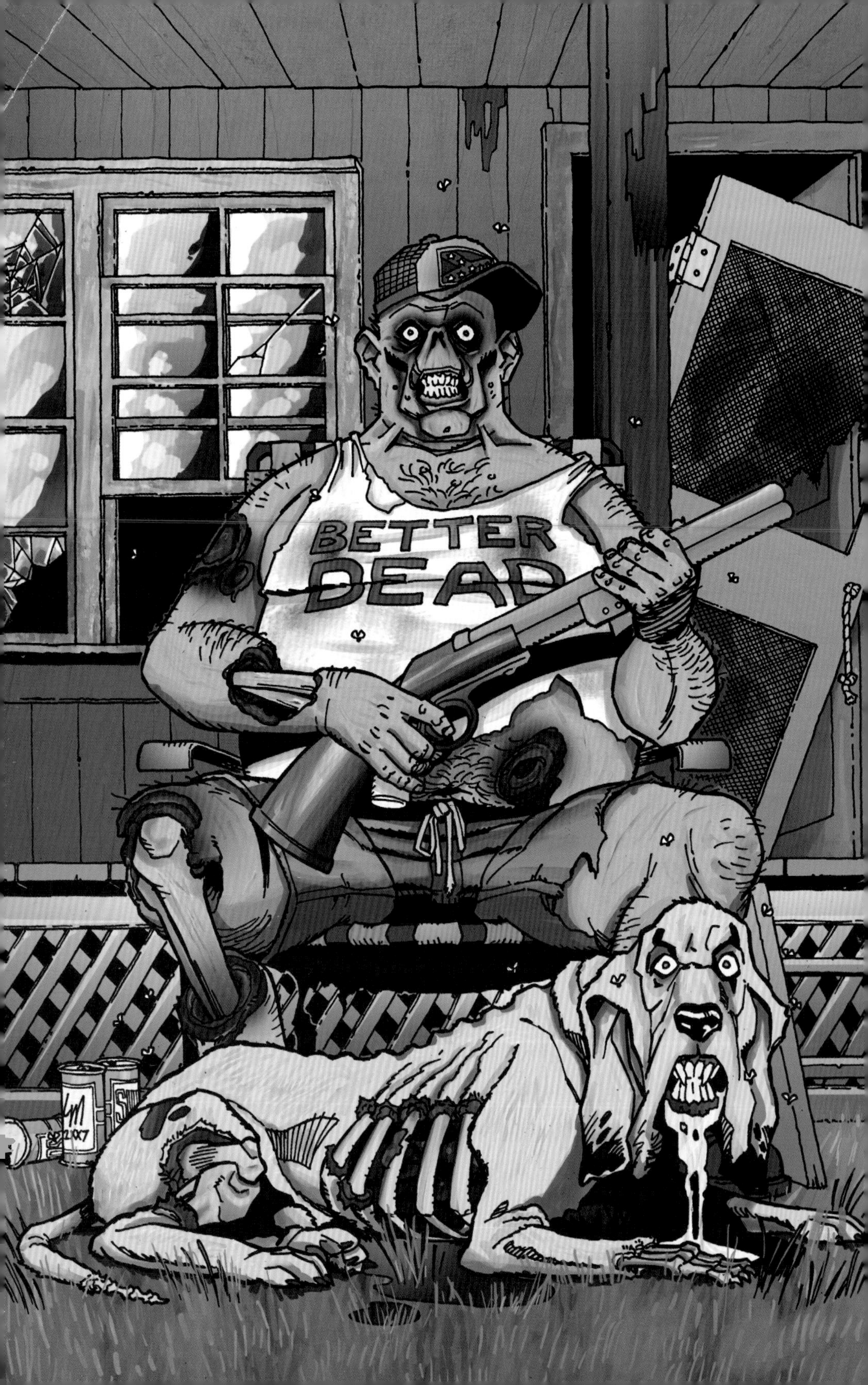
BETTER
DEAD

THE WAR AT HOME
Part Three:
THE ICE CREAM RIDE
Story: JOE R. LANSDALE
Art: EDUARDO BARRETO

LAST CALL IN
DEVIL'S BEND
Story: KARL KESEL
Art: JON REED

5 STARS
Story: WILLIAM MESSNER-LOEBS
Art: JON REED

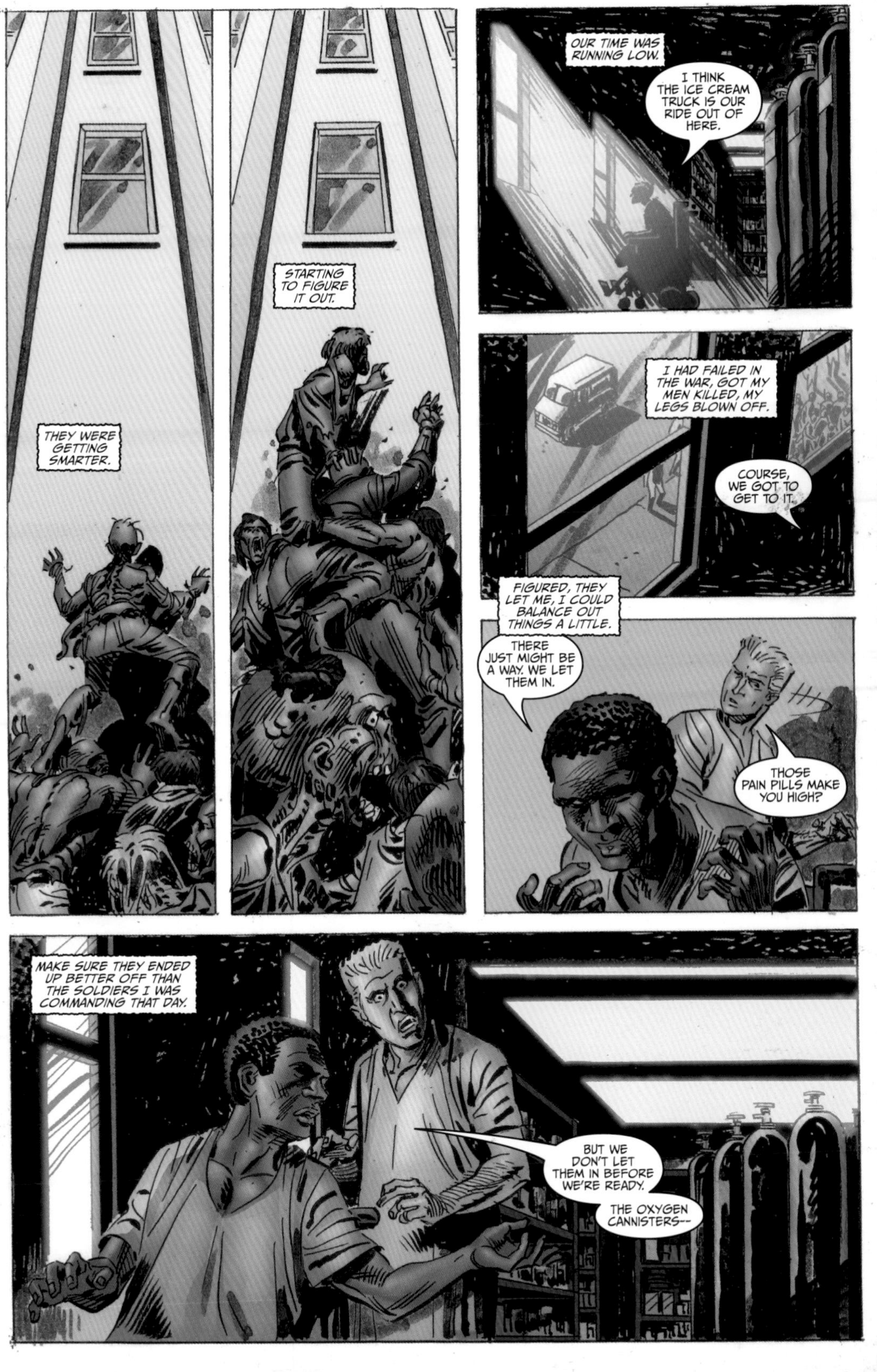
THEY WERE GETTING SMARTER.
STARTING TO FIGURE IT OUT.
OUR TIME WAS RUNNING LOW.
I THINK THE ICE CREAM TRUCK IS OUR RIDE OUT OF HERE.
I HAD FAILED IN THE WAR, GOT MY MEN KILLED, MY LEGS BLOWN OFF.
COURSE, WE GOT TO GET TO IT.
FIGURED, THEY LET ME, I COULD BALANCE OUT THINGS A LITTLE.
THERE JUST MIGHT BE A WAY. WE LET THEM IN.
THOSE PAIN PILLS MAKE YOU HIGH?
MAKE SURE THEY ENDED UP BETTER OFF THAN THE SOLDIERS I WAS COMMANDING THAT DAY.
BUT WE DON'T LET THEM IN BEFORE WE'RE READY.
THE OXYGEN CANNISTERS--

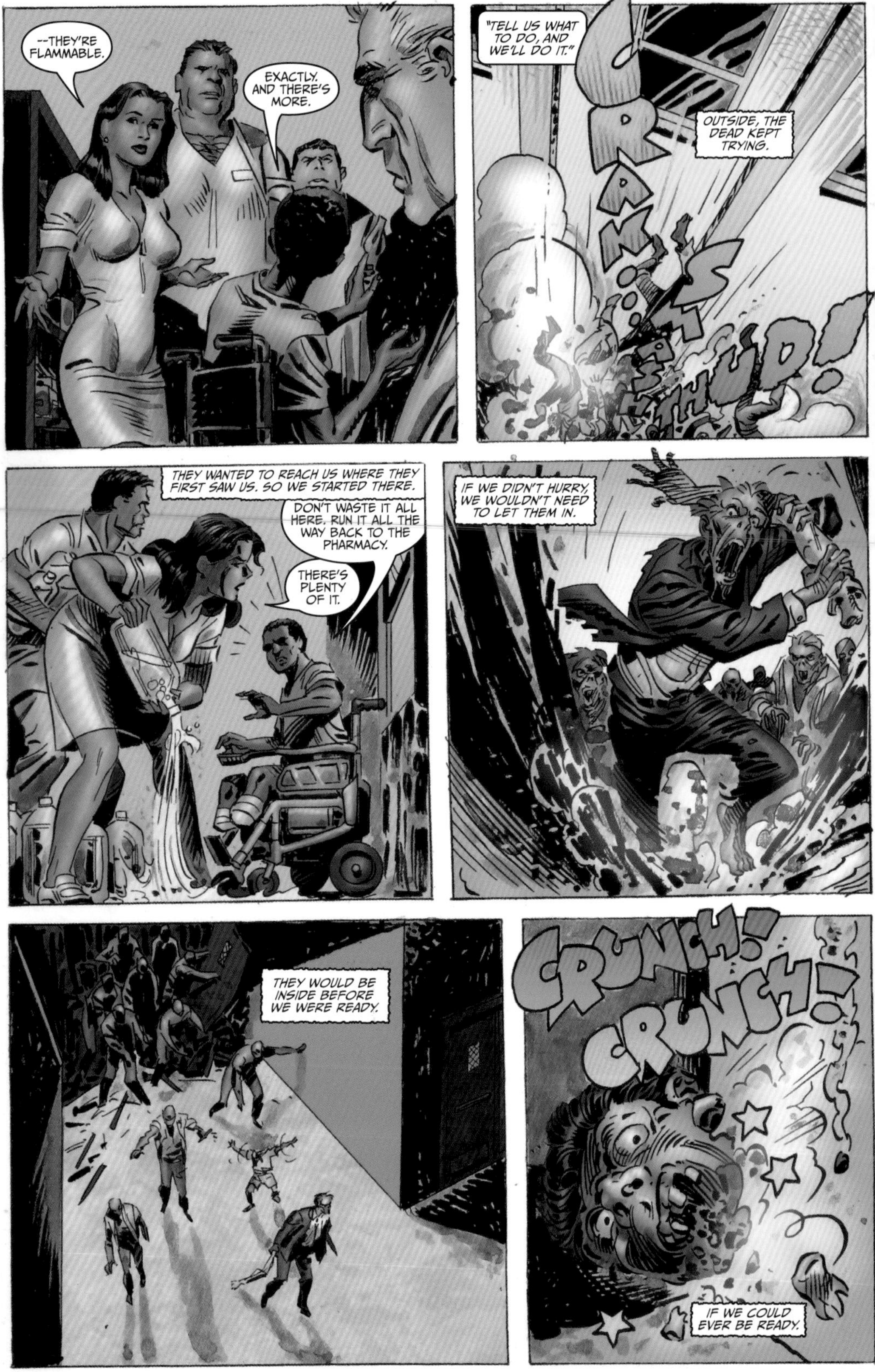

--THEY'RE FLAMMABLE.
EXACTLY. AND THERE'S MORE.
"TELL US WHAT TO DO, AND WE'LL DO IT."
OUTSIDE, THE DEAD KEPT TRYING.
THUD!
THEY WANTED TO REACH US WHERE THEY FIRST SAW US. SO WE STARTED THERE.
DON'T WASTE IT ALL HERE. RUN IT ALL THE WAY BACK TO THE PHARMACY.
THERE'S PLENTY OF IT.
IF WE DIDN'T HURRY, WE WOULDN'T NEED TO LET THEM IN.
THEY WOULD BE INSIDE BEFORE WE WERE READY.
CRUNCH! CRUNCH!
IF WE COULD EVER BE READY.

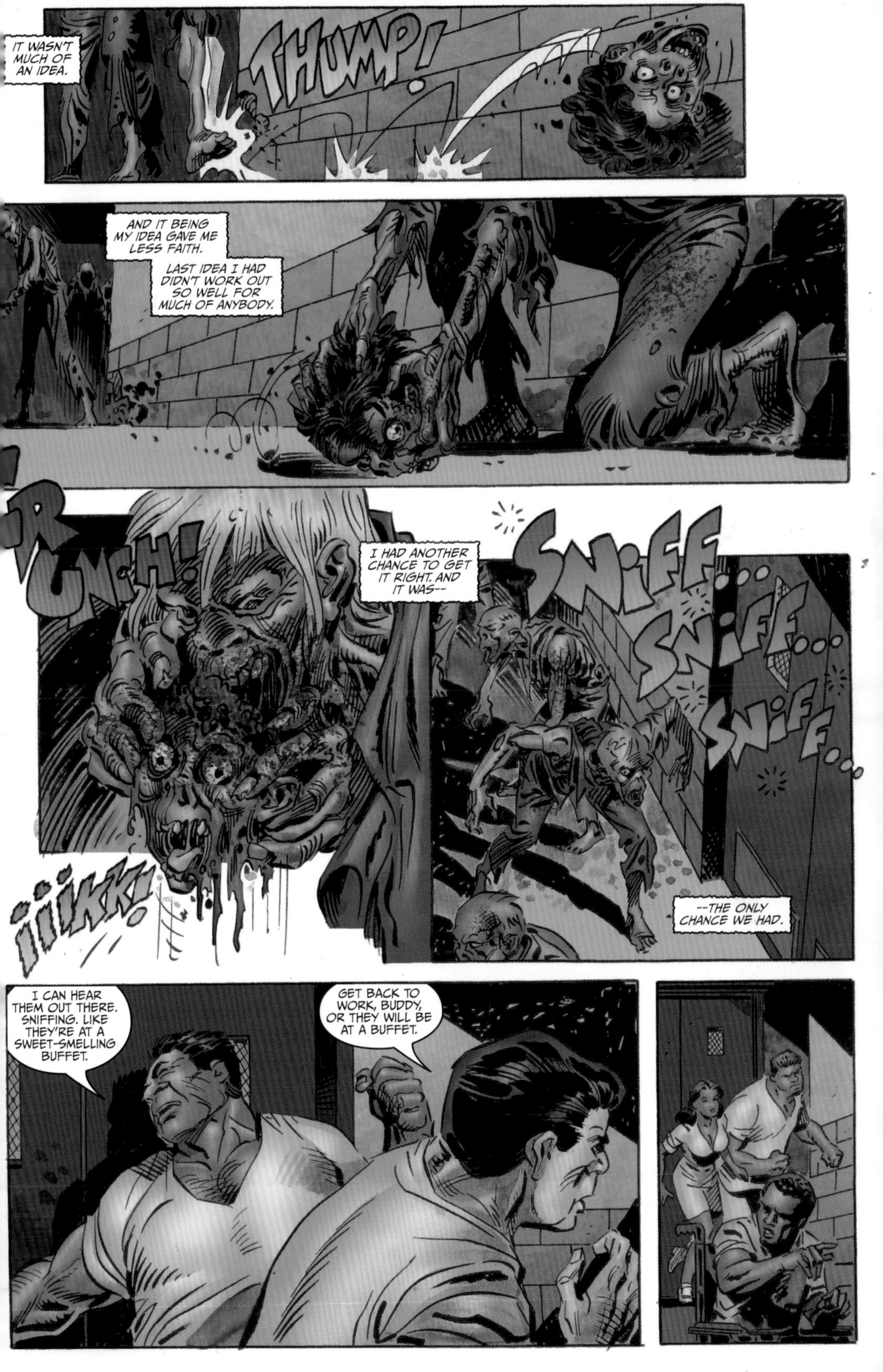
IT WASN'T MUCH OF AN IDEA.
THUMP!
AND IT BEING MY IDEA GAVE ME LESS FAITH.
LAST IDEA I HAD DIDN'T WORK OUT SO WELL FOR MUCH OF ANYBODY.
RUNCH!
iiiIKK!
I HAD ANOTHER CHANCE TO GET IT RIGHT. AND IT WAS--
SNIFF...
SNIFF...
SNIFF...
--THE ONLY CHANCE WE HAD.
I CAN HEAR THEM OUT THERE. SNIFFING. LIKE THEY'RE AT A SWEET-SMELLING BUFFET.
GET BACK TO WORK, BUDDY, OR THEY WILL BE AT A BUFFET.

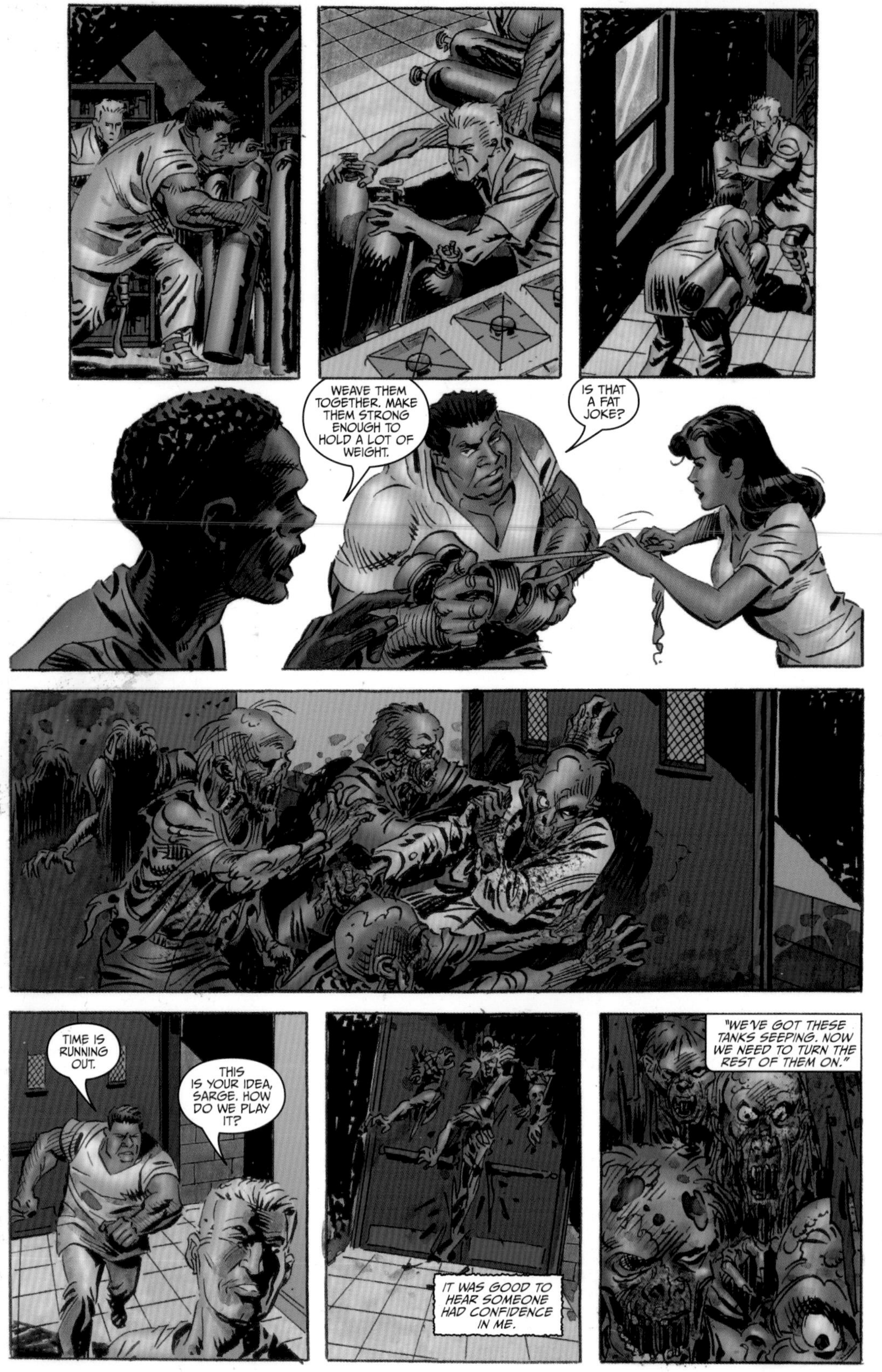
WEAVE THEM TOGETHER. MAKE THEM STRONG ENOUGH TO HOLD A LOT OF WEIGHT.
IS THAT A FAT JOKE?
TIME IS RUNNING OUT.
THIS IS YOUR IDEA, SARGE. HOW DO WE PLAY IT?
IT WAS GOOD TO HEAR SOMEONE HAD CONFIDENCE IN ME.
"WE'VE GOT THESE TANKS SEEPING. NOW WE NEED TO TURN THE REST OF THEM ON."

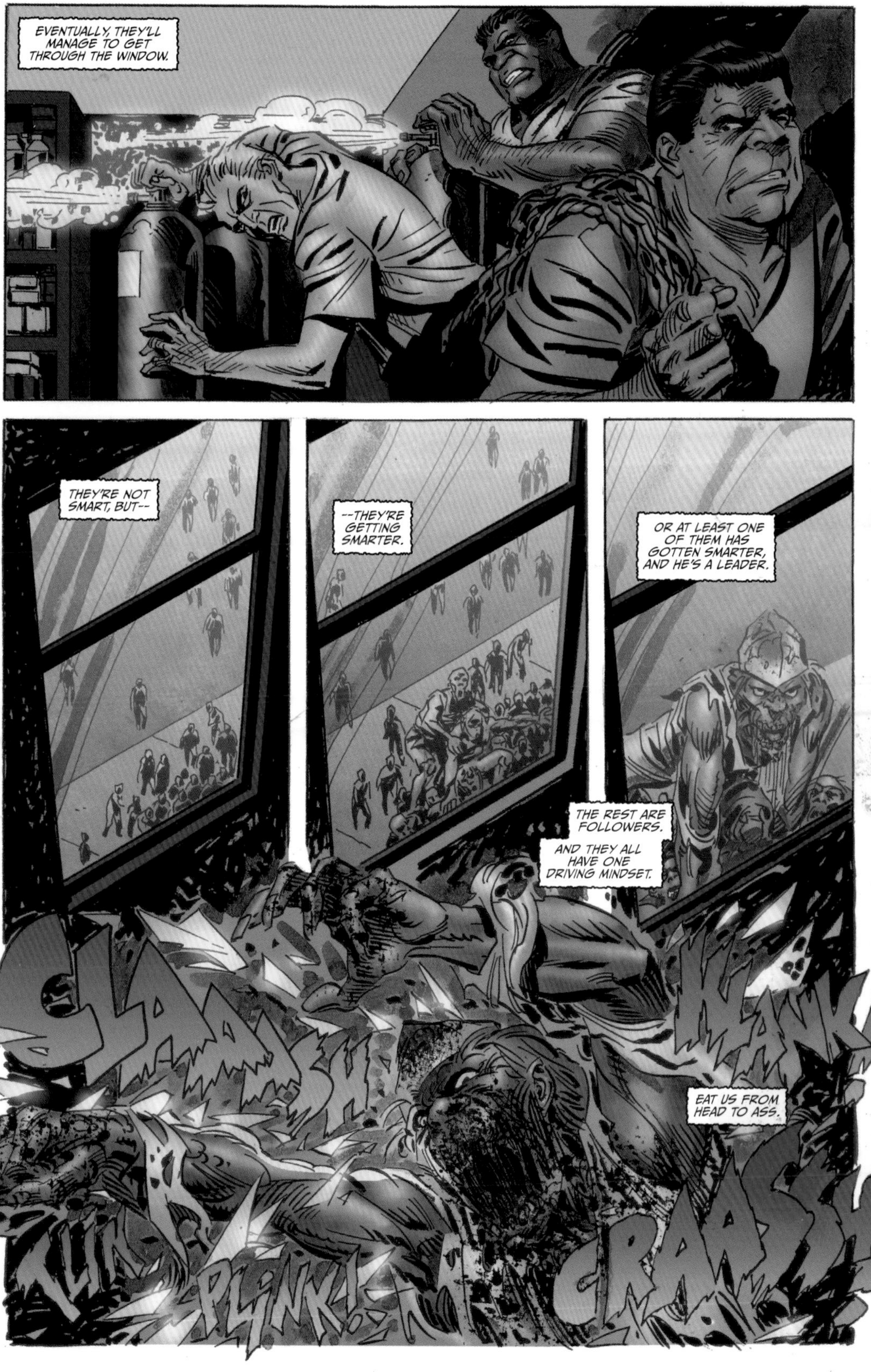
EVENTUALLY, THEY'LL MANAGE TO GET THROUGH THE WINDOW.
THEY'RE NOT SMART, BUT--
--THEY'RE GETTING SMARTER.
OR AT LEAST ONE OF THEM HAS GOTTEN SMARTER, AND HE'S A LEADER.
THE REST ARE FOLLOWERS.
AND THEY ALL HAVE ONE DRIVING MINDSET.
EAT US FROM HEAD TO ASS.
PLINK!

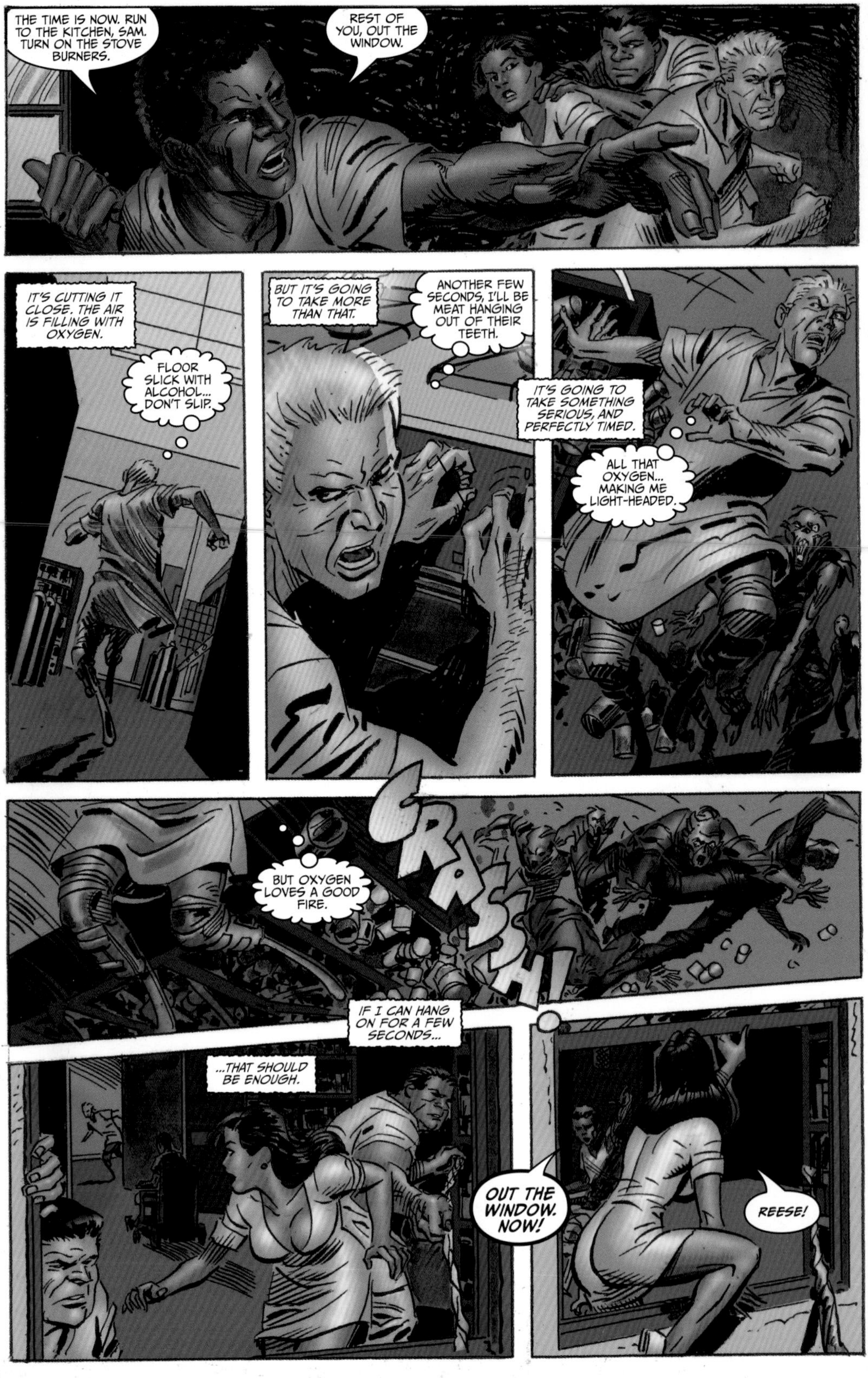
THE TIME IS NOW. RUN TO THE KITCHEN, SAM. TURN ON THE STOVE BURNERS.
REST OF YOU, OUT THE WINDOW.
IT'S CUTTING IT CLOSE. THE AIR IS FILLING WITH OXYGEN.
FLOOR SLICK WITH ALCOHOL... DON'T SLIP.
BUT IT'S GOING TO TAKE MORE THAN THAT.
ANOTHER FEW SECONDS, I'LL BE MEAT HANGING OUT OF THEIR TEETH.
IT'S GOING TO TAKE SOMETHING SERIOUS, AND PERFECTLY TIMED.
ALL THAT OXYGEN... MAKING ME LIGHT-HEADED.
BUT OXYGEN LOVES A GOOD FIRE.
CRASSH!
IF I CAN HANG ON FOR A FEW SECONDS...
...THAT SHOULD BE ENOUGH.
OUT THE WINDOW. NOW!
REESE!

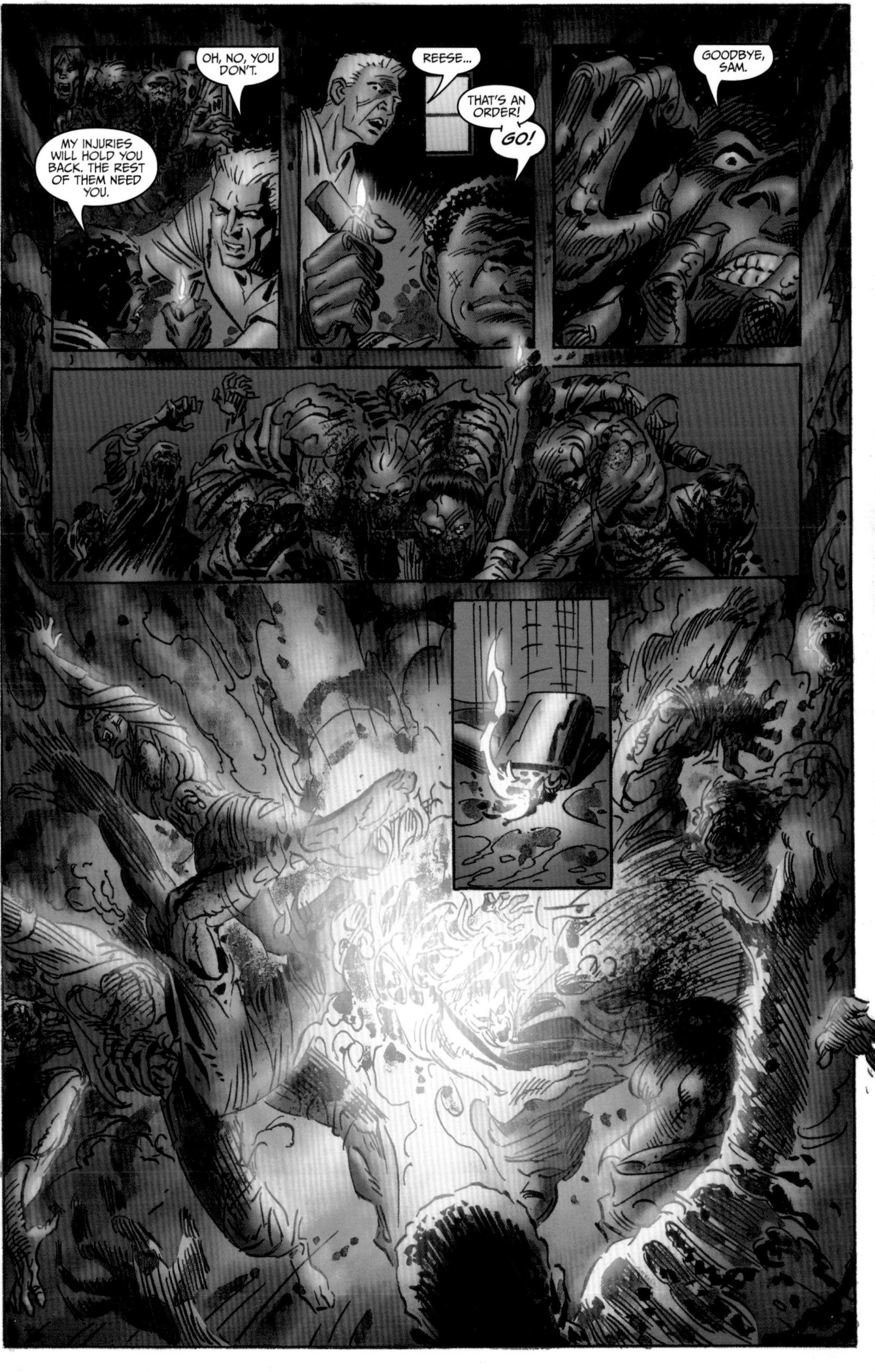
OH, NO, YOU DON'T.
MY INJURIES WILL HOLD YOU BACK. THE REST OF THEM NEED YOU.
REESE...
THAT'S AN ORDER!
GO!
GOODBYE, SAM.

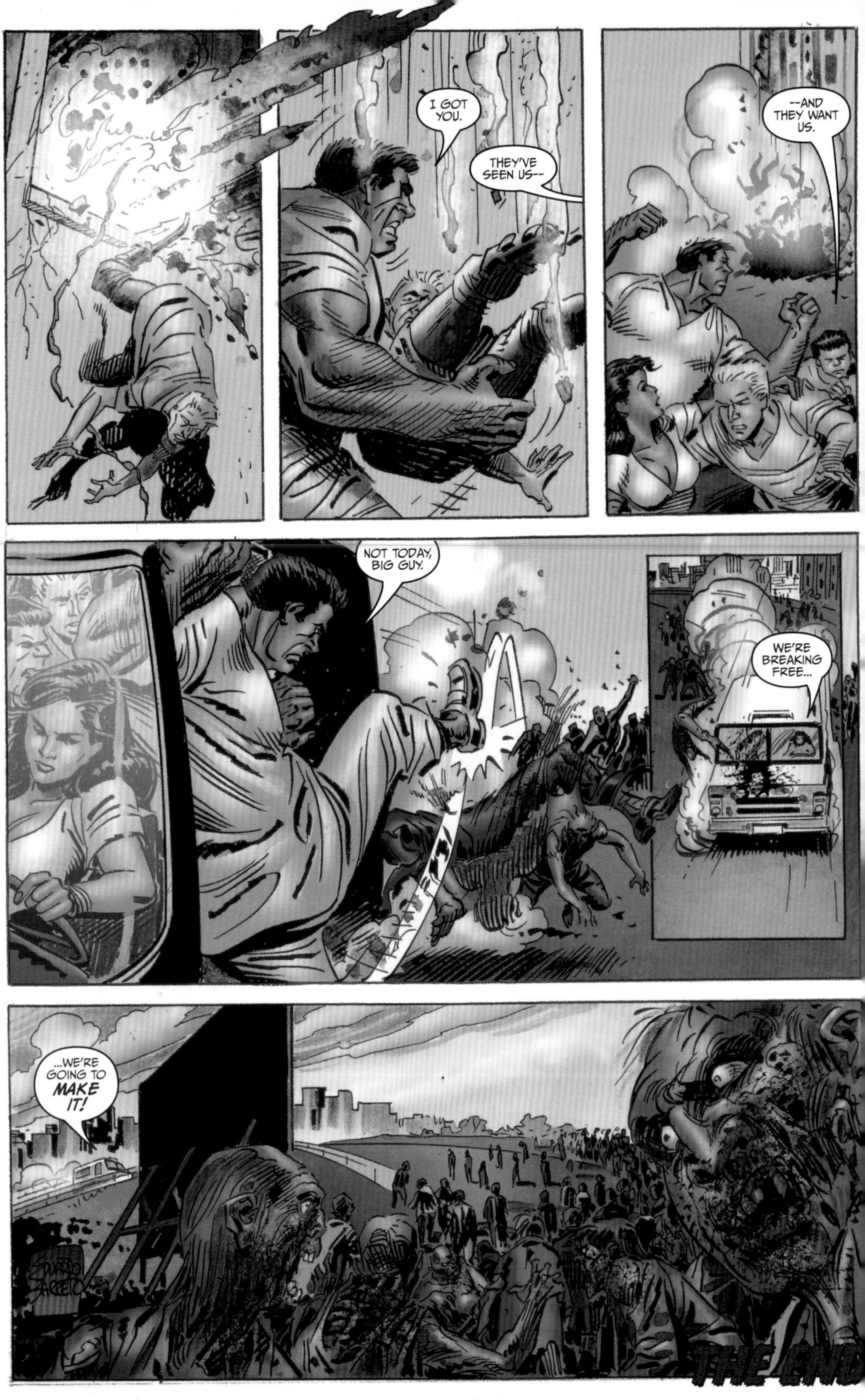
I GOT YOU.
THEY'VE SEEN US--
--AND THEY WANT US.
NOT TODAY, BIG GUY.
WE'RE BREAKING FREE...
...WE'RE GOING TO MAKE IT!
THE END

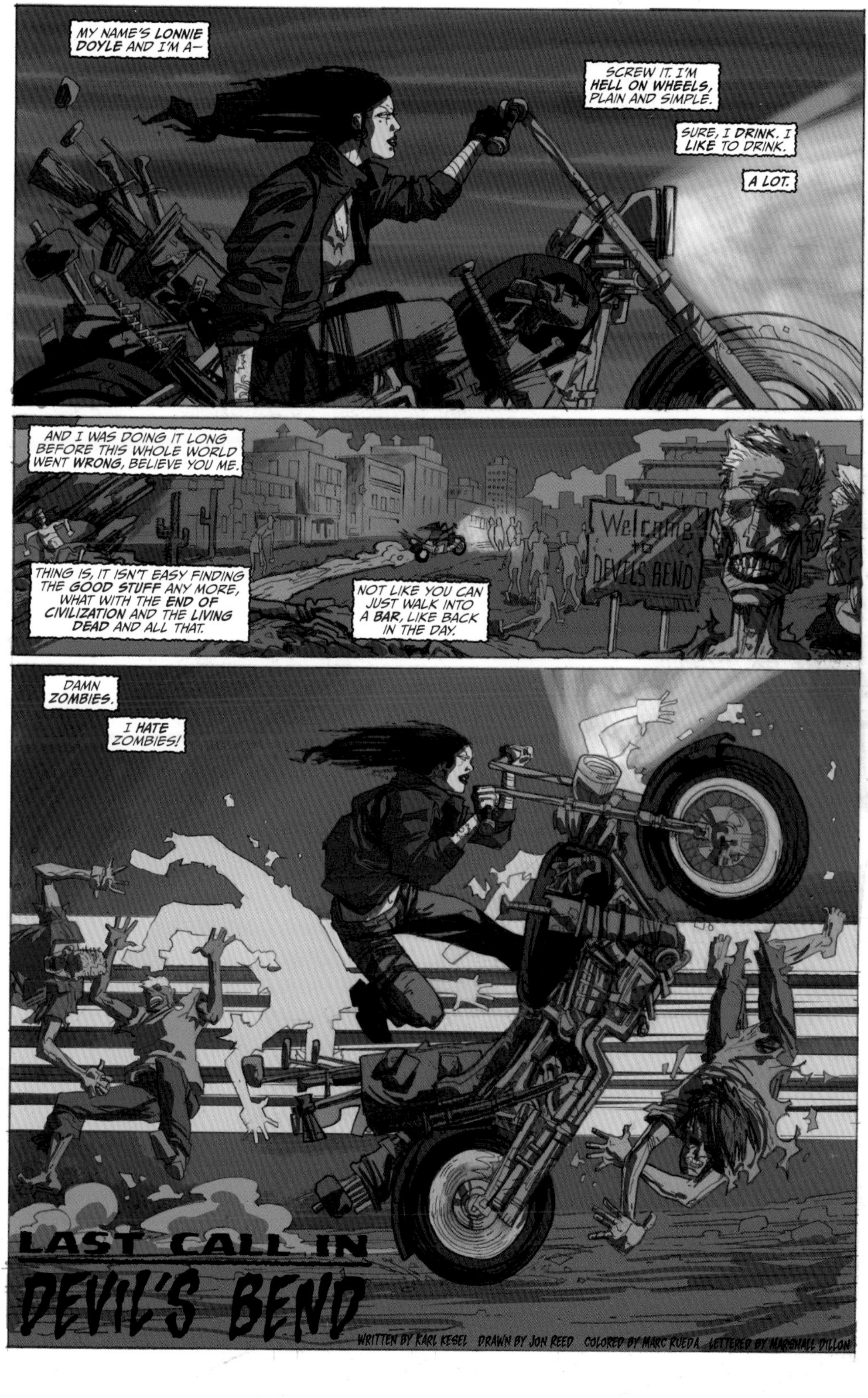
MY NAME'S LONNIE DOYLE AND I'M A—
SCREW IT. I'M HELL ON WHEELS, PLAIN AND SIMPLE.
SURE, I DRINK. I LIKE TO DRINK.
A LOT.
AND I WAS DOING IT LONG BEFORE THIS WHOLE WORLD WENT WRONG, BELIEVE YOU ME.
Welcome to DEVILS BEND
THING IS, IT ISN'T EASY FINDING THE GOOD STUFF ANY MORE, WHAT WITH THE END OF CIVILIZATION AND THE LIVING DEAD AND ALL THAT.
NOT LIKE YOU CAN JUST WALK INTO A BAR, LIKE BACK IN THE DAY.
DAMN ZOMBIES.
I HATE ZOMBIES!
LAST CALL IN
DEVIL'S BEND
WRITTEN BY KARL KESEL DRAWN BY JON REED COLORED BY MARC RUEDA LETTERED BY MARSHALL DILLON

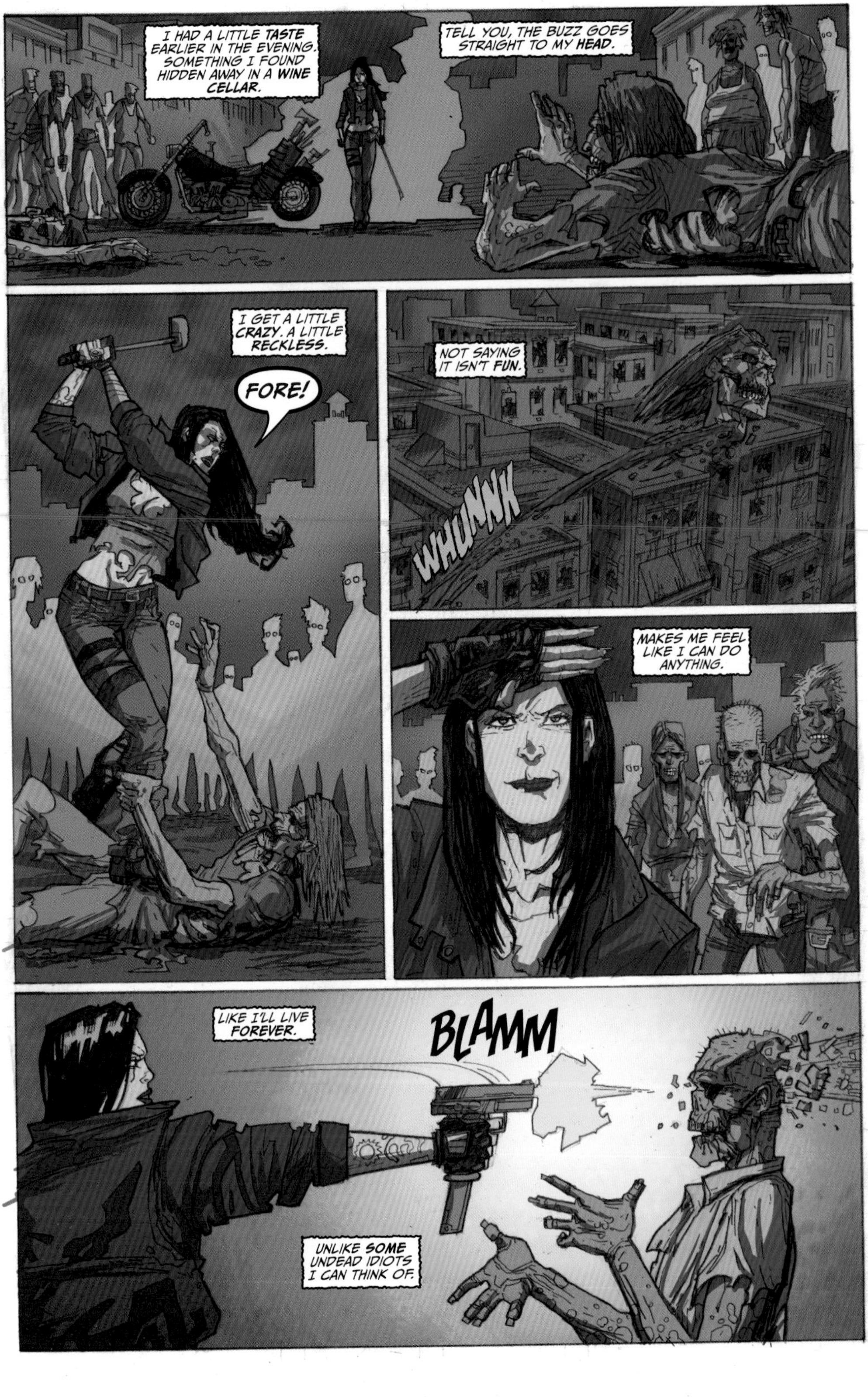
I HAD A LITTLE TASTE EARLIER IN THE EVENING. SOMETHING I FOUND HIDDEN AWAY IN A WINE CELLAR.
TELL YOU, THE BUZZ GOES STRAIGHT TO MY HEAD.
I GET A LITTLE CRAZY. A LITTLE RECKLESS.
FORE!
NOT SAYING IT ISN'T FUN.
WHUNNK
MAKES ME FEEL LIKE I CAN DO ANYTHING.
LIKE I'LL LIVE FOREVER.
BLAMM
UNLIKE SOME UNDEAD IDIOTS I CAN THINK OF.

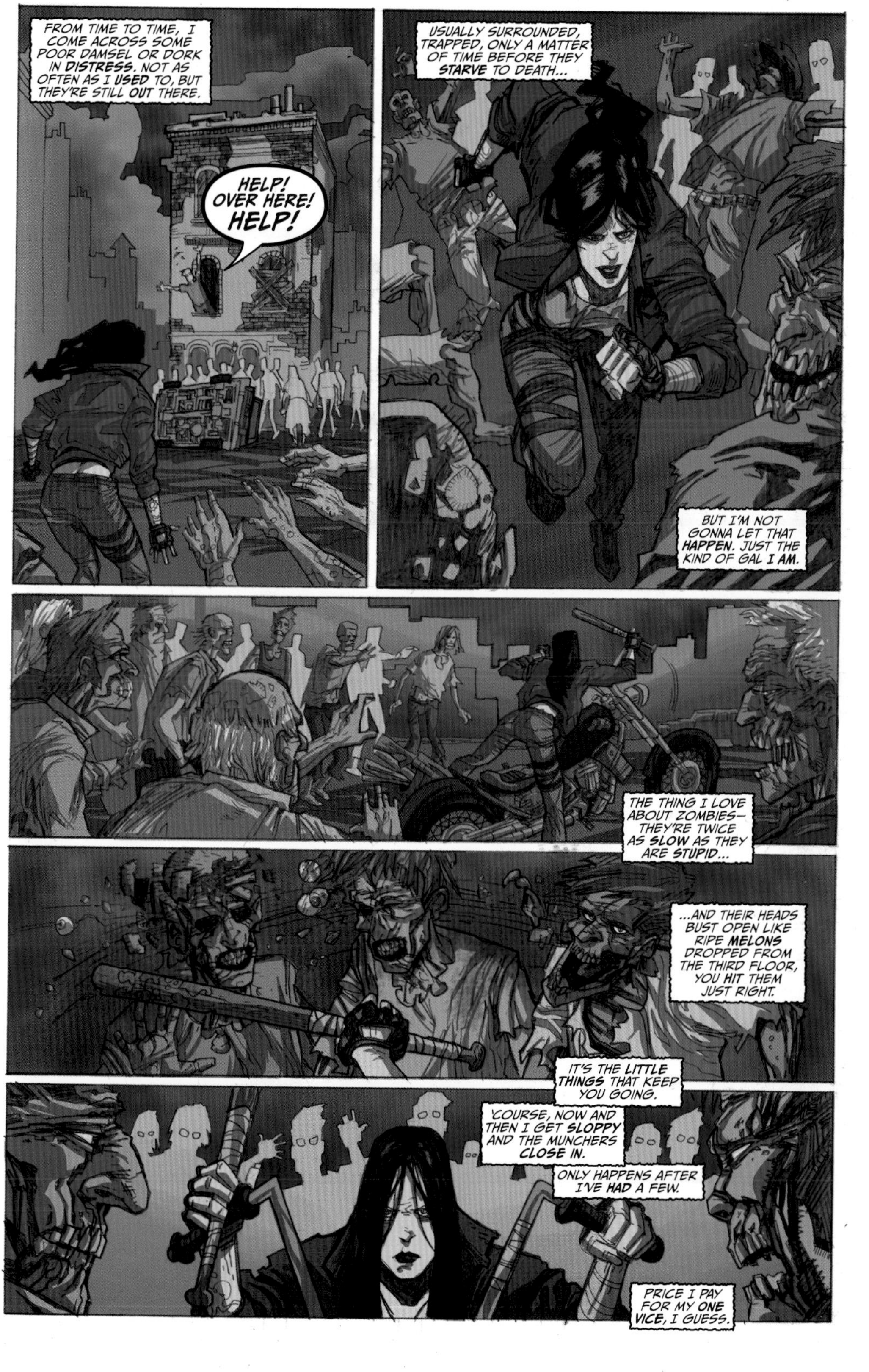
FROM TIME TO TIME, I COME ACROSS SOME POOR DAMSEL OR DORK IN DISTRESS. NOT AS OFTEN AS I USED TO, BUT THEY'RE STILL OUT THERE.
HELP! OVER HERE! HELP!
USUALLY SURROUNDED, TRAPPED, ONLY A MATTER OF TIME BEFORE THEY STARVE TO DEATH...
BUT I'M NOT GONNA LET THAT HAPPEN. JUST THE KIND OF GAL I AM.
THE THING I LOVE ABOUT ZOMBIES— THEY'RE TWICE AS SLOW AS THEY ARE STUPID...
...AND THEIR HEADS BUST OPEN LIKE RIPE MELONS DROPPED FROM THE THIRD FLOOR, YOU HIT THEM JUST RIGHT.
IT'S THE LITTLE THINGS THAT KEEP YOU GOING.
'COURSE, NOW AND THEN I GET SLOPPY AND THE MUNCHERS CLOSE IN.
ONLY HAPPENS AFTER I'VE HAD A FEW.
PRICE I PAY FOR MY ONE VICE, I GUESS.

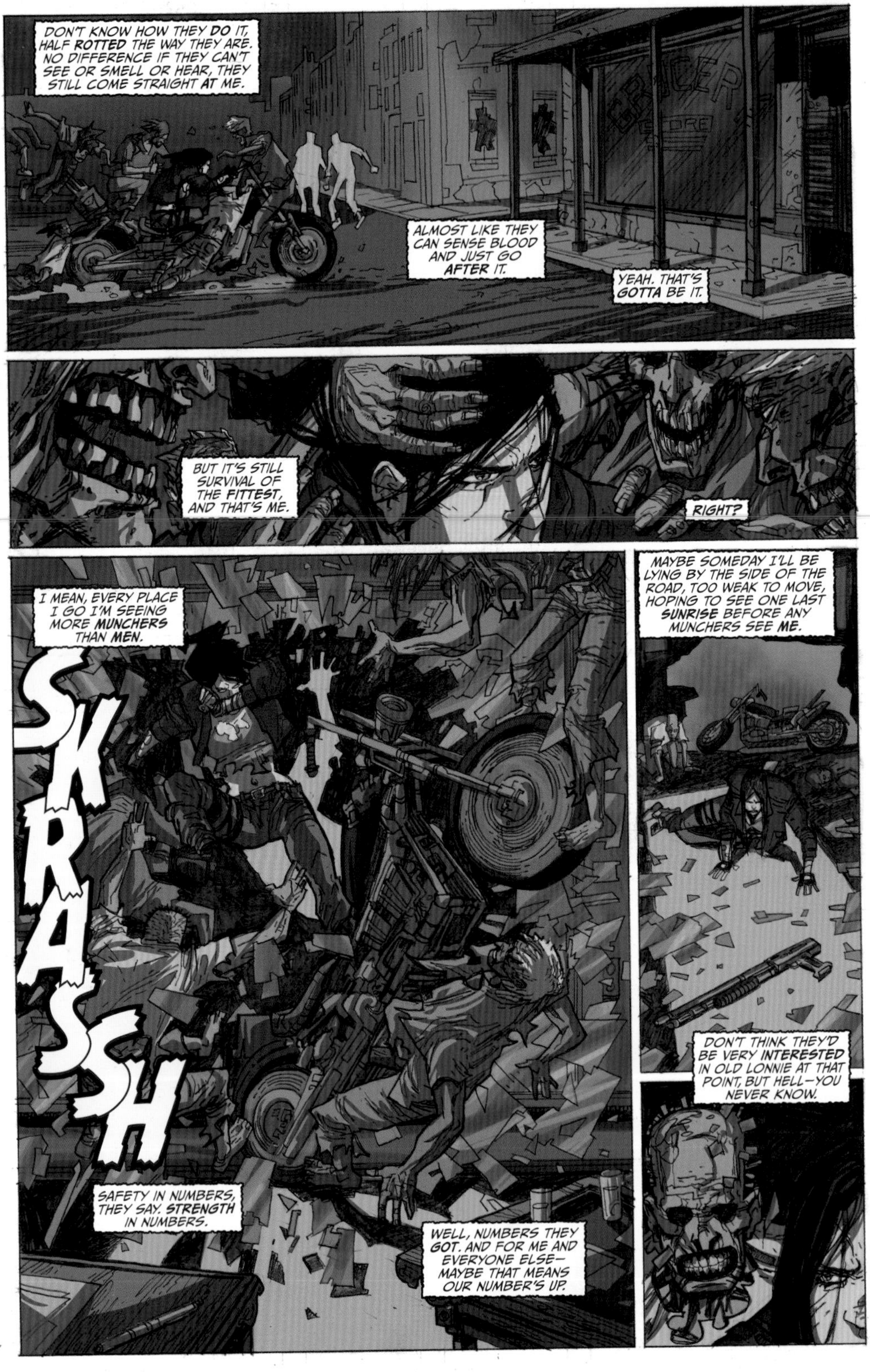

DON'T KNOW HOW THEY DO IT, HALF ROTTED THE WAY THEY ARE. NO DIFFERENCE IF THEY CAN'T SEE OR SMELL OR HEAR, THEY STILL COME STRAIGHT AT ME.
ALMOST LIKE THEY CAN SENSE BLOOD AND JUST GO AFTER IT.
YEAH. THAT'S GOTTA BE IT.
BUT IT'S STILL SURVIVAL OF THE FITTEST, AND THAT'S ME.
RIGHT?
I MEAN, EVERY PLACE I GO I'M SEEING MORE MUNCHERS THAN MEN.
SKRASSH
SAFETY IN NUMBERS, THEY SAY. STRENGTH IN NUMBERS.
WELL, NUMBERS THEY GOT. AND FOR ME AND EVERYONE ELSE— MAYBE THAT MEANS OUR NUMBER'S UP.
MAYBE SOMEDAY I'LL BE LYING BY THE SIDE OF THE ROAD, TOO WEAK TO MOVE, HOPING TO SEE ONE LAST SUNRISE BEFORE ANY MUNCHERS SEE ME.
DON'T THINK THEY'D BE VERY INTERESTED IN OLD LONNIE AT THAT POINT, BUT HELL—YOU NEVER KNOW.

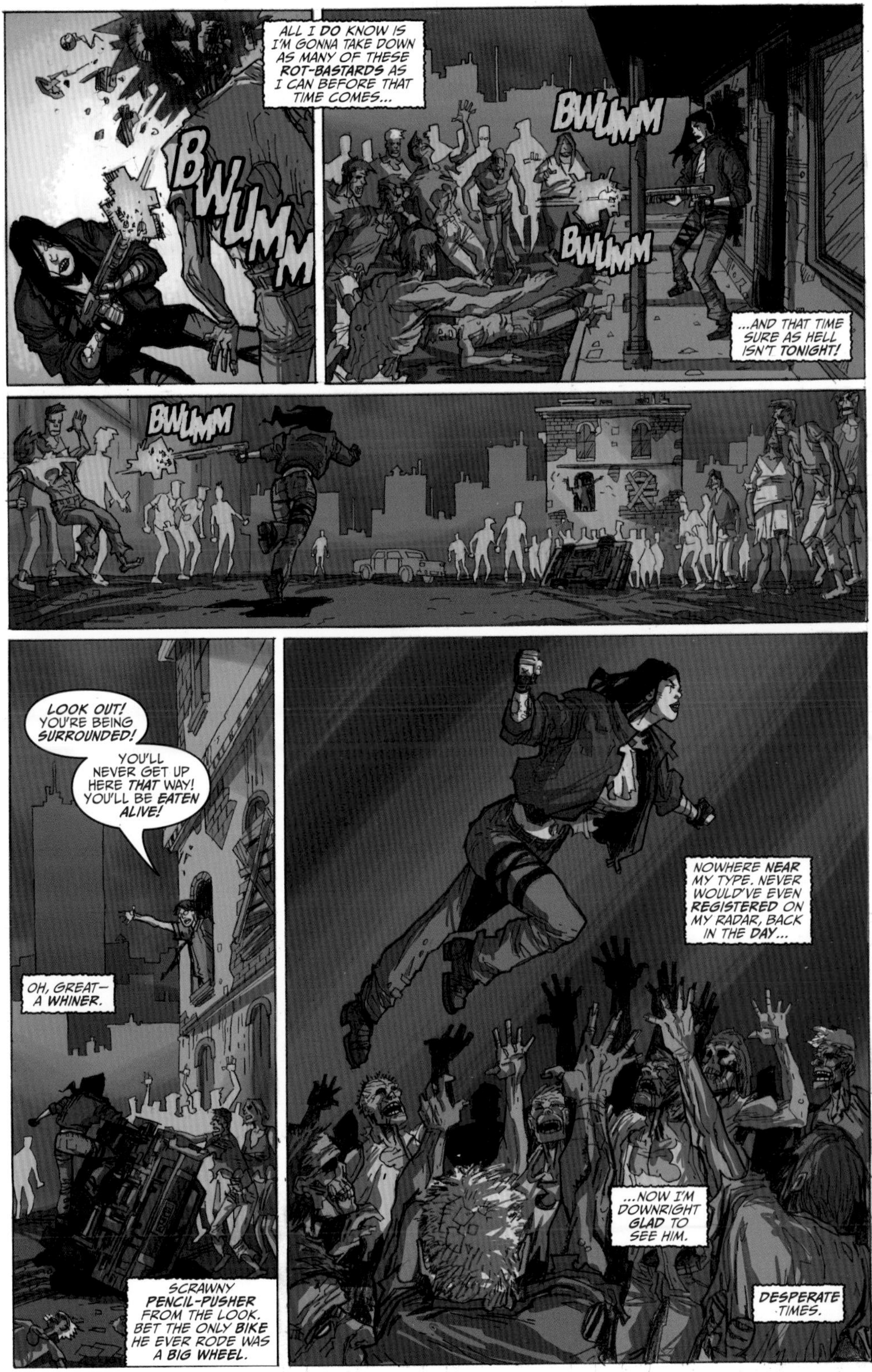
ALL I DO KNOW IS I'M GONNA TAKE DOWN AS MANY OF THESE ROT-BASTARDS AS I CAN BEFORE THAT TIME COMES...
BWUMM
BWUMM
BWUMM
...AND THAT TIME SURE AS HELL ISN'T TONIGHT!
BWUMM
LOOK OUT! YOU'RE BEING SURROUNDED!
YOU'LL NEVER GET UP HERE THAT WAY! YOU'LL BE EATEN ALIVE!
OH, GREAT— A WHINER.
SCRAWNY PENCIL-PUSHER FROM THE LOOK. BET THE ONLY BIKE HE EVER RODE WAS A BIG WHEEL.
NOWHERE NEAR MY TYPE. NEVER WOULD'VE EVEN REGISTERED ON MY RADAR, BACK IN THE DAY...
...NOW I'M DOWNRIGHT GLAD TO SEE HIM.
DESPERATE TIMES.

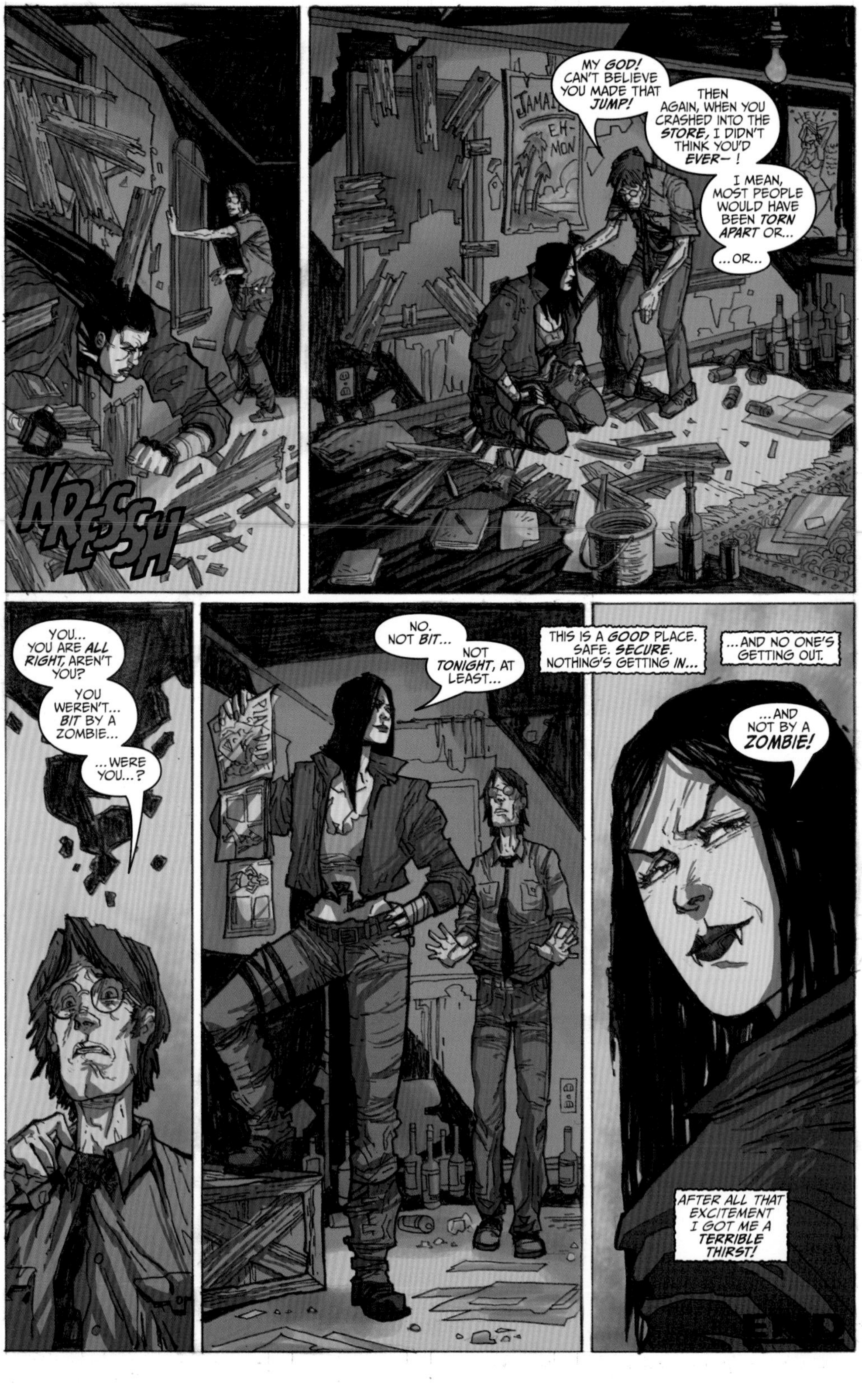
KRESSH
MY GOD! CAN'T BELIEVE YOU MADE THAT JUMP!
THEN AGAIN, WHEN YOU CRASHED INTO THE STORE, I DIDN'T THINK YOU'D EVER— !
I MEAN, MOST PEOPLE WOULD HAVE BEEN TORN APART OR...
...OR...
JAMAI
EH-MON
HEY!
YOU... YOU ARE ALL RIGHT, AREN'T YOU?
YOU WEREN'T... BIT BY A ZOMBIE...
...WERE YOU...?
NO. NOT BIT...
NOT TONIGHT, AT LEAST...
THIS IS A GOOD PLACE. SAFE. SECURE. NOTHING'S GETTING IN...
...AND NO ONE'S GETTING OUT.
...AND NOT BY A ZOMBIE!
AFTER ALL THAT EXCITEMENT I GOT ME A TERRIBLE THIRST!
END

5 STARS

WILLIAM MESSNER-LOEBS-SCRIPT JON REED-ART RENATO FACCINI-COLORS MARSHALL DILLON-LETTERS

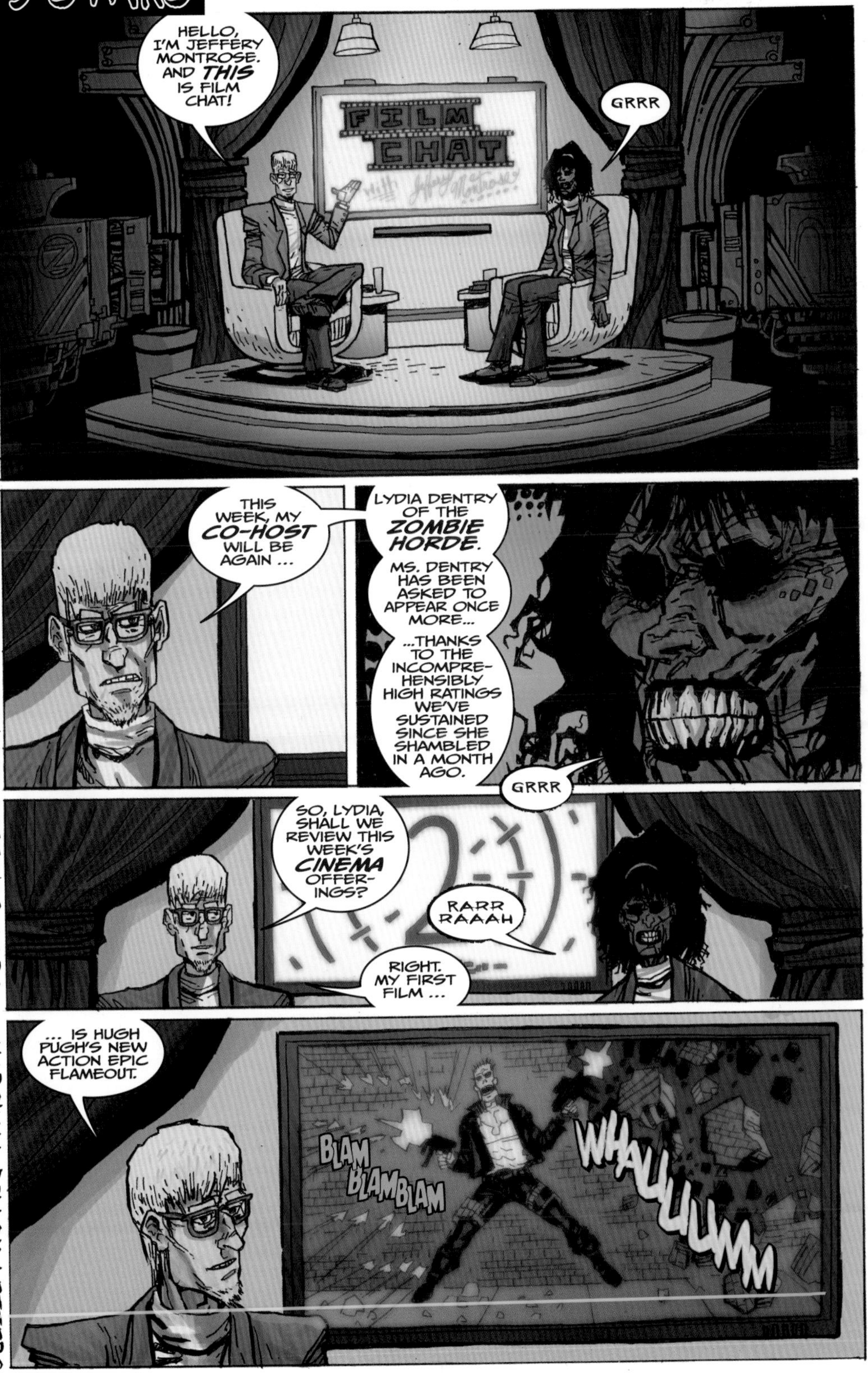
HELLO, I'M JEFFERY MONTROSE. AND THIS IS FILM CHAT!
FILM CHAT
GRRR
THIS WEEK, MY CO-HOST WILL BE AGAIN ...
LYDIA DENTRY OF THE ZOMBIE HORDE.
MS. DENTRY HAS BEEN ASKED TO APPEAR ONCE MORE...
...THANKS TO THE INCOMPREHENSIBLY HIGH RATINGS WE'VE SUSTAINED SINCE SHE SHAMBLED IN A MONTH AGO.
GRRR
SO, LYDIA, SHALL WE REVIEW THIS WEEK'S CINEMA OFFERINGS?
RARR RAAAH
RIGHT. MY FIRST FILM ...
... IS HUGH PUGH'S NEW ACTION EPIC FLAMEOUT.
BLAM BLAMBLAM
WHAUUUMM

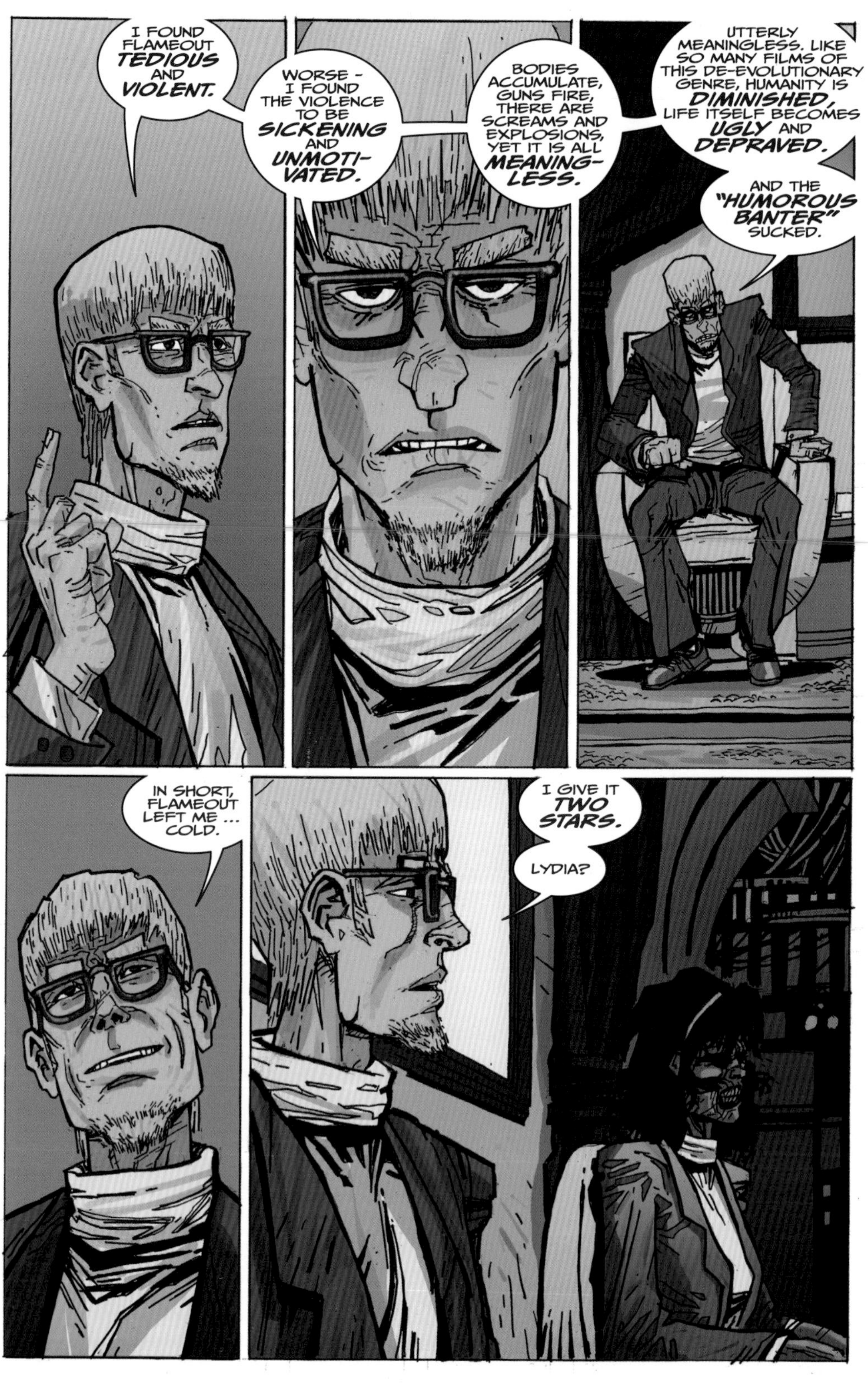
I FOUND FLAMEOUT TEDIOUS AND VIOLENT.
WORSE - I FOUND THE VIOLENCE TO BE SICKENING AND UNMOTI-VATED.
BODIES ACCUMULATE, GUNS FIRE, THERE ARE SCREAMS AND EXPLOSIONS, YET IT IS ALL MEANING-LESS.
UTTERLY MEANINGLESS. LIKE SO MANY FILMS OF THIS DE-EVOLUTIONARY GENRE, HUMANITY IS DIMINISHED, LIFE ITSELF BECOMES UGLY AND DEPRAVED.
AND THE "HUMOROUS BANTER" SUCKED.
IN SHORT, FLAMEOUT LEFT ME ... COLD.
I GIVE IT TWO STARS.
LYDIA?

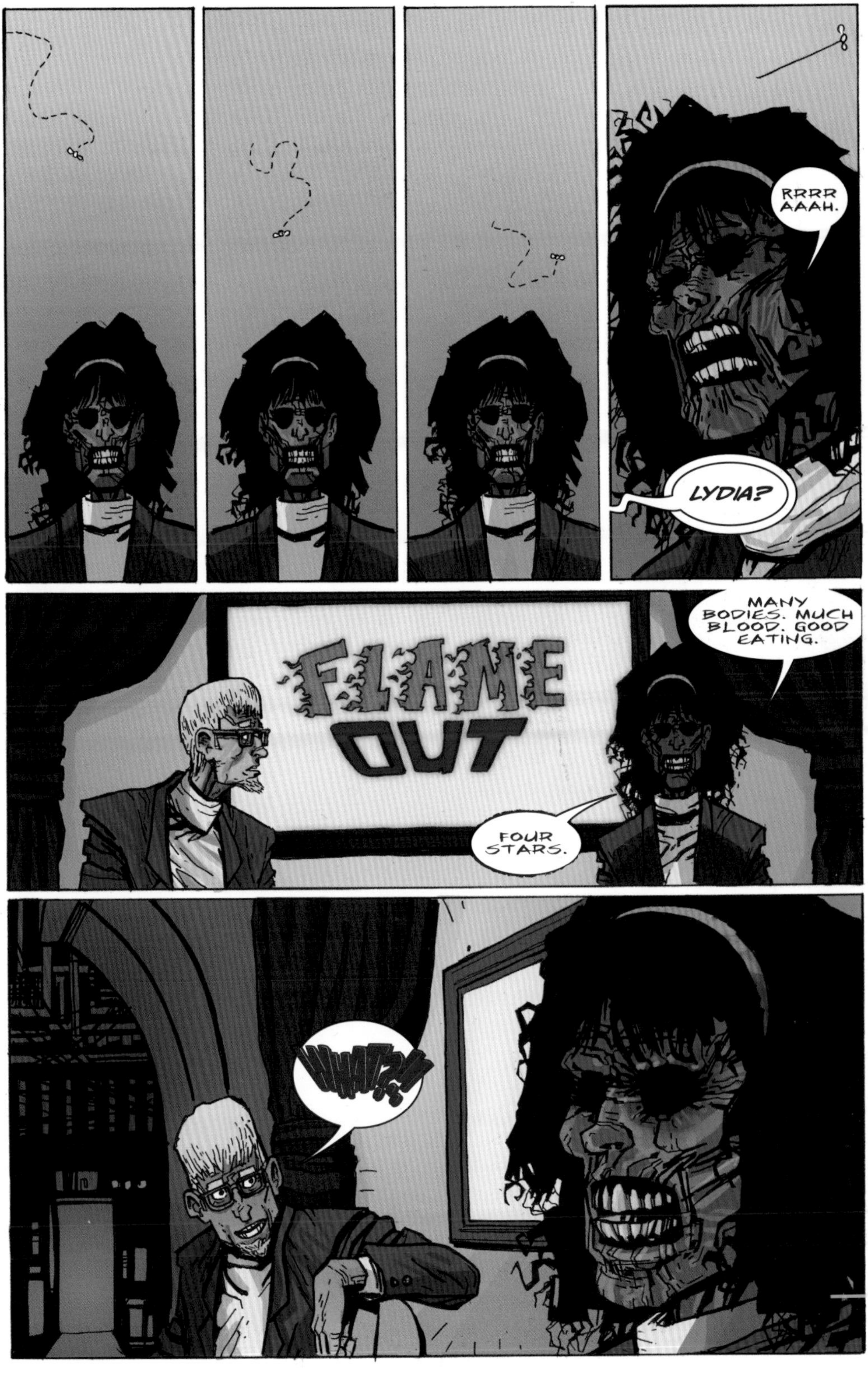
RRRR AAAH.
LYDIA?
FLAME OUT
MANY BODIES. MUCH BLOOD. GOOD EATING.
FOUR STARS.
WHAT?!!

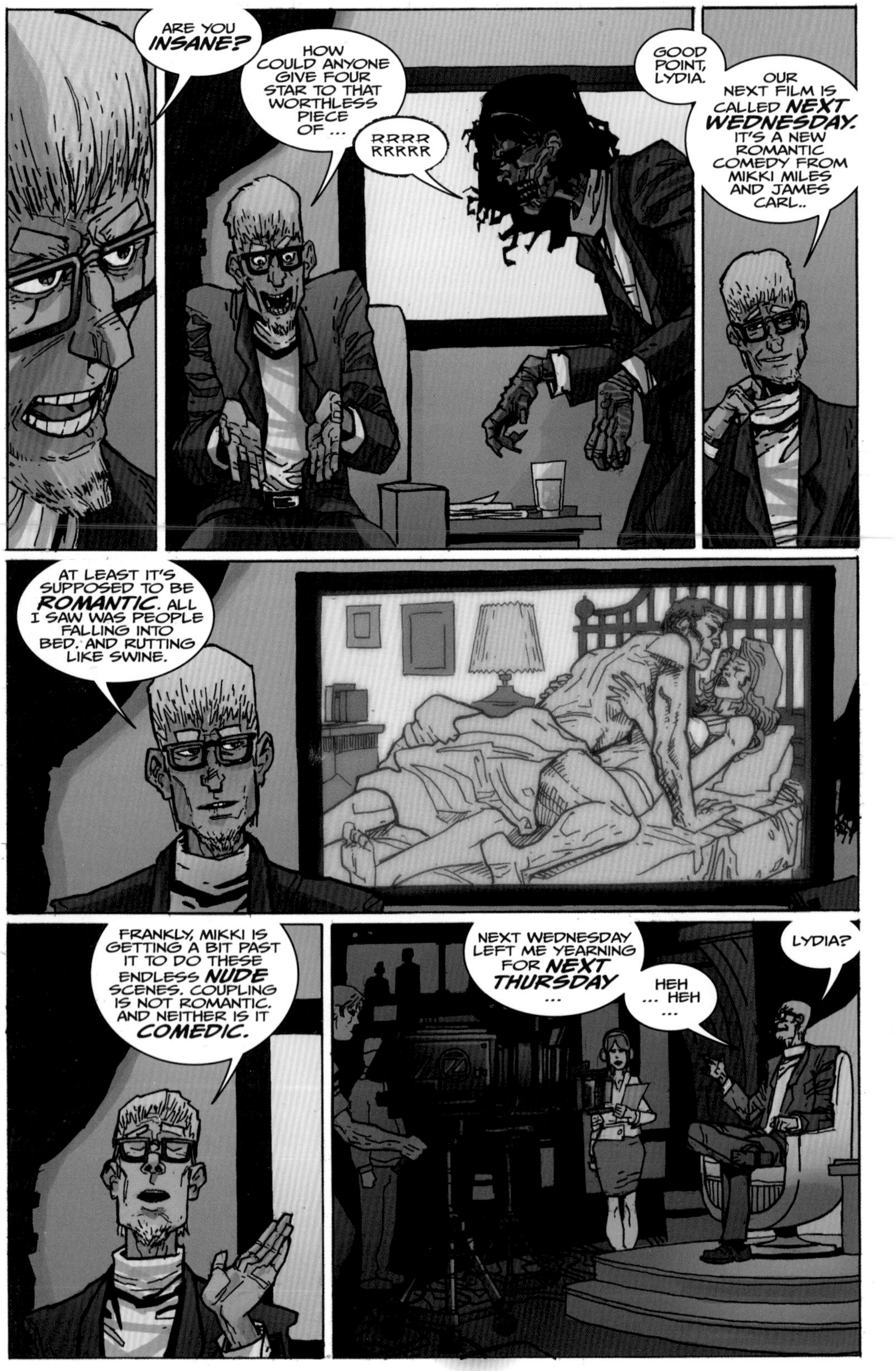
ARE YOU INSANE?
HOW COULD ANYONE GIVE FOUR STAR TO THAT WORTHLESS PIECE OF ...
RRRR RRRRR
GOOD POINT, LYDIA.
OUR NEXT FILM IS CALLED NEXT WEDNESDAY. IT'S A NEW ROMANTIC COMEDY FROM MIKKI MILES AND JAMES CARL..
AT LEAST IT'S SUPPOSED TO BE ROMANTIC. ALL I SAW WAS PEOPLE FALLING INTO BED. AND RUTTING LIKE SWINE.
FRANKLY, MIKKI IS GETTING A BIT PAST IT TO DO THESE ENDLESS NUDE SCENES. COUPLING IS NOT ROMANTIC. AND NEITHER IS IT COMEDIC.
NEXT WEDNESDAY LEFT ME YEARNING FOR NEXT THURSDAY ...
HEH ... HEH ...
LYDIA?

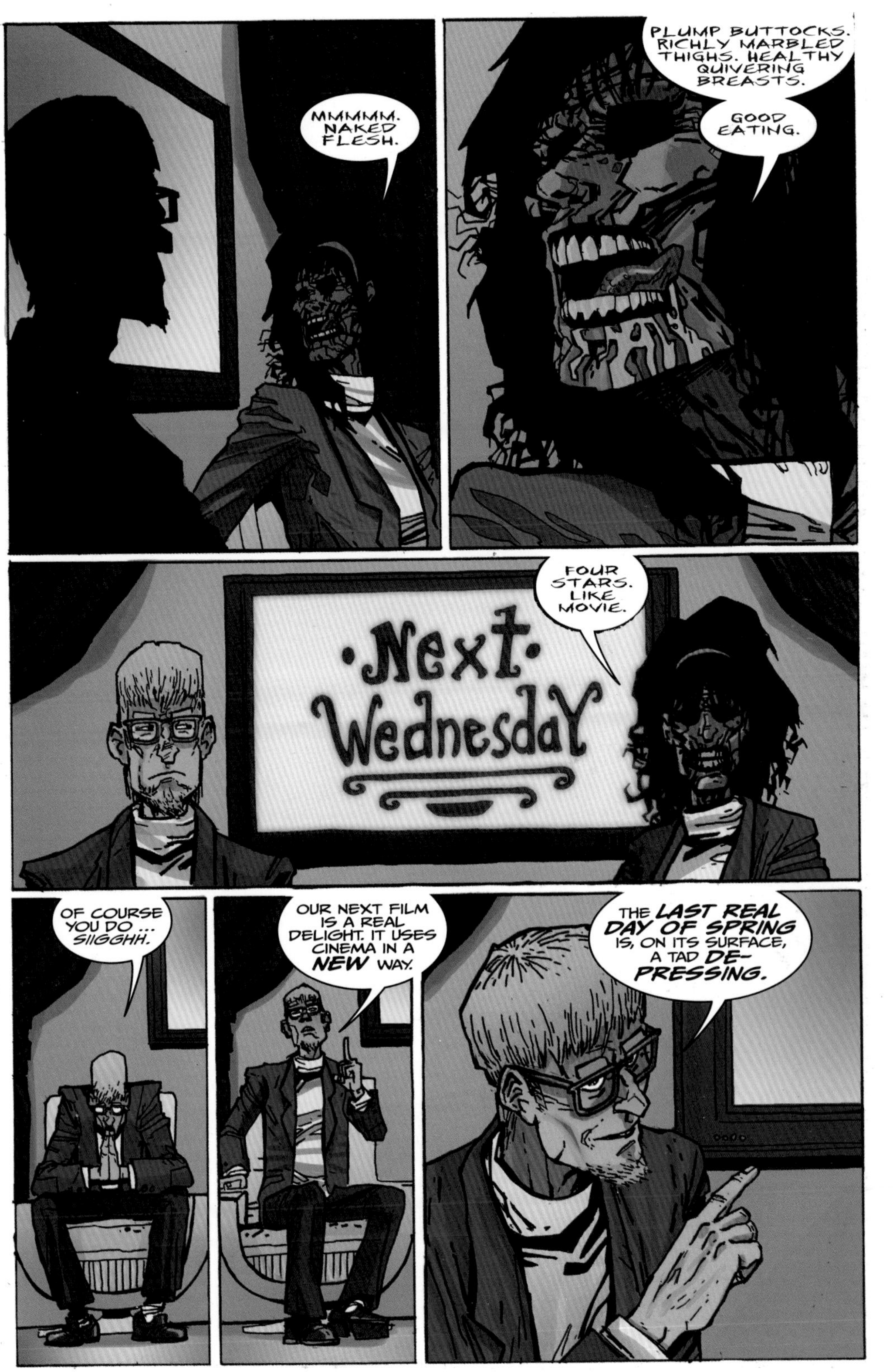

MMMMM. NAKED FLESH.
PLUMP BUTTOCKS. RICHLY MARBLED THIGHS. HEALTHY QUIVERING BREASTS.
GOOD EATING.
Next Wednesday
FOUR STARS. LIKE MOVIE.
OF COURSE YOU DO ... SIIGGHH.
OUR NEXT FILM IS A REAL DELIGHT. IT USES CINEMA IN A NEW WAY.
THE LAST REAL DAY OF SPRING IS, ON ITS SURFACE, A TAD DE-PRESSING.

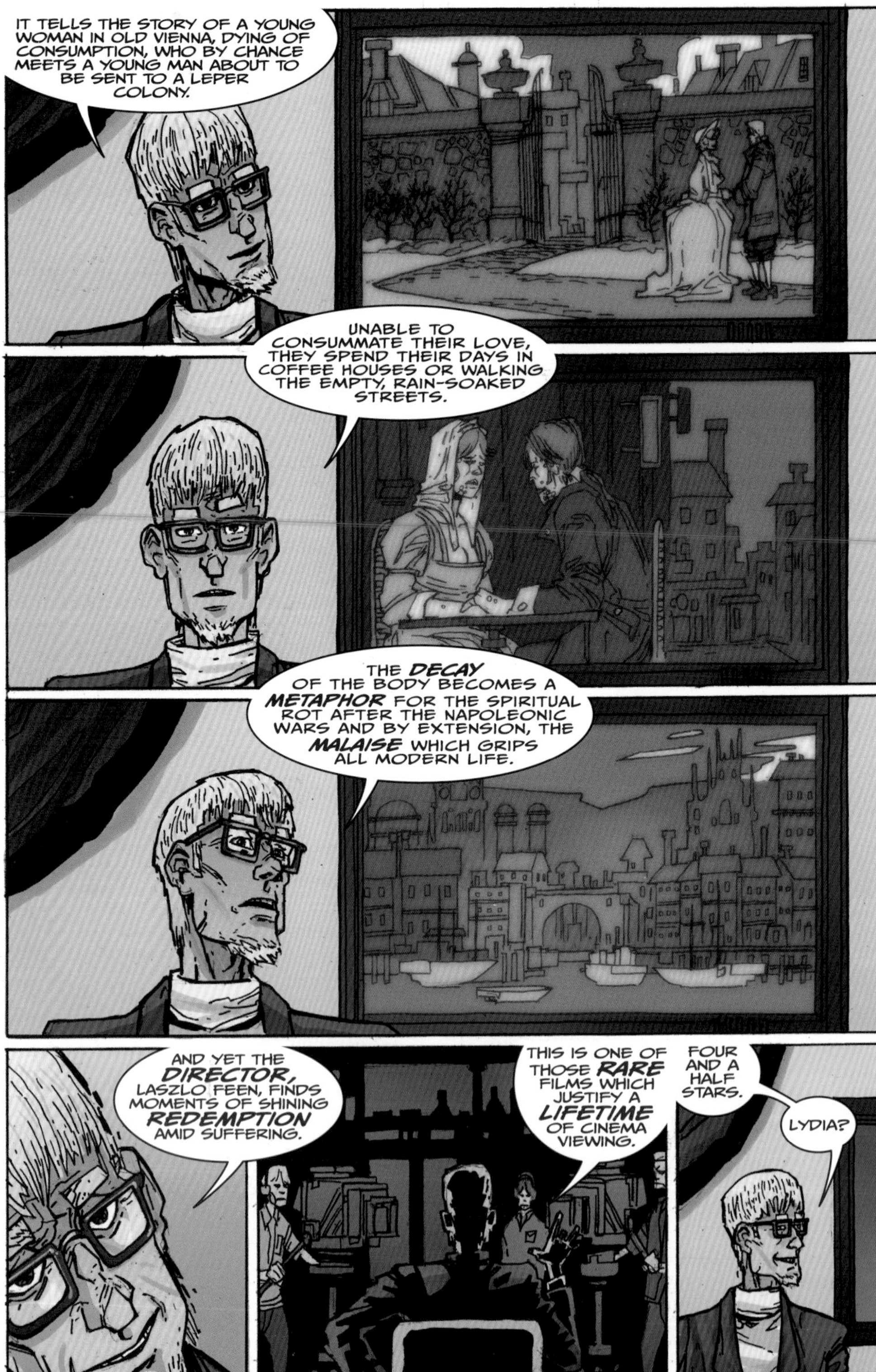
IT TELLS THE STORY OF A YOUNG WOMAN IN OLD VIENNA, DYING OF CONSUMPTION, WHO BY CHANCE MEETS A YOUNG MAN ABOUT TO BE SENT TO A LEPER COLONY.
UNABLE TO CONSUMMATE THEIR LOVE, THEY SPEND THEIR DAYS IN COFFEE HOUSES OR WALKING THE EMPTY, RAIN-SOAKED STREETS.
THE DECAY OF THE BODY BECOMES A METAPHOR FOR THE SPIRITUAL ROT AFTER THE NAPOLEONIC WARS AND BY EXTENSION, THE MALAISE WHICH GRIPS ALL MODERN LIFE.
AND YET THE DIRECTOR, LASZLO FEEN, FINDS MOMENTS OF SHINING REDEMPTION AMID SUFFERING.
THIS IS ONE OF THOSE RARE FILMS WHICH JUSTIFY A LIFETIME OF CINEMA VIEWING.
FOUR AND A HALF STARS.
LYDIA?

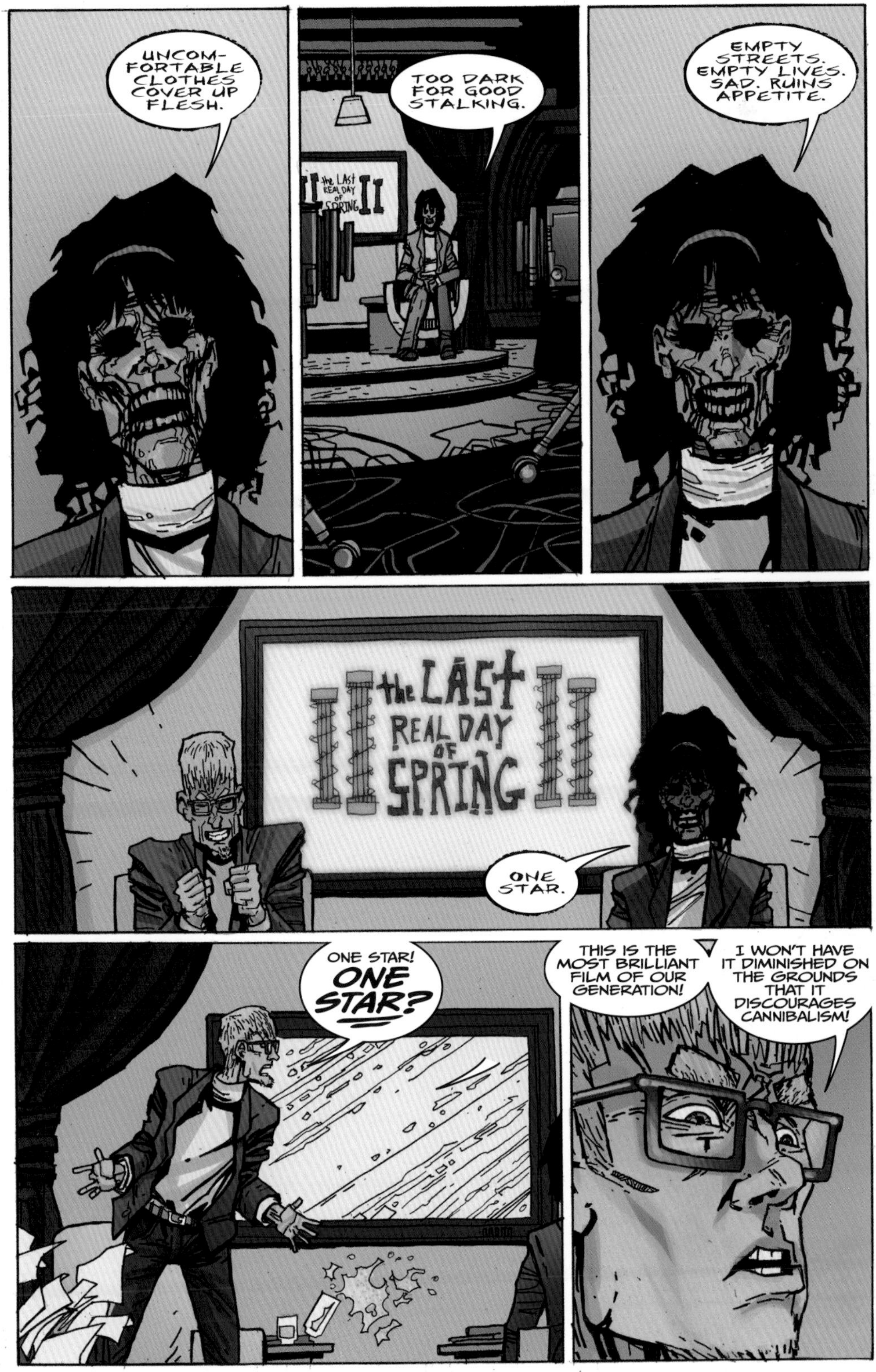
UNCOM-FORTABLE CLOTHES COVER UP FLESH.
TOO DARK FOR GOOD STALKING.
EMPTY STREETS. EMPTY LIVES. SAD. RUINS APPETITE.
the LAST REAL DAY OF SPRING
ONE STAR.
ONE STAR! ONE STAR?
THIS IS THE MOST BRILLIANT FILM OF OUR GENERATION!
I WON'T HAVE IT DIMINISHED ON THE GROUNDS THAT IT DISCOURAGES CANNIBALISM!

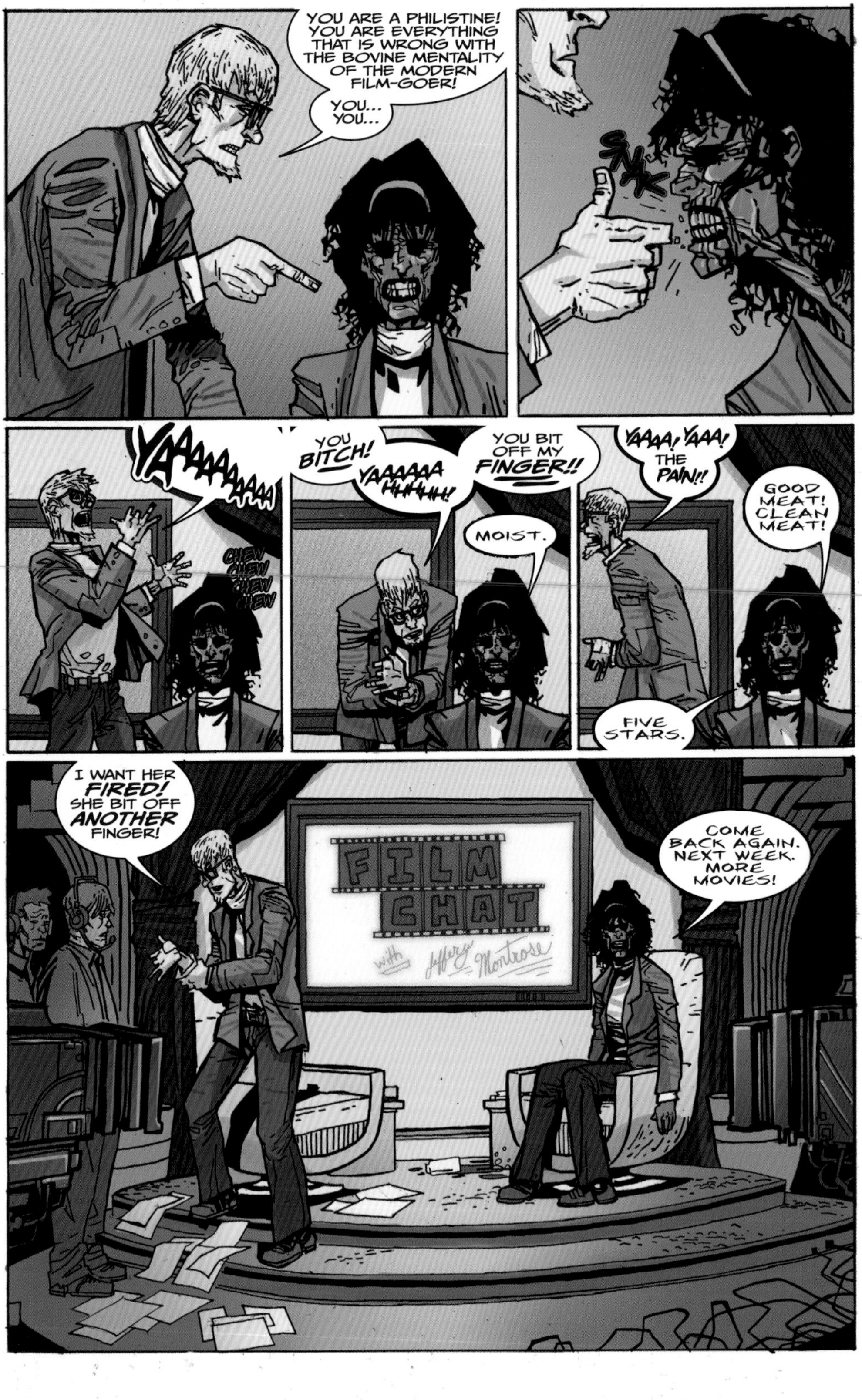
YOU ARE A PHILISTINE! YOU ARE EVERYTHING THAT IS WRONG WITH THE BOVINE MENTALITY OF THE MODERN FILM-GOER!
YOU... YOU...
SNAK
YAAAAAAAAAA
CHEW CHEW CHEW CHEW
YOU BITCH!
YAAAAAA HHHHH!
YOU BIT OFF MY FINGER!!
MOIST.
YAAAA! YAAA! THE PAIN!!
GOOD MEAT! CLEAN MEAT!
FIVE STARS.
I WANT HER FIRED! SHE BIT OFF ANOTHER FINGER!
FILM CHAT
with Jeffery Montrose
COME BACK AGAIN. NEXT WEEK. MORE MOVIES!

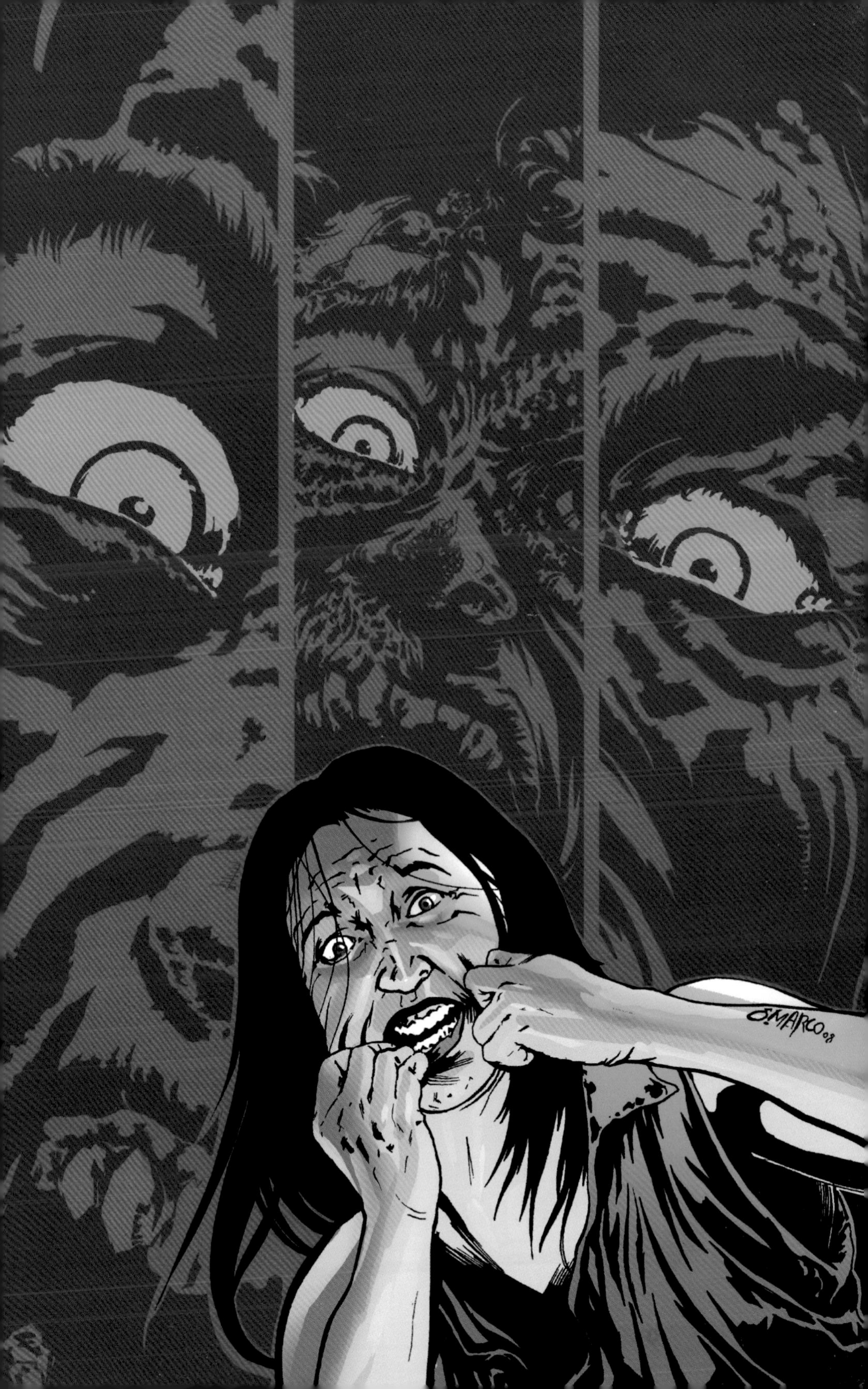

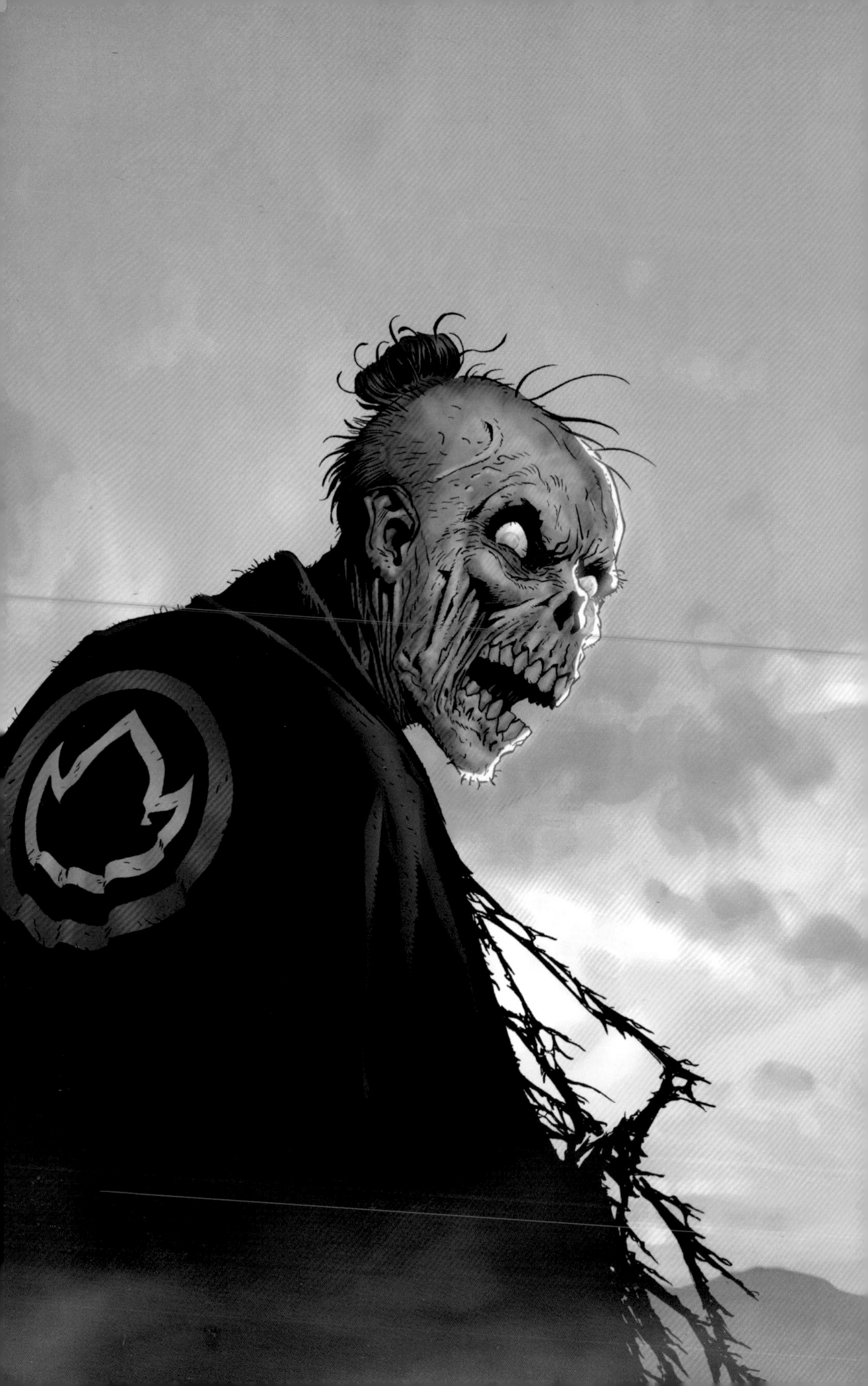

ZAAMBI

Story: TERRY MORGAN
and CHRIS MORGAN

Part 1 Art: GABRIEL HARDMAN
Part 2 Art: MINCK OOSTERVEER
Part 3 Art: JASON HO

Lettering: MARSHALL DILLON
Coloring: CRIS PETER

ZAAMBI

BY CHRIS MORGAN & TERRY MORGAN

PART I:
IN WHICH I BECOME A MAN.

YEAR OF OUR SORROWS 103

ART: GABRIEL HARDMAN

I KILLED THREE ZAAMBI TODAY BEFORE MY FATHER RETURNED TO HONCHU VILLAGE.

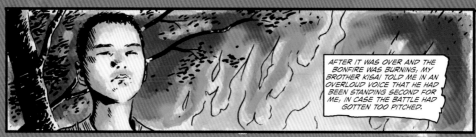

AFTER IT WAS OVER AND THE BONFIRE WAS BURNING, MY BROTHER KISAI TOLD ME IN AN OVERLOUD VOICE THAT HE HAD BEEN STANDING SECOND FOR ME, IN CASE THE BATTLE HAD GOTTEN TOO PITCHED.

UPON RETURNING HOME, KISAI WAITED NO MORE THAN FIVE SECONDS TO REGALE MOTHER AND HIROKO WITH OUR ADVENTURE, THE TELLING OF WHICH UPSET THEM NO LITTLE AMOUNT.

TODAY I, TOSHIRO, HAD PROVED MYSELF A MAN. MY FATHER WOULD HAVE TO RECOGNIZE ME AS SUCH WHEN I HANDED HIM MY KILL BAG WITH THE THREE HEADS IN IT.

IT HAD BEEN A VERY GOOD DAY.

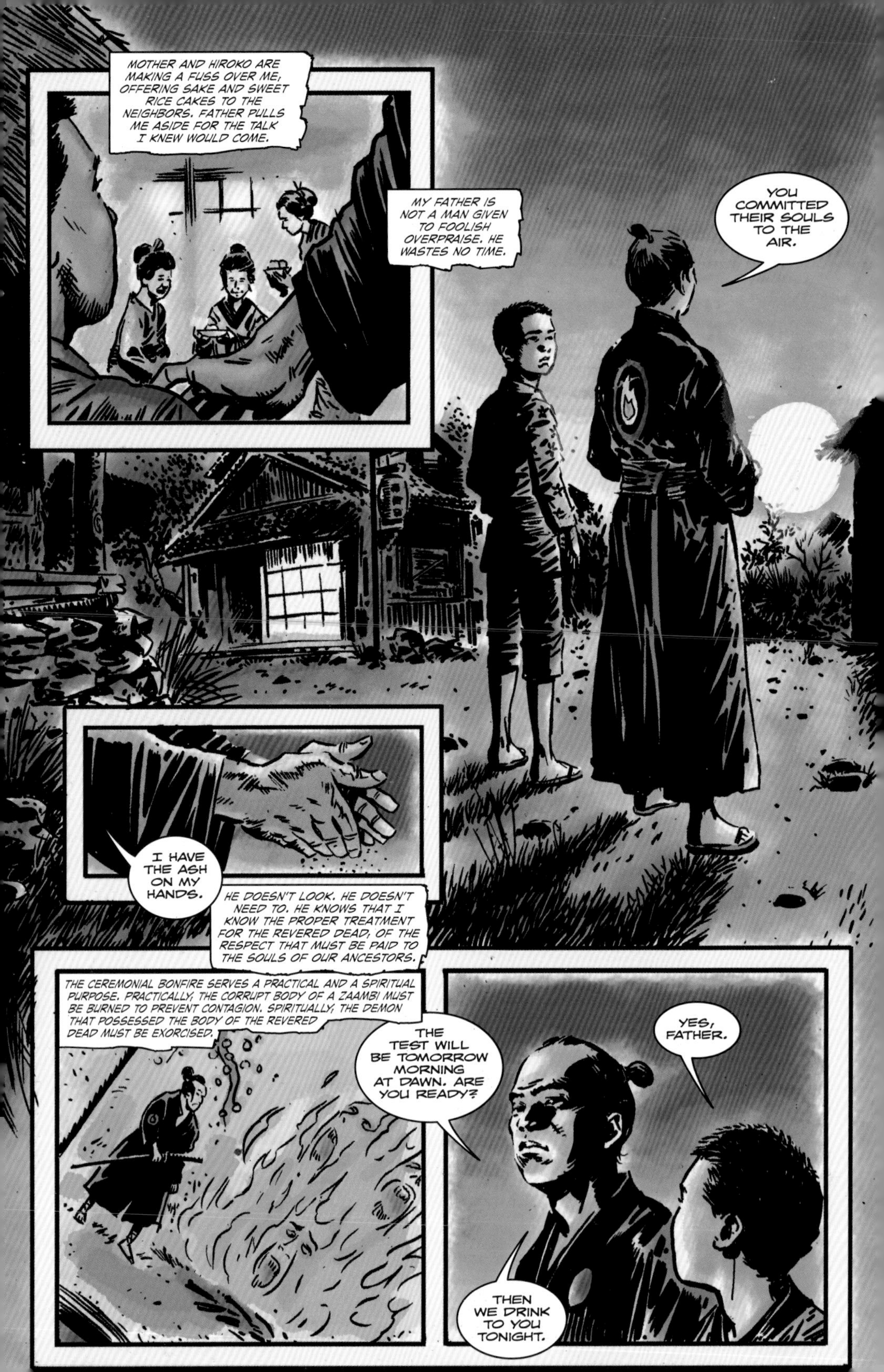
MOTHER AND HIROKO ARE MAKING A FUSS OVER ME, OFFERING SAKE AND SWEET RICE CAKES TO THE NEIGHBORS. FATHER PULLS ME ASIDE FOR THE TALK I KNEW WOULD COME.
MY FATHER IS NOT A MAN GIVEN TO FOOLISH OVERPRAISE. HE WASTES NO TIME.
YOU COMMITTED THEIR SOULS TO THE AIR.
I HAVE THE ASH ON MY HANDS.
HE DOESN'T LOOK. HE DOESN'T NEED TO. HE KNOWS THAT I KNOW THE PROPER TREATMENT FOR THE REVERED DEAD, OF THE RESPECT THAT MUST BE PAID TO THE SOULS OF OUR ANCESTORS.
THE CEREMONIAL BONFIRE SERVES A PRACTICAL AND A SPIRITUAL PURPOSE. PRACTICALLY, THE CORRUPT BODY OF A ZAAMBI MUST BE BURNED TO PREVENT CONTAGION. SPIRITUALLY, THE DEMON THAT POSSESSED THE BODY OF THE REVERED DEAD MUST BE EXORCISED.
THE TEST WILL BE TOMORROW MORNING AT DAWN. ARE YOU READY?
YES, FATHER.
THEN WE DRINK TO YOU TONIGHT.

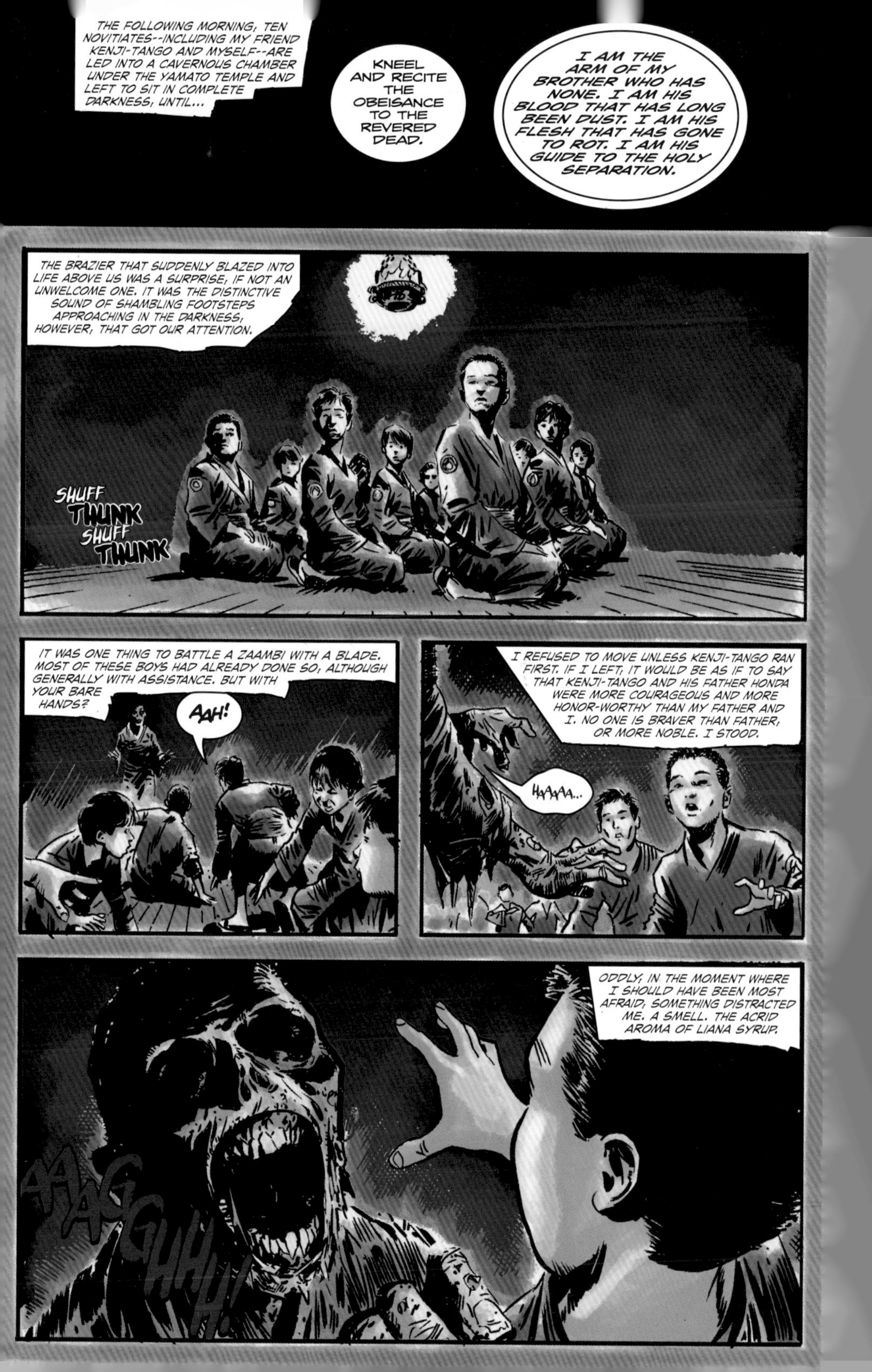
THE FOLLOWING MORNING, TEN NOVITIATES--INCLUDING MY FRIEND KENJI-TANGO AND MYSELF--ARE LED INTO A CAVERNOUS CHAMBER UNDER THE YAMATO TEMPLE AND LEFT TO SIT IN COMPLETE DARKNESS, UNTIL...
KNEEL AND RECITE THE OBEISANCE TO THE REVERED DEAD.
I AM THE ARM OF MY BROTHER WHO HAS NONE. I AM HIS BLOOD THAT HAS LONG BEEN DUST. I AM HIS FLESH THAT HAS GONE TO ROT. I AM HIS GUIDE TO THE HOLY SEPARATION.
THE BRAZIER THAT SUDDENLY BLAZED INTO LIFE ABOVE US WAS A SURPRISE, IF NOT AN UNWELCOME ONE. IT WAS THE DISTINCTIVE SOUND OF SHAMBLING FOOTSTEPS APPROACHING IN THE DARKNESS, HOWEVER, THAT GOT OUR ATTENTION.
SHUFF THUNK SHUFF THUNK
IT WAS ONE THING TO BATTLE A ZAAMBI WITH A BLADE. MOST OF THESE BOYS HAD ALREADY DONE SO, ALTHOUGH GENERALLY WITH ASSISTANCE. BUT WITH YOUR BARE HANDS?
AAH!
I REFUSED TO MOVE UNLESS KENJI-TANGO RAN FIRST. IF I LEFT, IT WOULD BE AS IF TO SAY THAT KENJI-TANGO AND HIS FATHER HONDA WERE MORE COURAGEOUS AND MORE HONOR-WORTHY THAN MY FATHER AND I. NO ONE IS BRAVER THAN FATHER, OR MORE NOBLE. I STOOD.
HAAAAA...
ODDLY, IN THE MOMENT WHERE I SHOULD HAVE BEEN MOST AFRAID, SOMETHING DISTRACTED ME. A SMELL. THE ACRID AROMA OF LIANA SYRUP.
AAAGGHHH!

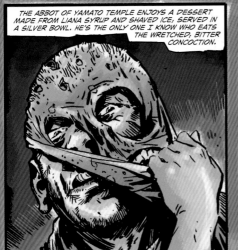

THE ABBOT OF YAMATO TEMPLE ENJOYS A DESSERT MADE FROM LIANA SYRUP AND SHAVED ICE, SERVED IN A SILVER BOWL. HE'S THE ONLY ONE I KNOW WHO EATS THE WRETCHED, BITTER CONCOCTION.

ENOUGH! YOU IN THE CORNERS DARE NOT LAUGH! LAUGHTER IS A PRIVILEGE FOR THE COURAGEOUS *ONLY*!

FEAR IS NOT A QUALITY WITH WHICH PATROL MEMBERS REGARD ZAAMBI.

WE FEEL ONLY ANGER FOR THE VIOLATION BY THE POSSESSING DEMON,

AND SORROW FOR OUR BRETHREN WHOSE SOULS AND BODIES ARE BEING RAVAGED.

YOU ARE NOW TO UNDERGO THE EXAMINATION FOR ENTRANCE INTO THE HOLY ANCESTOR GUILD. YOU ARE EACH ALLOWED TWO BOKKEN.

DEFEND YOURSELVES FROM THE GUILD MEMBERS WHO WILL ATTACK YOU. DO NOT HOLD BACK; THEY ARE WELL-PROTECTED.

THEY WILL ATTEMPT TO DRAG YOU FROM THIS ROOM.

IF THEY DO, YOU ARE DISQUALIFIED. USE ANY MEANS YOU MUST TO STAY IN THIS ROOM.

YOU WILL BE JUDGED ON TECHNIQUE AS WELL AS COURAGE. THAT IS ALL. GOOD LUCK.

WITH THAT, ABBOT YAMATO WALKED OUT OF OUR CIRCLE OF LIGHT AND INTO THE BLACKNESS.

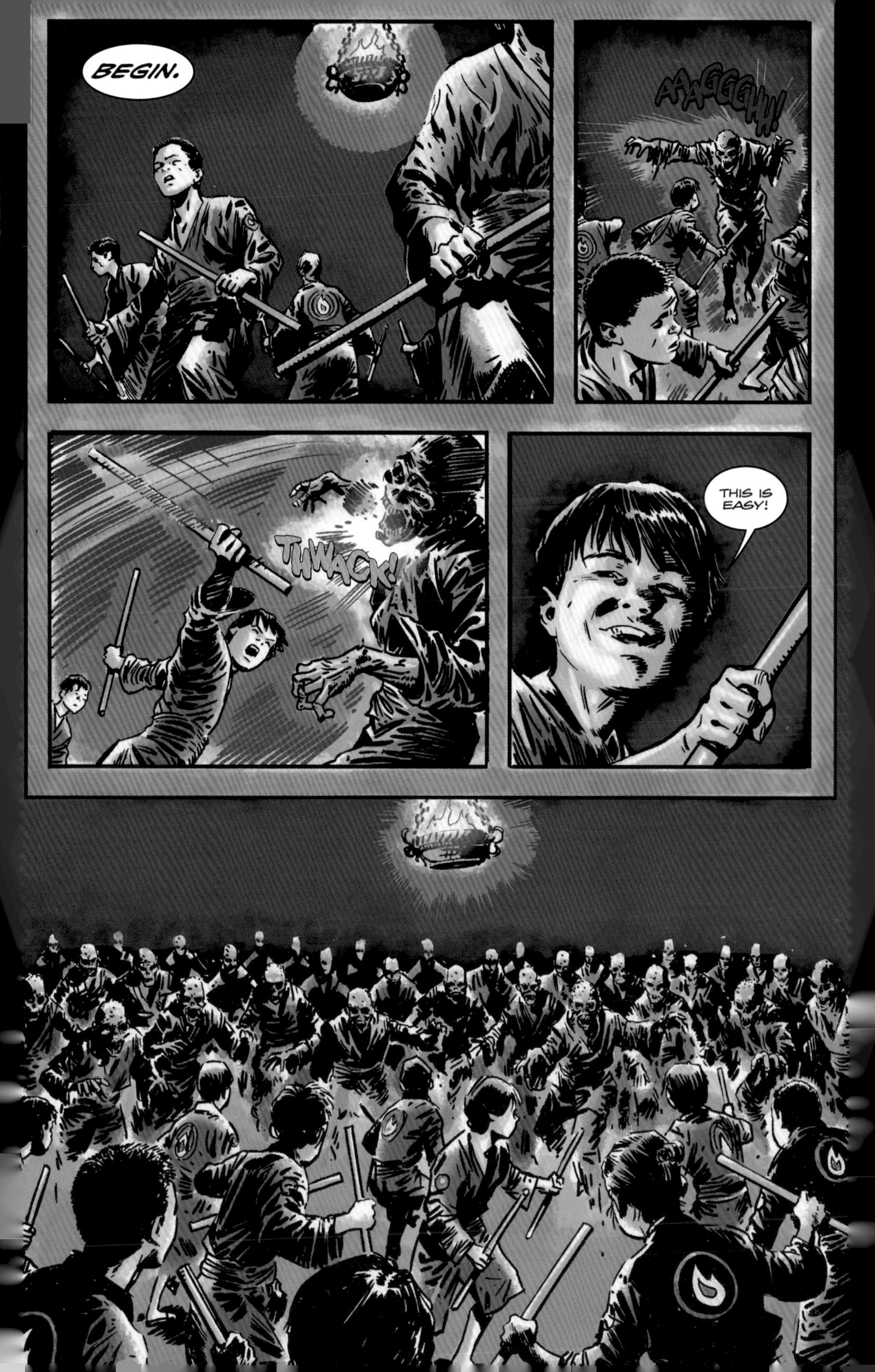
BEGIN.
AAAGGGHH!
THWACK!
THIS IS EASY!

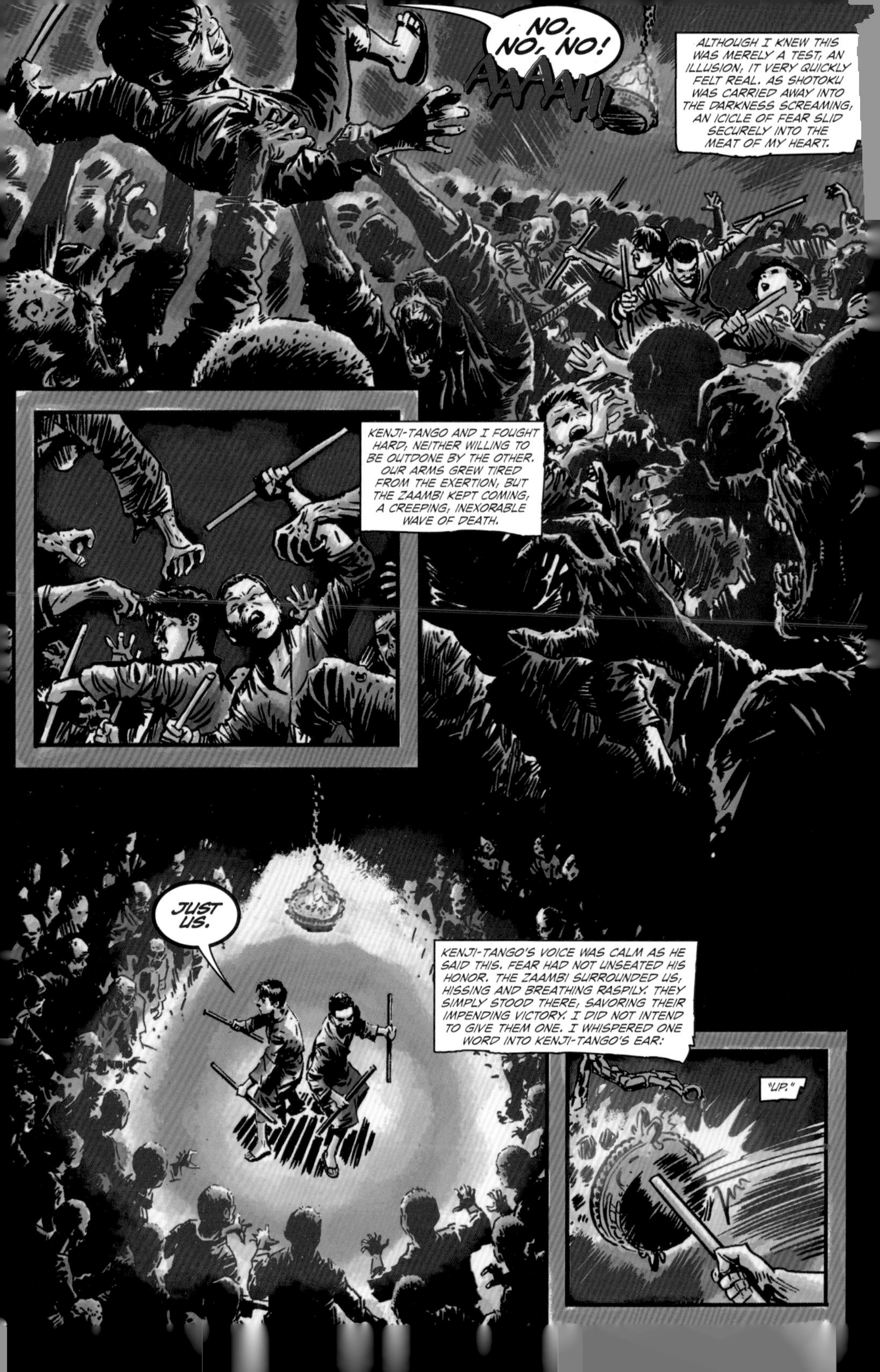
NO, NO, NO!
AAAAAH!
ALTHOUGH I KNEW THIS WAS MERELY A TEST, AN ILLUSION, IT VERY QUICKLY FELT REAL. AS SHOTOKU WAS CARRIED AWAY INTO THE DARKNESS SCREAMING, AN ICICLE OF FEAR SLID SECURELY INTO THE MEAT OF MY HEART.
KENJI-TANGO AND I FOUGHT HARD, NEITHER WILLING TO BE OUTDONE BY THE OTHER. OUR ARMS GREW TIRED FROM THE EXERTION, BUT THE ZAAMBI KEPT COMING, A CREEPING, INEXORABLE WAVE OF DEATH.
JUST US.
KENJI-TANGO'S VOICE WAS CALM AS HE SAID THIS. FEAR HAD NOT UNSEATED HIS HONOR. THE ZAAMBI SURROUNDED US, HISSING AND BREATHING RASPILY. THEY SIMPLY STOOD THERE, SAVORING THEIR IMPENDING VICTORY. I DID NOT INTEND TO GIVE THEM ONE. I WHISPERED ONE WORD INTO KENJI-TANGO'S EAR:
"UP."

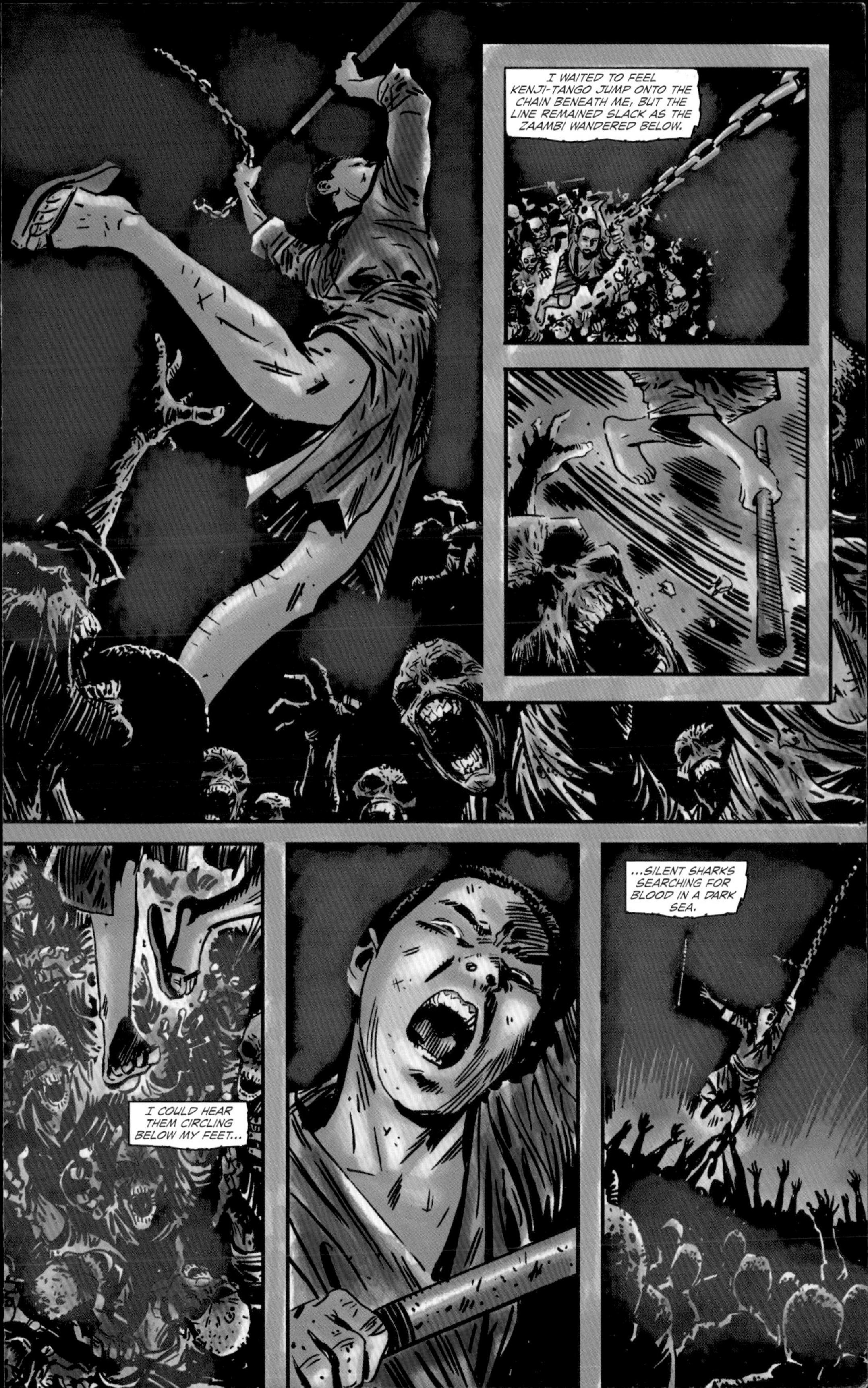
I WAITED TO FEEL KENJI-TANGO JUMP ONTO THE CHAIN BENEATH ME, BUT THE LINE REMAINED SLACK AS THE ZAAMBI WANDERED BELOW.
I COULD HEAR THEM CIRCLING BELOW MY FEET...
...SILENT SHARKS SEARCHING FOR BLOOD IN A DARK SEA.

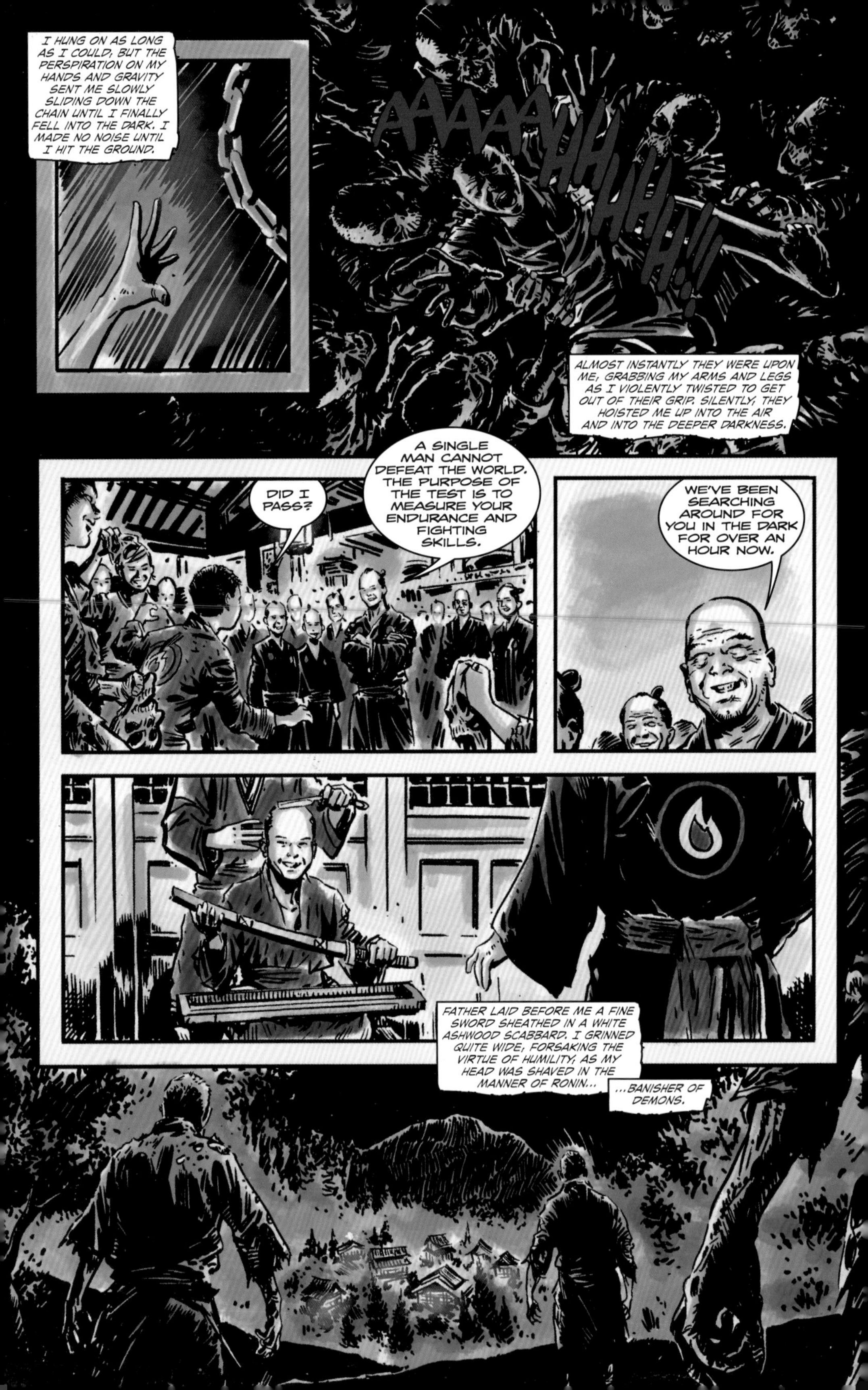
I HUNG ON AS LONG AS I COULD, BUT THE PERSPIRATION ON MY HANDS AND GRAVITY SENT ME SLOWLY SLIDING DOWN THE CHAIN UNTIL I FINALLY FELL INTO THE DARK. I MADE NO NOISE UNTIL I HIT THE GROUND.
AAAAAAHHHHHHHH!!!
ALMOST INSTANTLY THEY WERE UPON ME, GRABBING MY ARMS AND LEGS AS I VIOLENTLY TWISTED TO GET OUT OF THEIR GRIP. SILENTLY, THEY HOISTED ME UP INTO THE AIR AND INTO THE DEEPER DARKNESS.
DID I PASS?
A SINGLE MAN CANNOT DEFEAT THE WORLD. THE PURPOSE OF THE TEST IS TO MEASURE YOUR ENDURANCE AND FIGHTING SKILLS.
WE'VE BEEN SEARCHING AROUND FOR YOU IN THE DARK FOR OVER AN HOUR NOW.
FATHER LAID BEFORE ME A FINE SWORD SHEATHED IN A WHITE ASHWOOD SCABBARD. I GRINNED QUITE WIDE, FORSAKING THE VIRTUE OF HUMILITY, AS MY HEAD WAS SHAVED IN THE MANNER OF RONIN...
...BANISHER OF DEMONS.

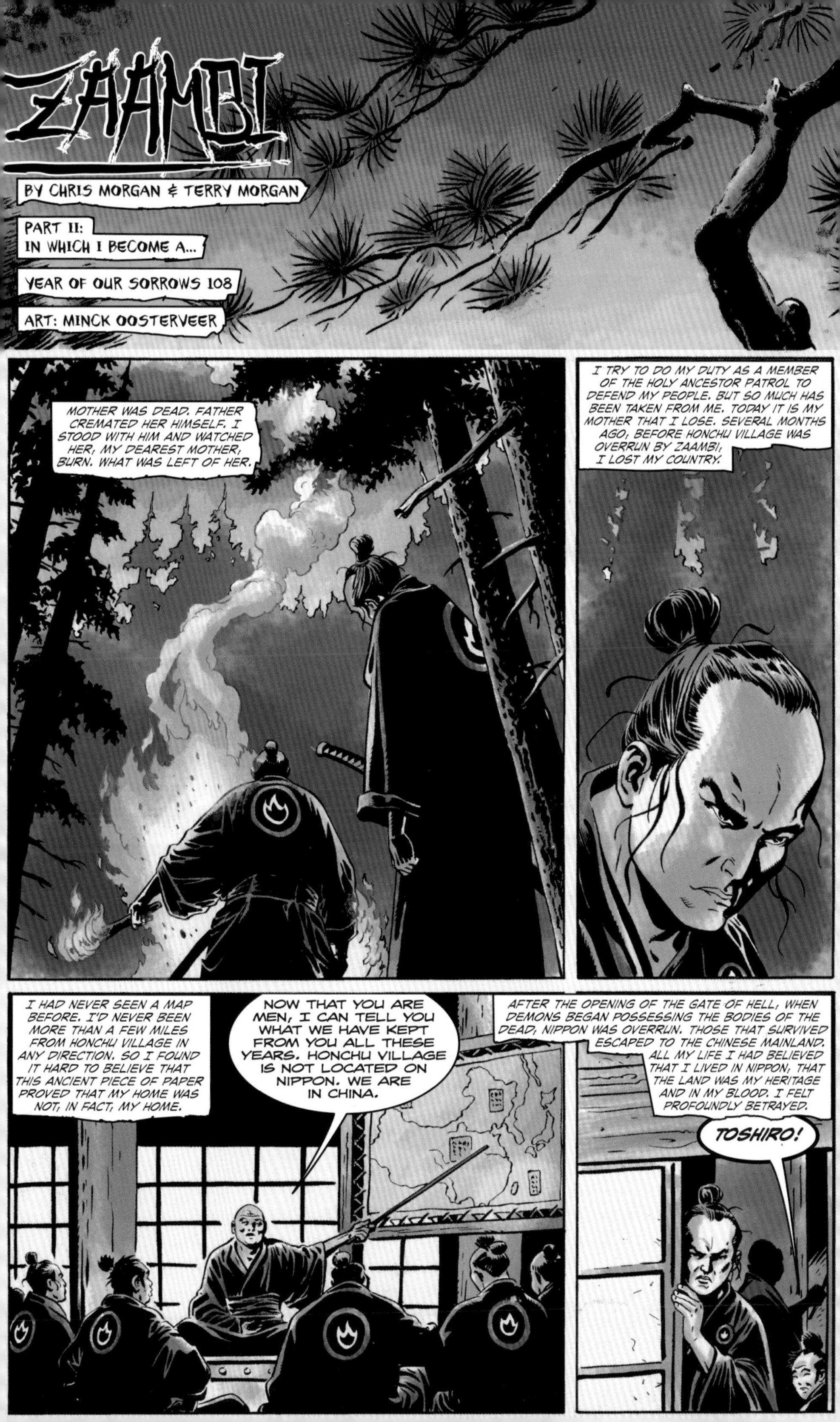
ZAAMBI
BY CHRIS MORGAN & TERRY MORGAN
PART II:
IN WHICH I BECOME A...
YEAR OF OUR SORROWS 108
ART: MINCK OOSTERVEER
MOTHER WAS DEAD. FATHER CREMATED HER HIMSELF. I STOOD WITH HIM AND WATCHED HER, MY DEAREST MOTHER, BURN. WHAT WAS LEFT OF HER.
I TRY TO DO MY DUTY AS A MEMBER OF THE HOLY ANCESTOR PATROL TO DEFEND MY PEOPLE. BUT SO MUCH HAS BEEN TAKEN FROM ME. TODAY IT IS MY MOTHER THAT I LOSE. SEVERAL MONTHS AGO, BEFORE HONCHU VILLAGE WAS OVERRUN BY ZAAMBI, I LOST MY COUNTRY.
I HAD NEVER SEEN A MAP BEFORE. I'D NEVER BEEN MORE THAN A FEW MILES FROM HONCHU VILLAGE IN ANY DIRECTION. SO I FOUND IT HARD TO BELIEVE THAT THIS ANCIENT PIECE OF PAPER PROVED THAT MY HOME WAS NOT, IN FACT, MY HOME.
NOW THAT YOU ARE MEN, I CAN TELL YOU WHAT WE HAVE KEPT FROM YOU ALL THESE YEARS. HONCHU VILLAGE IS NOT LOCATED ON NIPPON. WE ARE IN CHINA.
AFTER THE OPENING OF THE GATE OF HELL, WHEN DEMONS BEGAN POSSESSING THE BODIES OF THE DEAD, NIPPON WAS OVERRUN. THOSE THAT SURVIVED ESCAPED TO THE CHINESE MAINLAND.
ALL MY LIFE I HAD BELIEVED THAT I LIVED IN NIPPON, THAT THE LAND WAS MY HERITAGE AND IN MY BLOOD. I FELT PROFOUNDLY BETRAYED.
TOSHIRO!

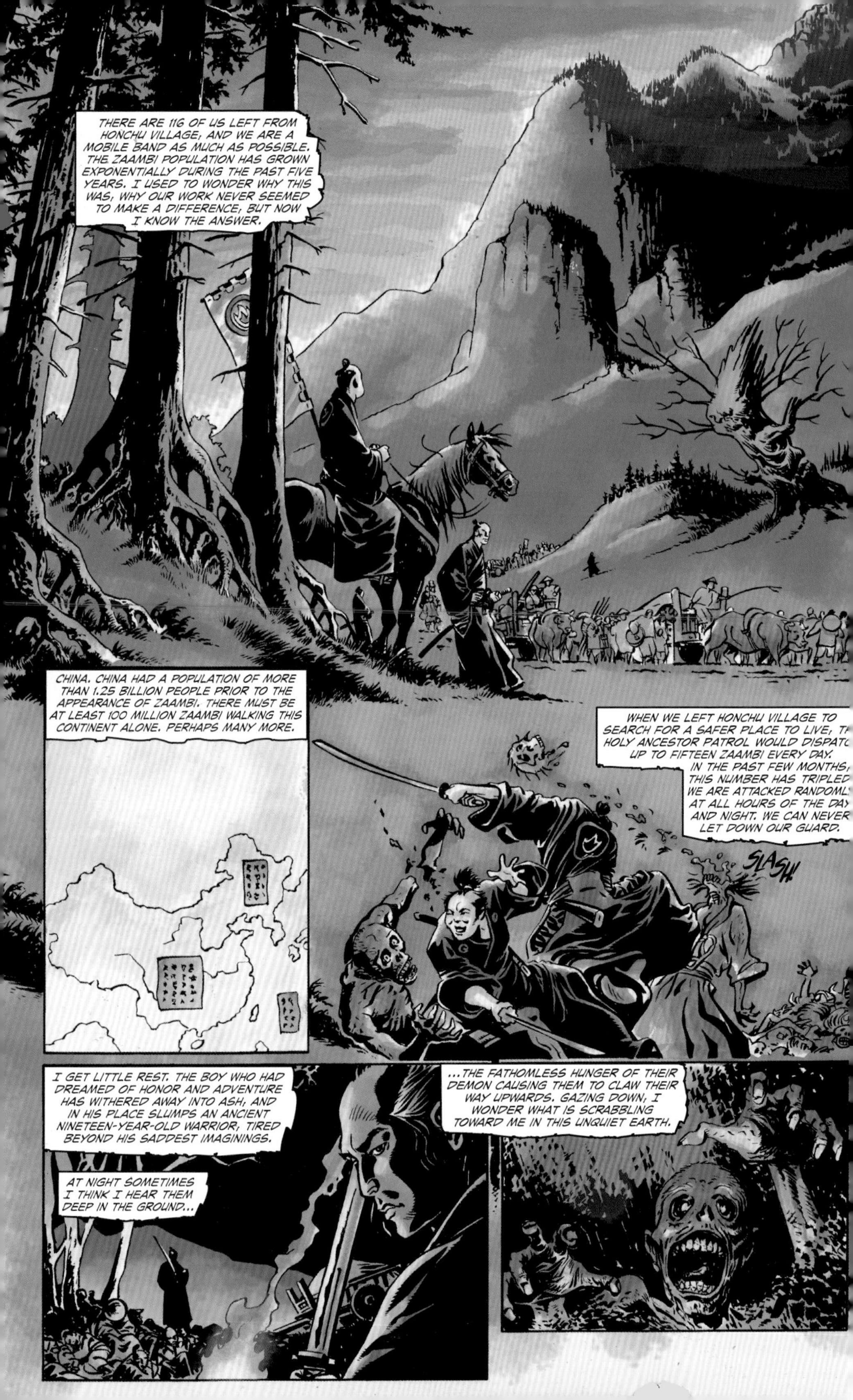

THERE ARE 116 OF US LEFT FROM HONCHU VILLAGE, AND WE ARE A MOBILE BAND AS MUCH AS POSSIBLE. THE ZAAMBI POPULATION HAS GROWN EXPONENTIALLY DURING THE PAST FIVE YEARS. I USED TO WONDER WHY THIS WAS, WHY OUR WORK NEVER SEEMED TO MAKE A DIFFERENCE, BUT NOW I KNOW THE ANSWER.
CHINA. CHINA HAD A POPULATION OF MORE THAN 1.25 BILLION PEOPLE PRIOR TO THE APPEARANCE OF ZAAMBI. THERE MUST BE AT LEAST 100 MILLION ZAAMBI WALKING THIS CONTINENT ALONE. PERHAPS MANY MORE.
WHEN WE LEFT HONCHU VILLAGE TO SEARCH FOR A SAFER PLACE TO LIVE, T HOLY ANCESTOR PATROL WOULD DISPATC UP TO FIFTEEN ZAAMBI EVERY DAY.
IN THE PAST FEW MONTHS, THIS NUMBER HAS TRIPLED WE ARE ATTACKED RANDOML AT ALL HOURS OF THE DAY AND NIGHT. WE CAN NEVER LET DOWN OUR GUARD.
SLASH!
I GET LITTLE REST. THE BOY WHO HAD DREAMED OF HONOR AND ADVENTURE HAS WITHERED AWAY INTO ASH, AND IN HIS PLACE SLUMPS AN ANCIENT NINETEEN-YEAR-OLD WARRIOR, TIRED BEYOND HIS SADDEST IMAGININGS.
AT NIGHT SOMETIMES I THINK I HEAR THEM DEEP IN THE GROUND...
...THE FATHOMLESS HUNGER OF THEIR DEMON CAUSING THEM TO CLAW THEIR WAY UPWARDS. GAZING DOWN, I WONDER WHAT IS SCRABBLING TOWARD ME IN THIS UNQUIET EARTH.

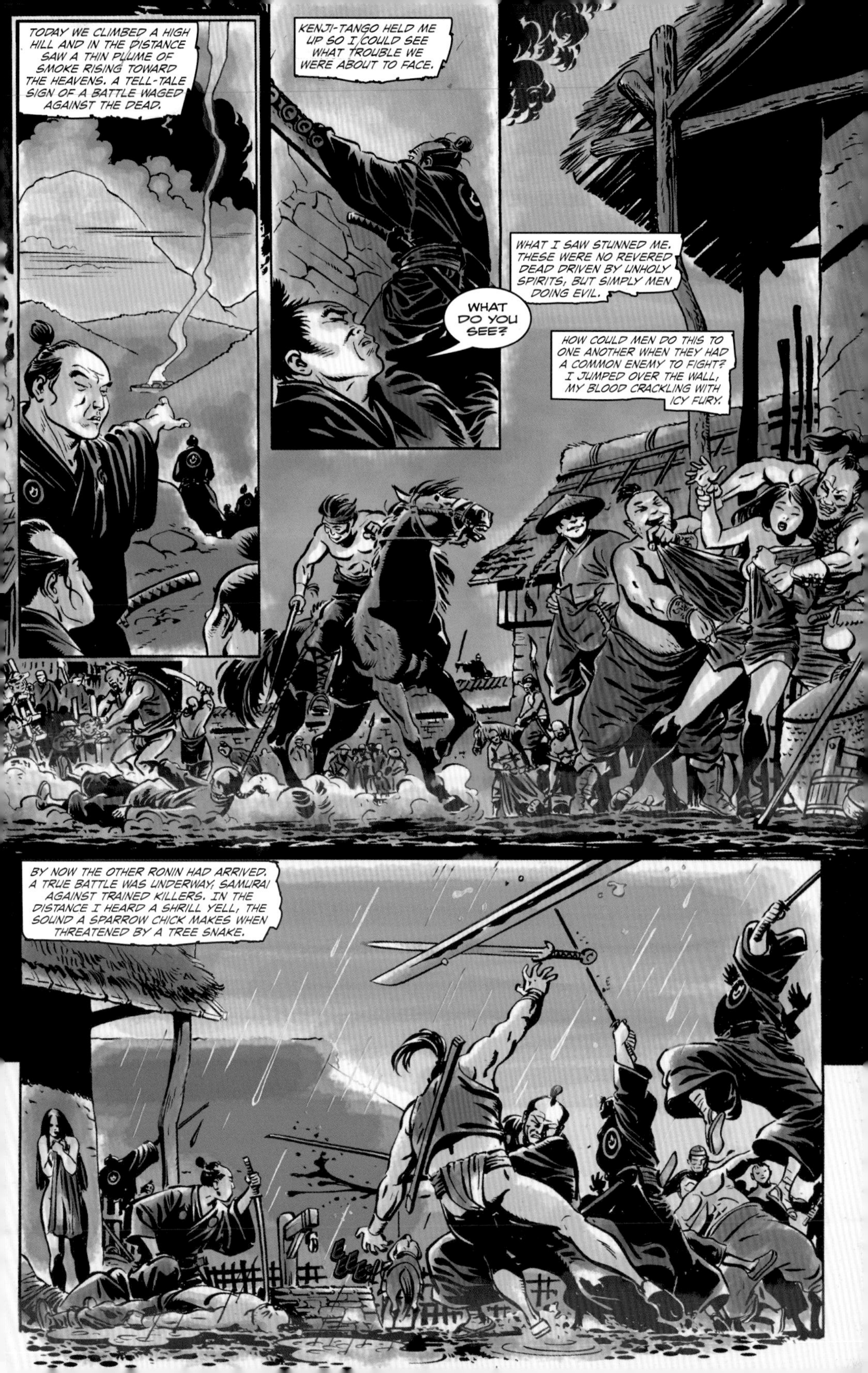
TODAY WE CLIMBED A HIGH HILL AND IN THE DISTANCE SAW A THIN PLUME OF SMOKE RISING TOWARD THE HEAVENS. A TELL-TALE SIGN OF A BATTLE WAGED AGAINST THE DEAD.
KENJI-TANGO HELD ME UP SO I COULD SEE WHAT TROUBLE WE WERE ABOUT TO FACE.
WHAT DO YOU SEE?
WHAT I SAW STUNNED ME. THESE WERE NO REVERED DEAD DRIVEN BY UNHOLY SPIRITS, BUT SIMPLY MEN DOING EVIL.
HOW COULD MEN DO THIS TO ONE ANOTHER WHEN THEY HAD A COMMON ENEMY TO FIGHT? I JUMPED OVER THE WALL, MY BLOOD CRACKLING WITH ICY FURY.
BY NOW THE OTHER RONIN HAD ARRIVED. A TRUE BATTLE WAS UNDERWAY, SAMURAI AGAINST TRAINED KILLERS. IN THE DISTANCE I HEARD A SHRILL YELL, THE SOUND A SPARROW CHICK MAKES WHEN THREATENED BY A TREE SNAKE.

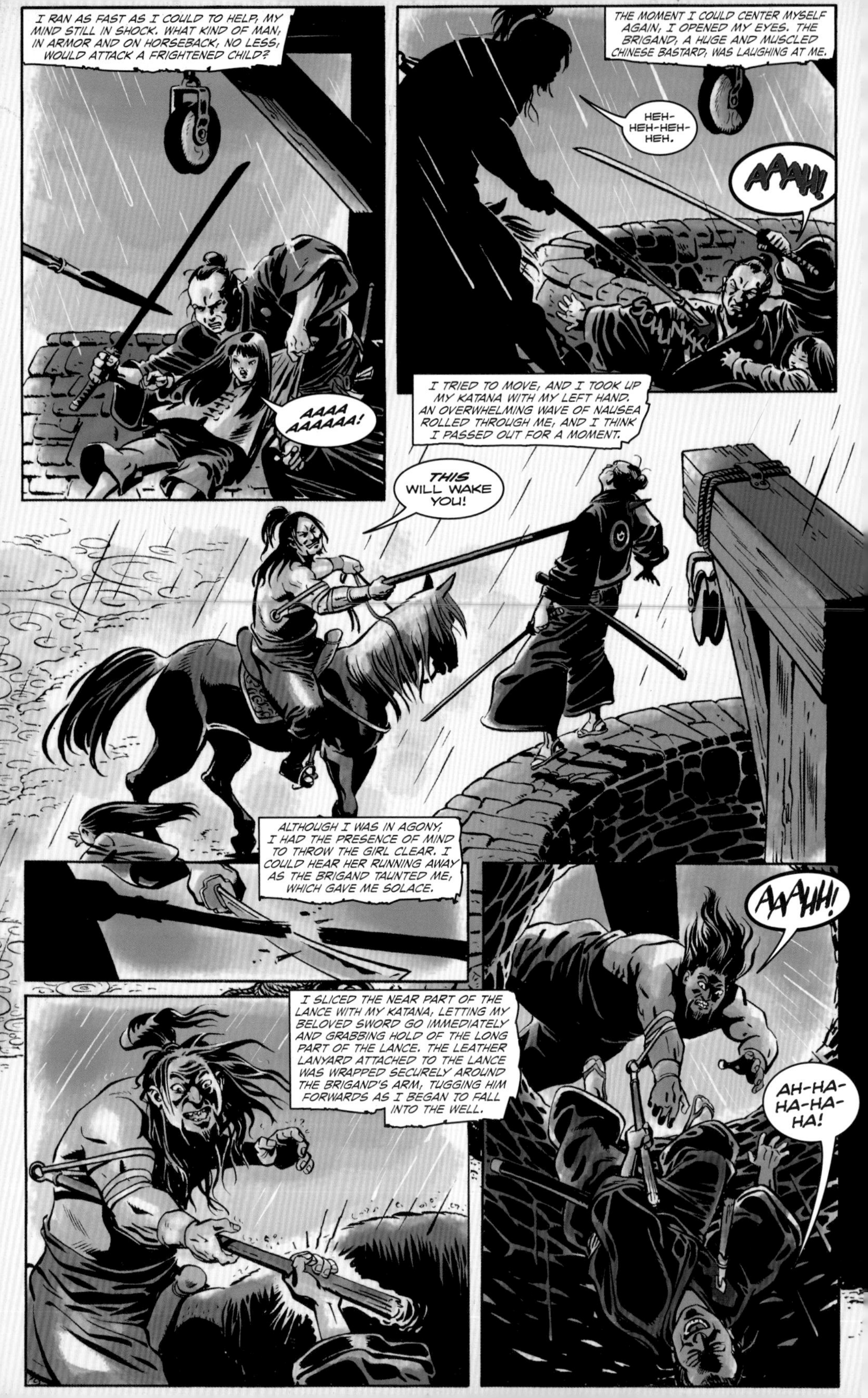
I RAN AS FAST AS I COULD TO HELP, MY MIND STILL IN SHOCK. WHAT KIND OF MAN, IN ARMOR AND ON HORSEBACK, NO LESS, WOULD ATTACK A FRIGHTENED CHILD?
AAAA AAAAAA!
THE MOMENT I COULD CENTER MYSELF AGAIN, I OPENED MY EYES. THE BRIGAND, A HUGE AND MUSCLED CHINESE BASTARD, WAS LAUGHING AT ME.
HEH-HEH-HEH-HEH.
AAAH!
SCHUNKK
I TRIED TO MOVE, AND I TOOK UP MY KATANA WITH MY LEFT HAND. AN OVERWHELMING WAVE OF NAUSEA ROLLED THROUGH ME, AND I THINK I PASSED OUT FOR A MOMENT.
THIS WILL WAKE YOU!
ALTHOUGH I WAS IN AGONY, I HAD THE PRESENCE OF MIND TO THROW THE GIRL CLEAR. I COULD HEAR HER RUNNING AWAY AS THE BRIGAND TAUNTED ME, WHICH GAVE ME SOLACE.
AAAHH!
I SLICED THE NEAR PART OF THE LANCE WITH MY KATANA, LETTING MY BELOVED SWORD GO IMMEDIATELY AND GRABBING HOLD OF THE LONG PART OF THE LANCE. THE LEATHER LANYARD ATTACHED TO THE LANCE WAS WRAPPED SECURELY AROUND THE BRIGAND'S ARM, TUGGING HIM FORWARDS AS I BEGAN TO FALL INTO THE WELL.
AH-HA-HA-HA-HA!

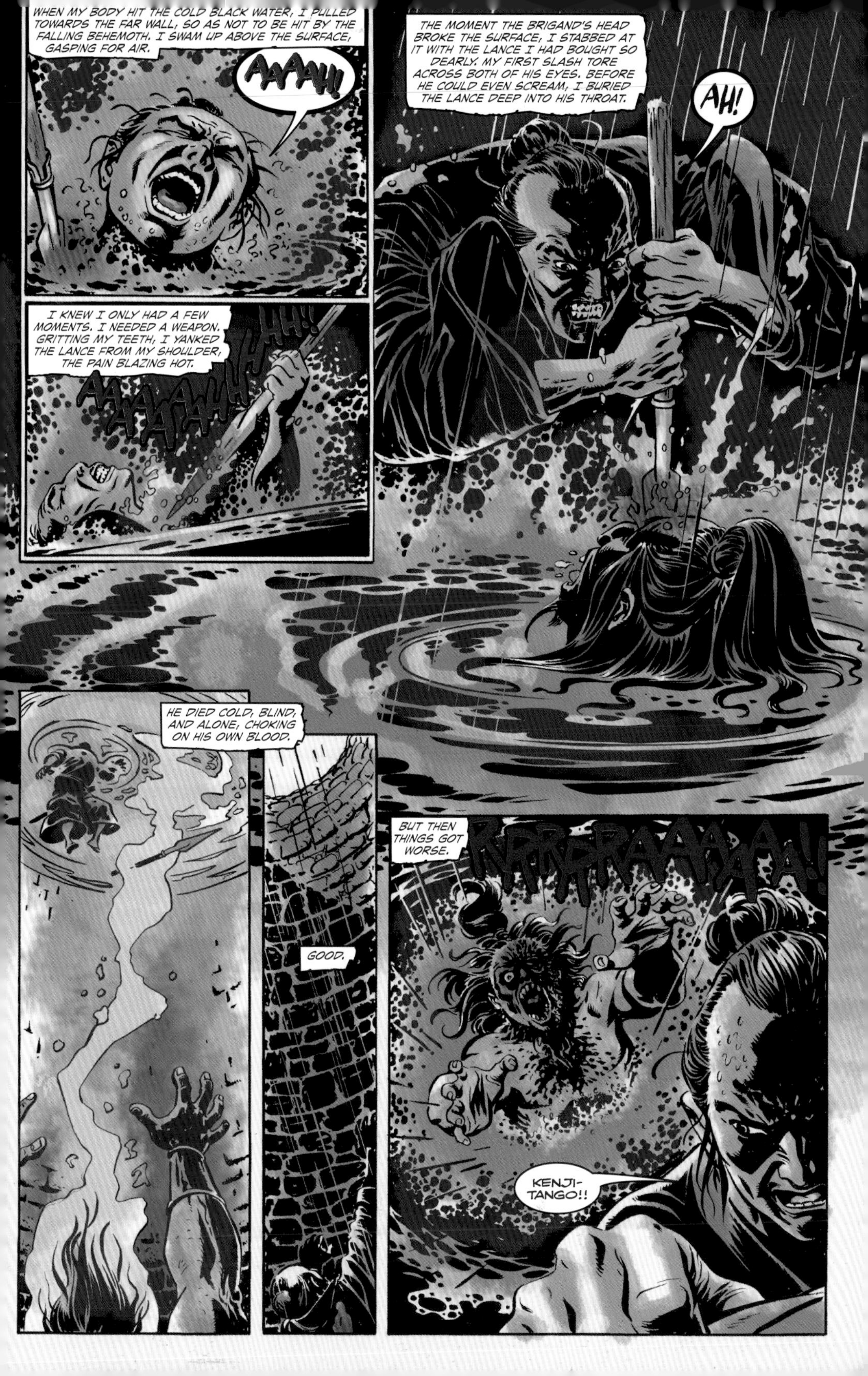
WHEN MY BODY HIT THE COLD BLACK WATER, I PULLED TOWARDS THE FAR WALL, SO AS NOT TO BE HIT BY THE FALLING BEHEMOTH. I SWAM UP ABOVE THE SURFACE, GASPING FOR AIR.
AAAAH!
I KNEW I ONLY HAD A FEW MOMENTS. I NEEDED A WEAPON. GRITTING MY TEETH, I YANKED THE LANCE FROM MY SHOULDER, THE PAIN BLAZING HOT.
AAAAAAHHHHH!!
THE MOMENT THE BRIGAND'S HEAD BROKE THE SURFACE, I STABBED AT IT WITH THE LANCE I HAD BOUGHT SO DEARLY. MY FIRST SLASH TORE ACROSS BOTH OF HIS EYES. BEFORE HE COULD EVEN SCREAM, I BURIED THE LANCE DEEP INTO HIS THROAT.
AH!
HE DIED COLD, BLIND, AND ALONE, CHOKING ON HIS OWN BLOOD.
GOOD.
BUT THEN THINGS GOT WORSE.
KRRRRRAAAAAAA!!
KENJI-TANGO!!

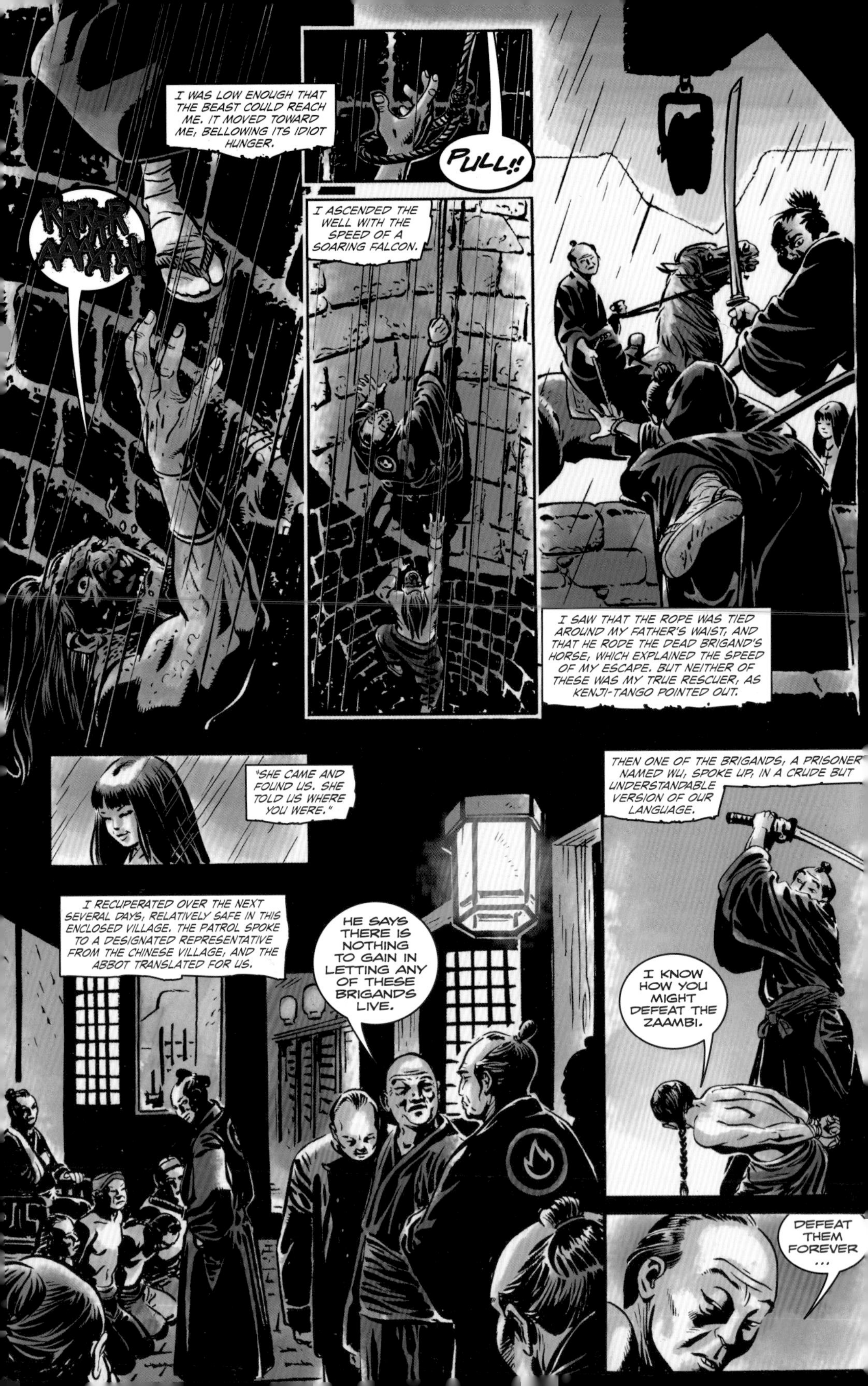
I WAS LOW ENOUGH THAT THE BEAST COULD REACH ME. IT MOVED TOWARD ME, BELLOWING ITS IDIOT HUNGER.
RARRR AAAAAA!
PULL!!
I ASCENDED THE WELL WITH THE SPEED OF A SOARING FALCON.
I SAW THAT THE ROPE WAS TIED AROUND MY FATHER'S WAIST, AND THAT HE RODE THE DEAD BRIGAND'S HORSE, WHICH EXPLAINED THE SPEED OF MY ESCAPE. BUT NEITHER OF THESE WAS MY TRUE RESCUER, AS KENJI-TANGO POINTED OUT.
"SHE CAME AND FOUND US. SHE TOLD US WHERE YOU WERE."
I RECUPERATED OVER THE NEXT SEVERAL DAYS, RELATIVELY SAFE IN THIS ENCLOSED VILLAGE. THE PATROL SPOKE TO A DESIGNATED REPRESENTATIVE FROM THE CHINESE VILLAGE, AND THE ABBOT TRANSLATED FOR US.
HE SAYS THERE IS NOTHING TO GAIN IN LETTING ANY OF THESE BRIGANDS LIVE.
THEN ONE OF THE BRIGANDS, A PRISONER NAMED WU, SPOKE UP, IN A CRUDE BUT UNDERSTANDABLE VERSION OF OUR LANGUAGE.
I KNOW HOW YOU MIGHT DEFEAT THE ZAAMBI.
DEFEAT THEM FOREVER ...

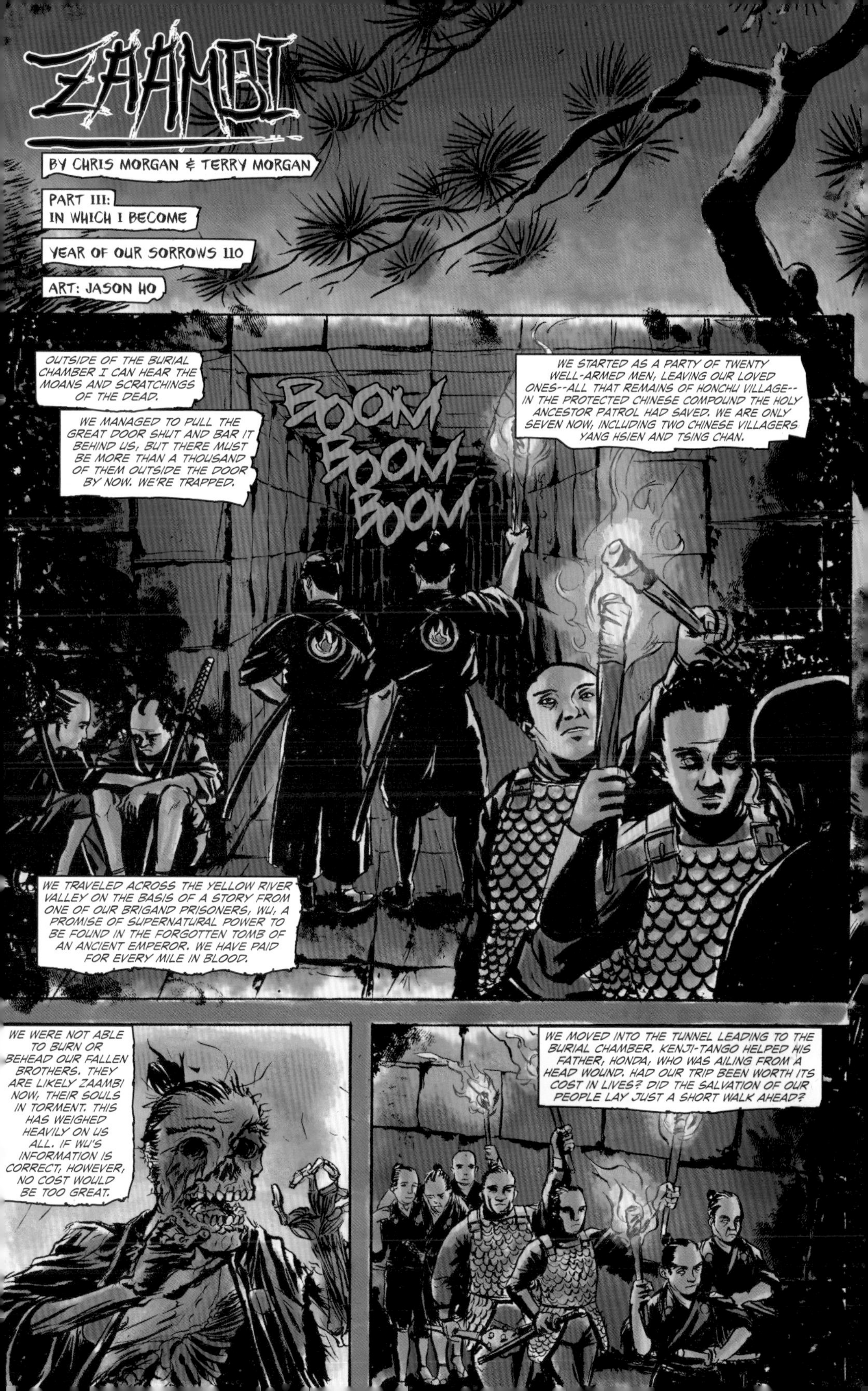
ZAAMBI
BY CHRIS MORGAN & TERRY MORGAN
PART III: IN WHICH I BECOME
YEAR OF OUR SORROWS 110
ART: JASON HO
OUTSIDE OF THE BURIAL CHAMBER I CAN HEAR THE MOANS AND SCRATCHINGS OF THE DEAD.
WE MANAGED TO PULL THE GREAT DOOR SHUT AND BAR IT BEHIND US, BUT THERE MUST BE MORE THAN A THOUSAND OF THEM OUTSIDE THE DOOR BY NOW. WE'RE TRAPPED.
BOOM BOOM BOOM
WE STARTED AS A PARTY OF TWENTY WELL-ARMED MEN, LEAVING OUR LOVED ONES--ALL THAT REMAINS OF HONCHU VILLAGE--IN THE PROTECTED CHINESE COMPOUND THE HOLY ANCESTOR PATROL HAD SAVED. WE ARE ONLY SEVEN NOW, INCLUDING TWO CHINESE VILLAGERS YANG HSIEN AND TSING CHAN.
WE TRAVELED ACROSS THE YELLOW RIVER VALLEY ON THE BASIS OF A STORY FROM ONE OF OUR BRIGAND PRISONERS, WU, A PROMISE OF SUPERNATURAL POWER TO BE FOUND IN THE FORGOTTEN TOMB OF AN ANCIENT EMPEROR. WE HAVE PAID FOR EVERY MILE IN BLOOD.
WE WERE NOT ABLE TO BURN OR BEHEAD OUR FALLEN BROTHERS. THEY ARE LIKELY ZAAMBI NOW, THEIR SOULS IN TORMENT. THIS HAS WEIGHED HEAVILY ON US ALL. IF WU'S INFORMATION IS CORRECT, HOWEVER, NO COST WOULD BE TOO GREAT.
WE MOVED INTO THE TUNNEL LEADING TO THE BURIAL CHAMBER. KENJI-TANGO HELPED HIS FATHER, HONDA, WHO WAS AILING FROM A HEAD WOUND. HAD OUR TRIP BEEN WORTH ITS COST IN LIVES? DID THE SALVATION OF OUR PEOPLE LAY JUST A SHORT WALK AHEAD?

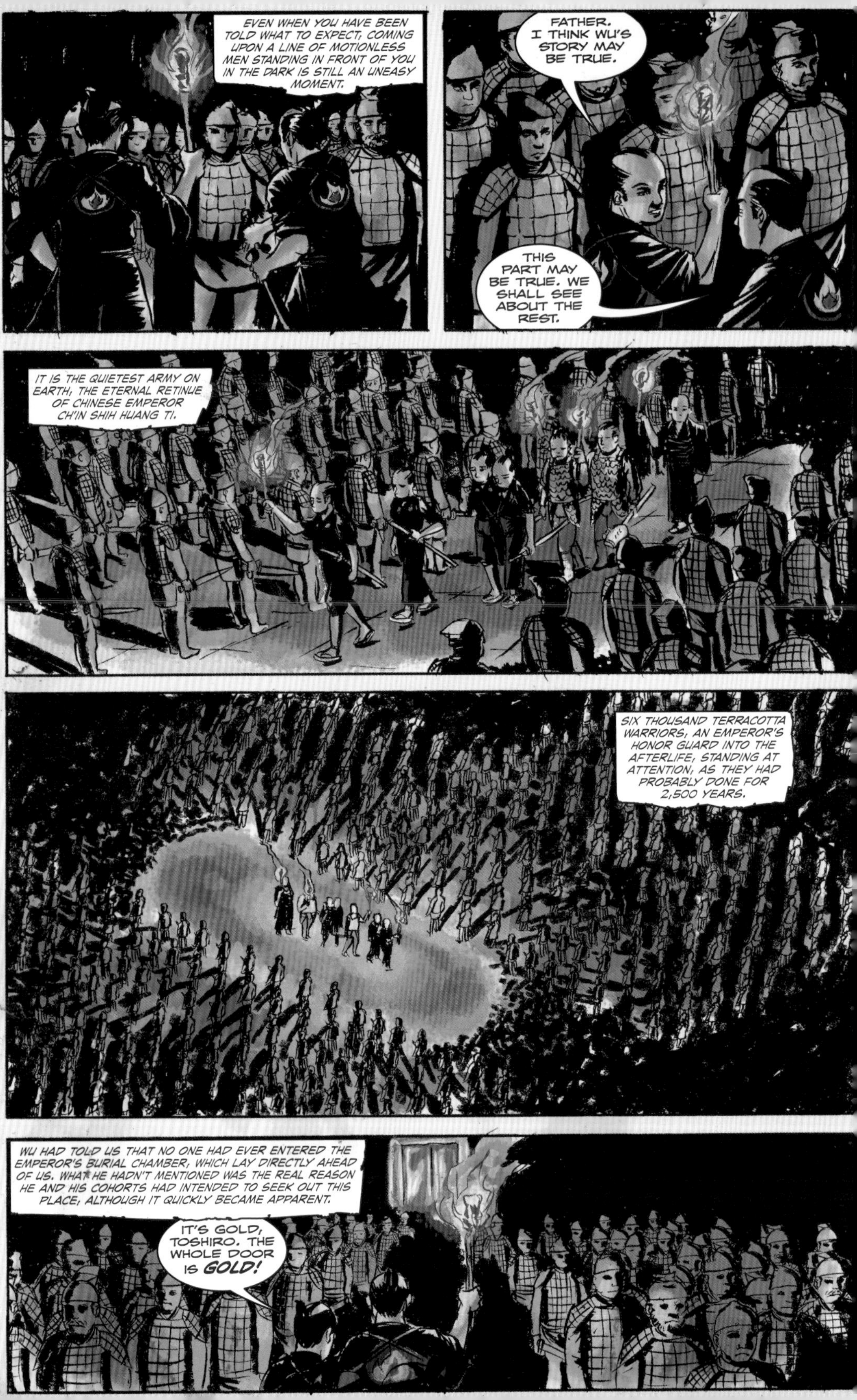
EVEN WHEN YOU HAVE BEEN TOLD WHAT TO EXPECT, COMING UPON A LINE OF MOTIONLESS MEN STANDING IN FRONT OF YOU IN THE DARK IS STILL AN UNEASY MOMENT.
FATHER. I THINK WU'S STORY MAY BE TRUE.
THIS PART MAY BE TRUE. WE SHALL SEE ABOUT THE REST.
IT IS THE QUIETEST ARMY ON EARTH, THE ETERNAL RETINUE OF CHINESE EMPEROR CH'IN SHIH HUANG TI.
SIX THOUSAND TERRACOTTA WARRIORS, AN EMPEROR'S HONOR GUARD INTO THE AFTERLIFE, STANDING AT ATTENTION, AS THEY HAD PROBABLY DONE FOR 2,500 YEARS.
WU HAD TOLD US THAT NO ONE HAD EVER ENTERED THE EMPEROR'S BURIAL CHAMBER, WHICH LAY DIRECTLY AHEAD OF US. WHAT HE HADN'T MENTIONED WAS THE REAL REASON HE AND HIS COHORTS HAD INTENDED TO SEEK OUT THIS PLACE, ALTHOUGH IT QUICKLY BECAME APPARENT.
IT'S GOLD, TOSHIRO. THE WHOLE DOOR IS GOLD!

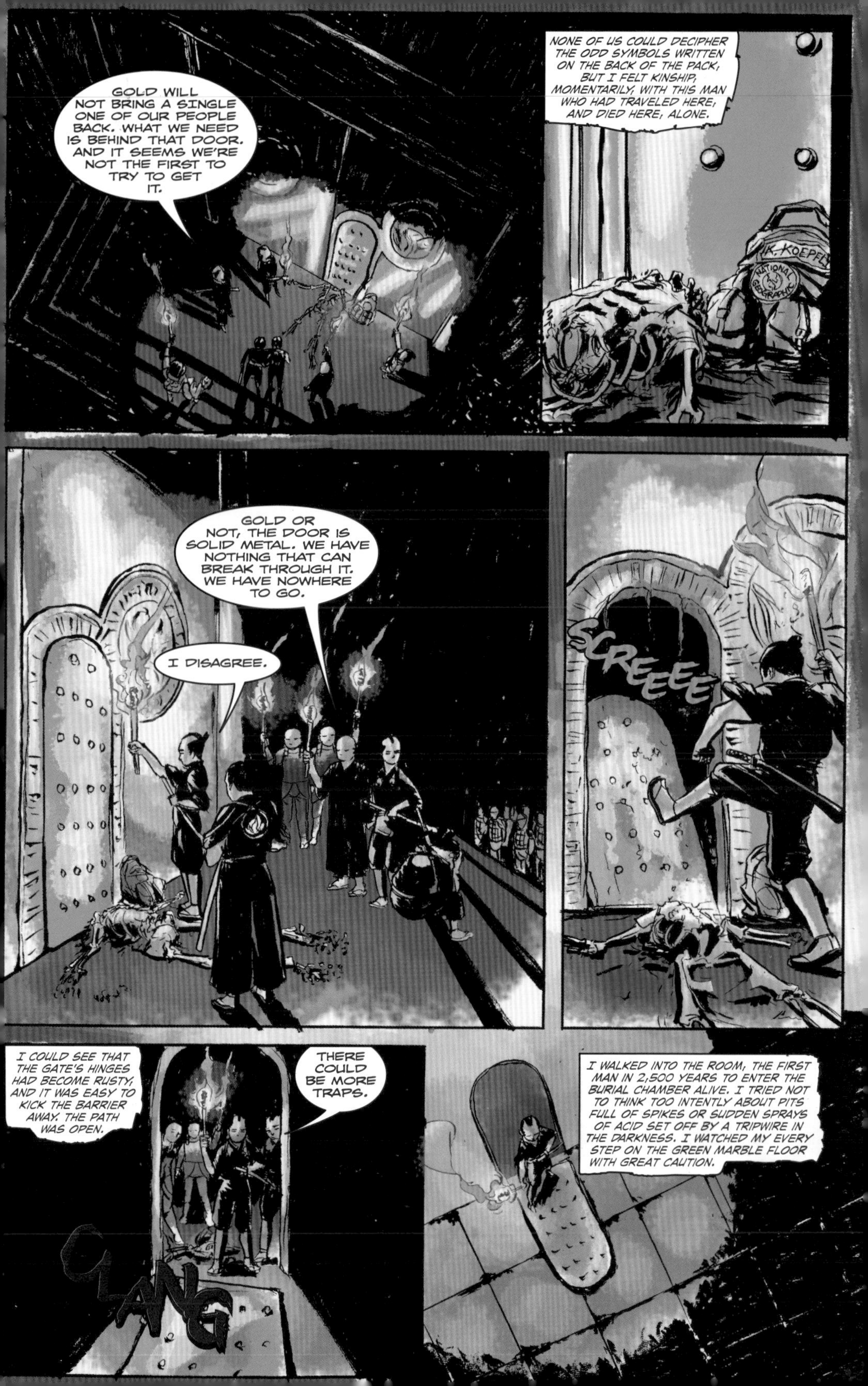
GOLD WILL NOT BRING A SINGLE ONE OF OUR PEOPLE BACK. WHAT WE NEED IS BEHIND THAT DOOR. AND IT SEEMS WE'RE NOT THE FIRST TO TRY TO GET IT.
NONE OF US COULD DECIPHER THE ODD SYMBOLS WRITTEN ON THE BACK OF THE PACK, BUT I FELT KINSHIP, MOMENTARILY, WITH THIS MAN WHO HAD TRAVELED HERE, AND DIED HERE, ALONE.
K. KOEPFL
NATIONAL GEOGRAPHIC
GOLD OR NOT, THE DOOR IS SOLID METAL. WE HAVE NOTHING THAT CAN BREAK THROUGH IT. WE HAVE NOWHERE TO GO.
I DISAGREE.
SCREEEE
I COULD SEE THAT THE GATE'S HINGES HAD BECOME RUSTY, AND IT WAS EASY TO KICK THE BARRIER AWAY. THE PATH WAS OPEN.
THERE COULD BE MORE TRAPS.
CLANG
I WALKED INTO THE ROOM, THE FIRST MAN IN 2,500 YEARS TO ENTER THE BURIAL CHAMBER ALIVE. I TRIED NOT TO THINK TOO INTENTLY ABOUT PITS FULL OF SPIKES OR SUDDEN SPRAYS OF ACID SET OFF BY A TRIPWIRE IN THE DARKNESS. I WATCHED MY EVERY STEP ON THE GREEN MARBLE FLOOR WITH GREAT CAUTION.

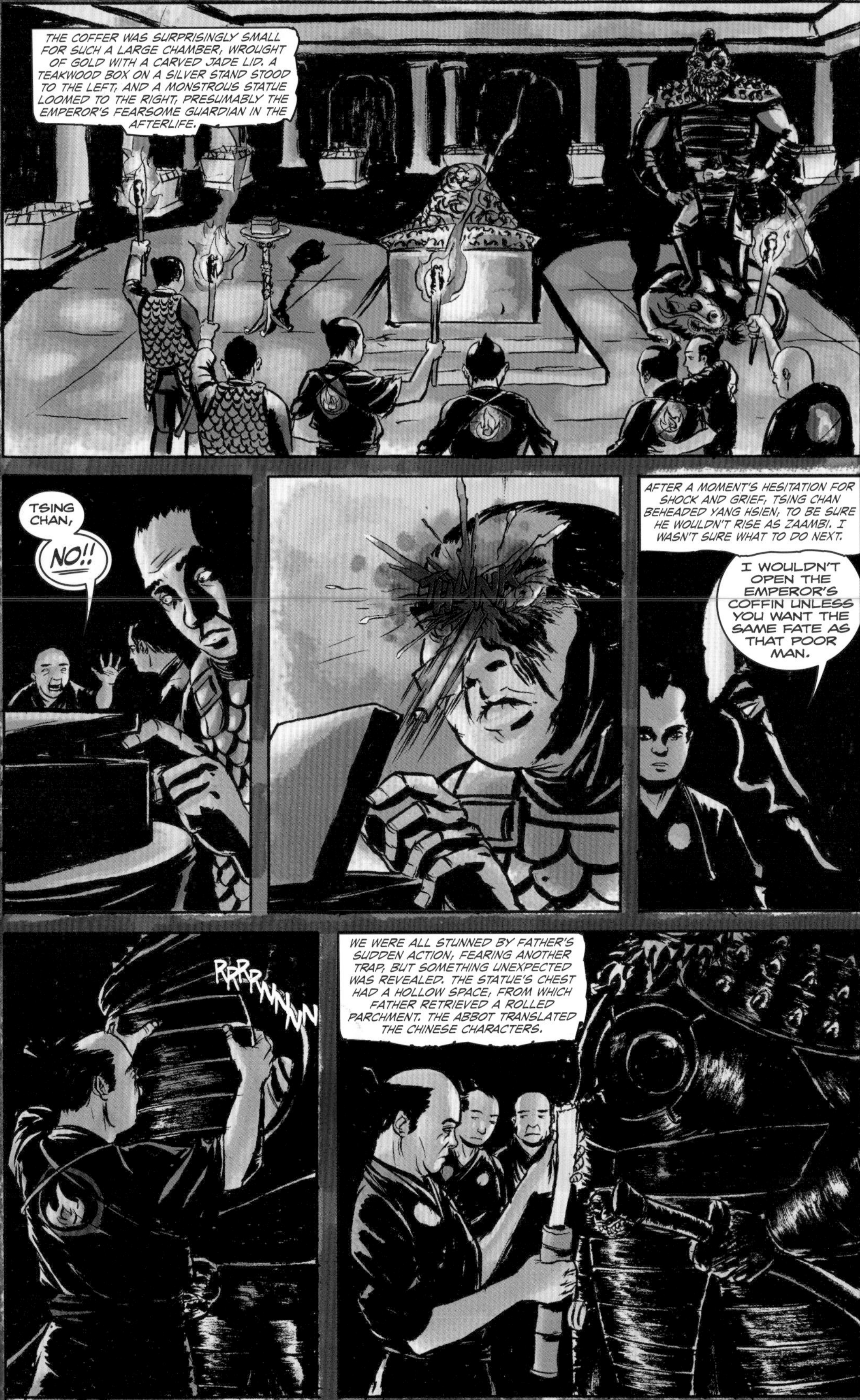
THE COFFER WAS SURPRISINGLY SMALL FOR SUCH A LARGE CHAMBER, WROUGHT OF GOLD WITH A CARVED JADE LID. A TEAKWOOD BOX ON A SILVER STAND STOOD TO THE LEFT, AND A MONSTROUS STATUE LOOMED TO THE RIGHT, PRESUMABLY THE EMPEROR'S FEARSOME GUARDIAN IN THE AFTERLIFE.
TSING CHAN, NO!!
AFTER A MOMENT'S HESITATION FOR SHOCK AND GRIEF, TSING CHAN BEHEADED YANG HSIEN, TO BE SURE HE WOULDN'T RISE AS ZAAMBI. I WASN'T SURE WHAT TO DO NEXT.
I WOULDN'T OPEN THE EMPEROR'S COFFIN UNLESS YOU WANT THE SAME FATE AS THAT POOR MAN.
RRRRNNNN
WE WERE ALL STUNNED BY FATHER'S SUDDEN ACTION, FEARING ANOTHER TRAP, BUT SOMETHING UNEXPECTED WAS REVEALED. THE STATUE'S CHEST HAD A HOLLOW SPACE, FROM WHICH FATHER RETRIEVED A ROLLED PARCHMENT. THE ABBOT TRANSLATED THE CHINESE CHARACTERS.

THE GREAT WARRIOR THAT STANDS BEFORE THE EMPEROR WAS MEANT TO HOUSE HIS SPIRIT AND LEAD HIS ARMY INTO WORLD CONQUEST, BUT SOMEONE ASSASSINATED HIM BEFORE HE COULD BECOME IMMORTAL. THIS SCROLL EXPLAINS THE PROCESS OF THE SUPERNATURAL TRANSFER.

WHAT IS REQUIRED FOR THE TRANSFER?

ONE OF US MUST TAKE HIS OWN BEATING HEART FROM HIS CHEST AND PLACE IT IN THE CHEST OF THE GREAT WARRIOR.

AS YOU SEE, THERE IS A SPOT SET ASIDE FOR THAT.

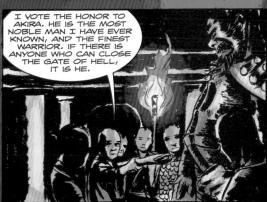

I VOTE THE HONOR TO AKIRA. HE IS THE MOST NOBLE MAN I HAVE EVER KNOWN, AND THE FINEST WARRIOR. IF THERE IS ANYONE WHO CAN CLOSE THE GATE OF HELL, IT IS HE.

I KNEW IT WOULD BE WRONG TO ADVOCATE FOR MY FATHER BY SPEAKING ALOUD, SO I BOWED DEEPLY TO SHOW MY RESPECT AND ASSENT FOR THE ABBOT'S PRAISE.

I CANNOT DO THIS, TO MY GREAT SHAME. THIS LIFE IS...HATEFUL TO ME. I CANNOT BEAR THE THOUGHT OF IMMORTALITY. NOT IN THIS CHARNEL HOUSE OF A WORLD. I AM SORRY.

CRACK WHUMP

I WAITED FOR OTHERS TO SPEAK UP, FEELING ANY OF THEM DESERVED THE HONOR BEFORE ME, BUT NONE SPOKE. KENJI-TANGO LOOKED TORN, BUT IT WAS CLEAR HIS FATHER WOULD CONTINUE TO NEED HELP. I LOOKED TO FATHER, BUT HE WOULD NOT MEET MY EYES. MY MOMENT OF INDECISION WAS BROKEN BY A DISTANT SOUND.

THE BREAKING OF A DOOR.

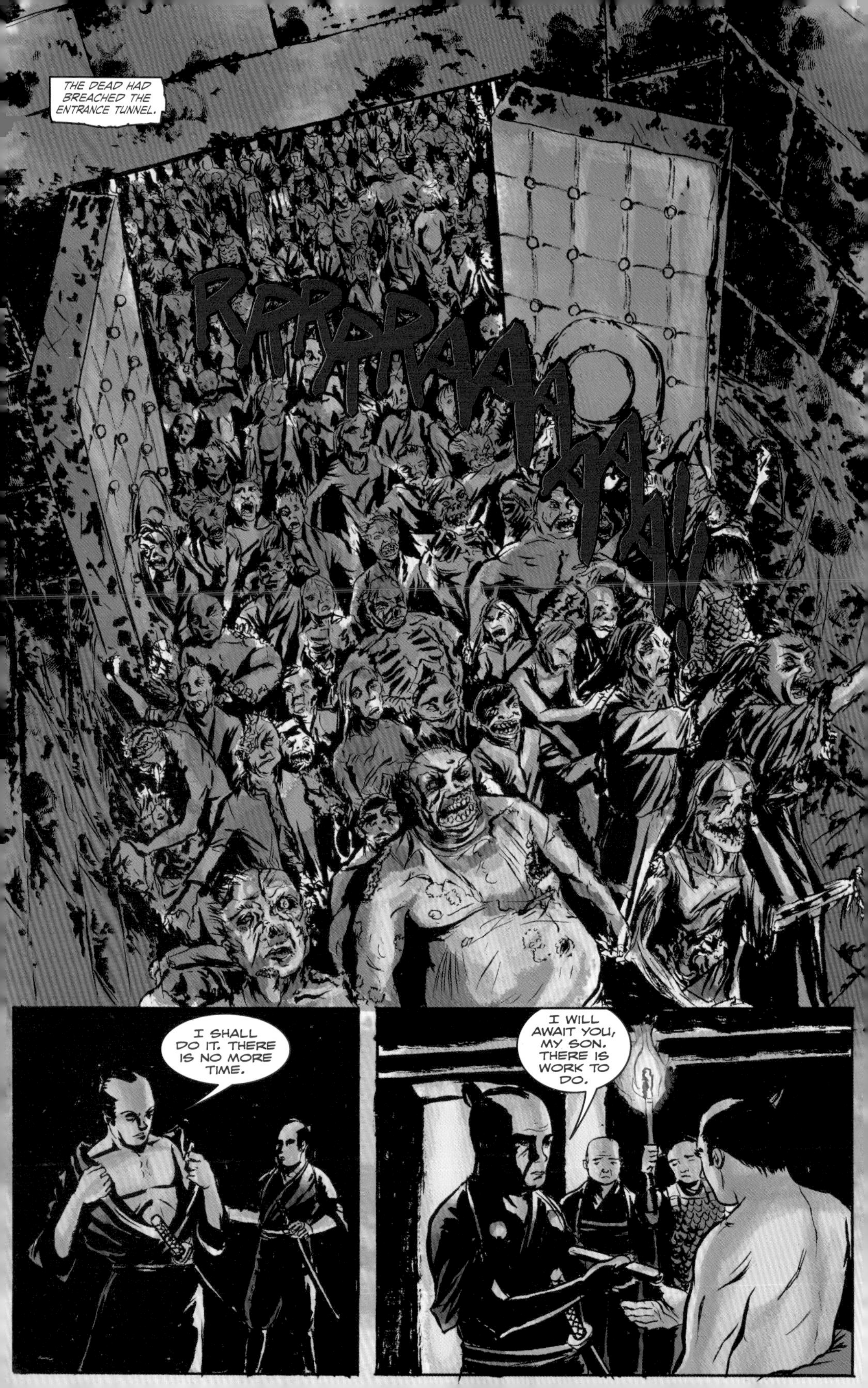
THE DEAD HAD BREACHED THE ENTRANCE TUNNEL.
RRRRRAAAAAAAA!!
I SHALL DO IT. THERE IS NO MORE TIME.
I WILL AWAIT YOU, MY SON. THERE IS WORK TO DO.

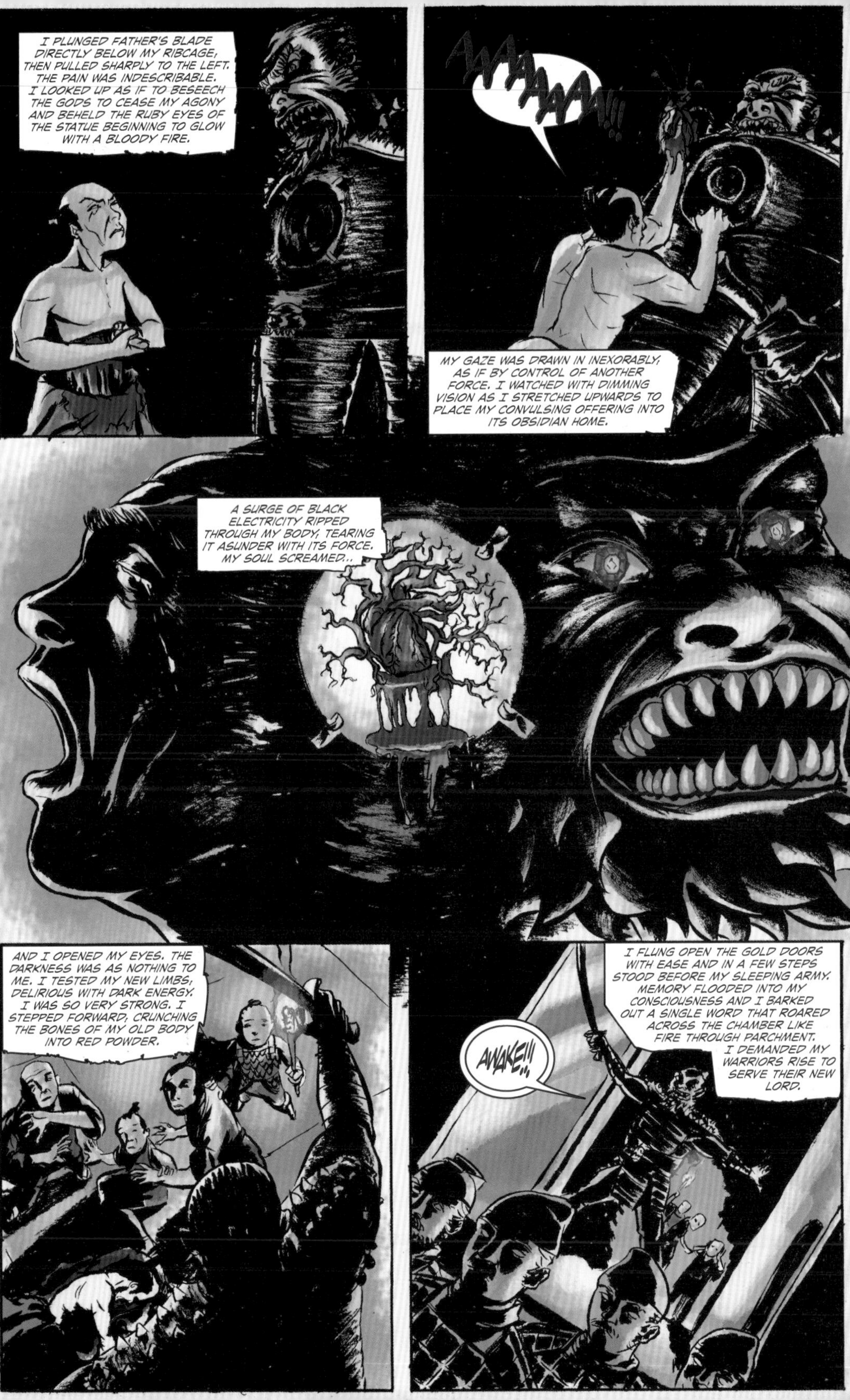
I PLUNGED FATHER'S BLADE DIRECTLY BELOW MY RIBCAGE, THEN PULLED SHARPLY TO THE LEFT. THE PAIN WAS INDESCRIBABLE. I LOOKED UP AS IF TO BESEECH THE GODS TO CEASE MY AGONY AND BEHELD THE RUBY EYES OF THE STATUE BEGINNING TO GLOW WITH A BLOODY FIRE.
AAAAAAAAAA!!!
MY GAZE WAS DRAWN IN INEXORABLY, AS IF BY CONTROL OF ANOTHER FORCE. I WATCHED WITH DIMMING VISION AS I STRETCHED UPWARDS TO PLACE MY CONVULSING OFFERING INTO ITS OBSIDIAN HOME.
A SURGE OF BLACK ELECTRICITY RIPPED THROUGH MY BODY, TEARING IT ASUNDER WITH ITS FORCE. MY SOUL SCREAMED...
AND I OPENED MY EYES. THE DARKNESS WAS AS NOTHING TO ME. I TESTED MY NEW LIMBS, DELIRIOUS WITH DARK ENERGY. I WAS SO VERY STRONG. I STEPPED FORWARD, CRUNCHING THE BONES OF MY OLD BODY INTO RED POWDER.
I FLUNG OPEN THE GOLD DOORS WITH EASE AND IN A FEW STEPS STOOD BEFORE MY SLEEPING ARMY. MEMORY FLOODED INTO MY CONSCIOUSNESS AND I BARKED OUT A SINGLE WORD THAT ROARED ACROSS THE CHAMBER LIKE FIRE THROUGH PARCHMENT.
AWAKE!!!
I DEMANDED MY WARRIORS RISE TO SERVE THEIR NEW LORD.

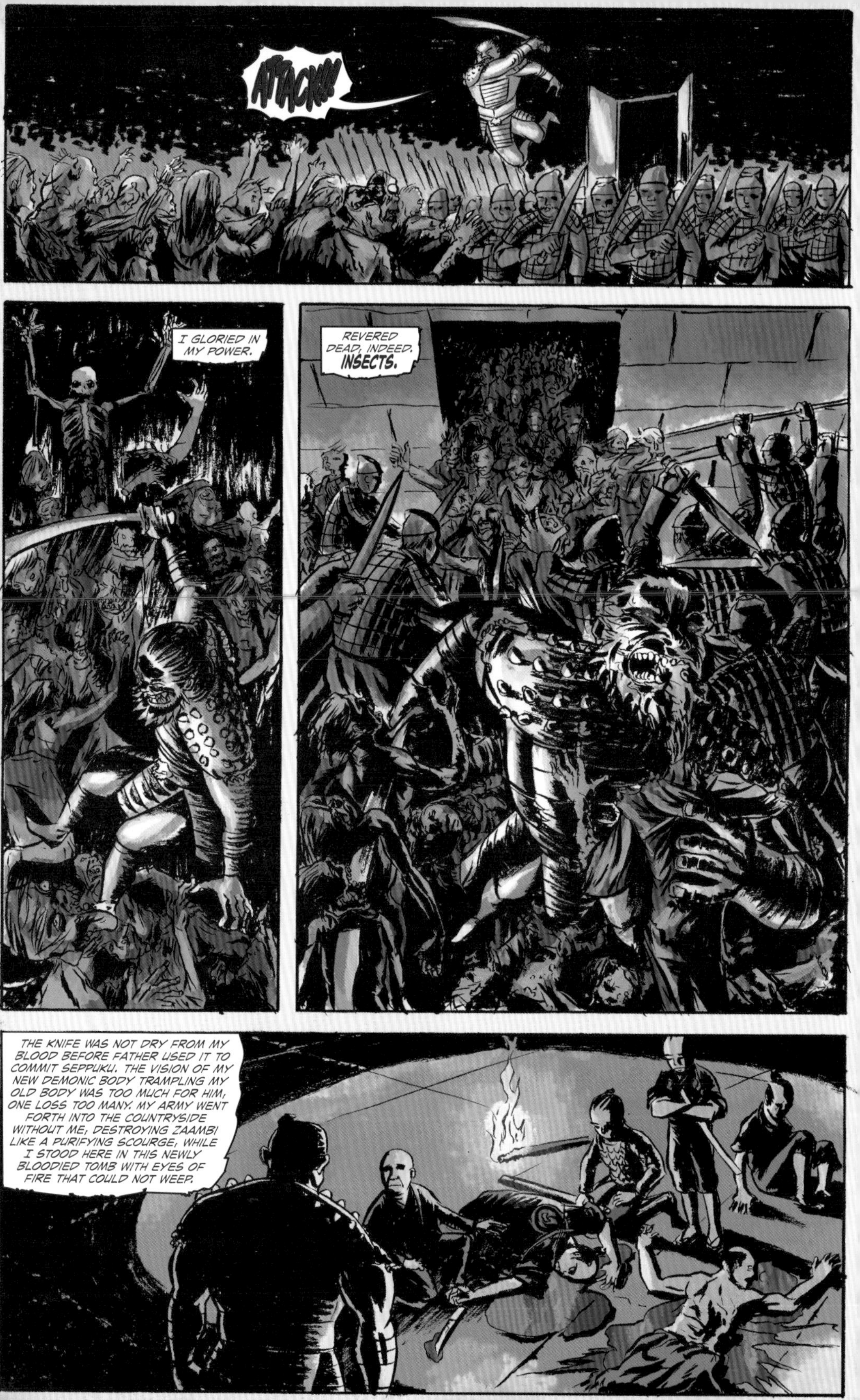
ATTACK!!!
I GLORIED IN MY POWER.
REVERED DEAD, INDEED. INSECTS.
THE KNIFE WAS NOT DRY FROM MY BLOOD BEFORE FATHER USED IT TO COMMIT SEPPUKU. THE VISION OF MY NEW DEMONIC BODY TRAMPLING MY OLD BODY WAS TOO MUCH FOR HIM, ONE LOSS TOO MANY. MY ARMY WENT FORTH INTO THE COUNTRYSIDE WITHOUT ME, DESTROYING ZAAMBI LIKE A PURIFYING SCOURGE, WHILE I STOOD HERE IN THIS NEWLY BLOODIED TOMB WITH EYES OF FIRE THAT COULD NOT WEEP.

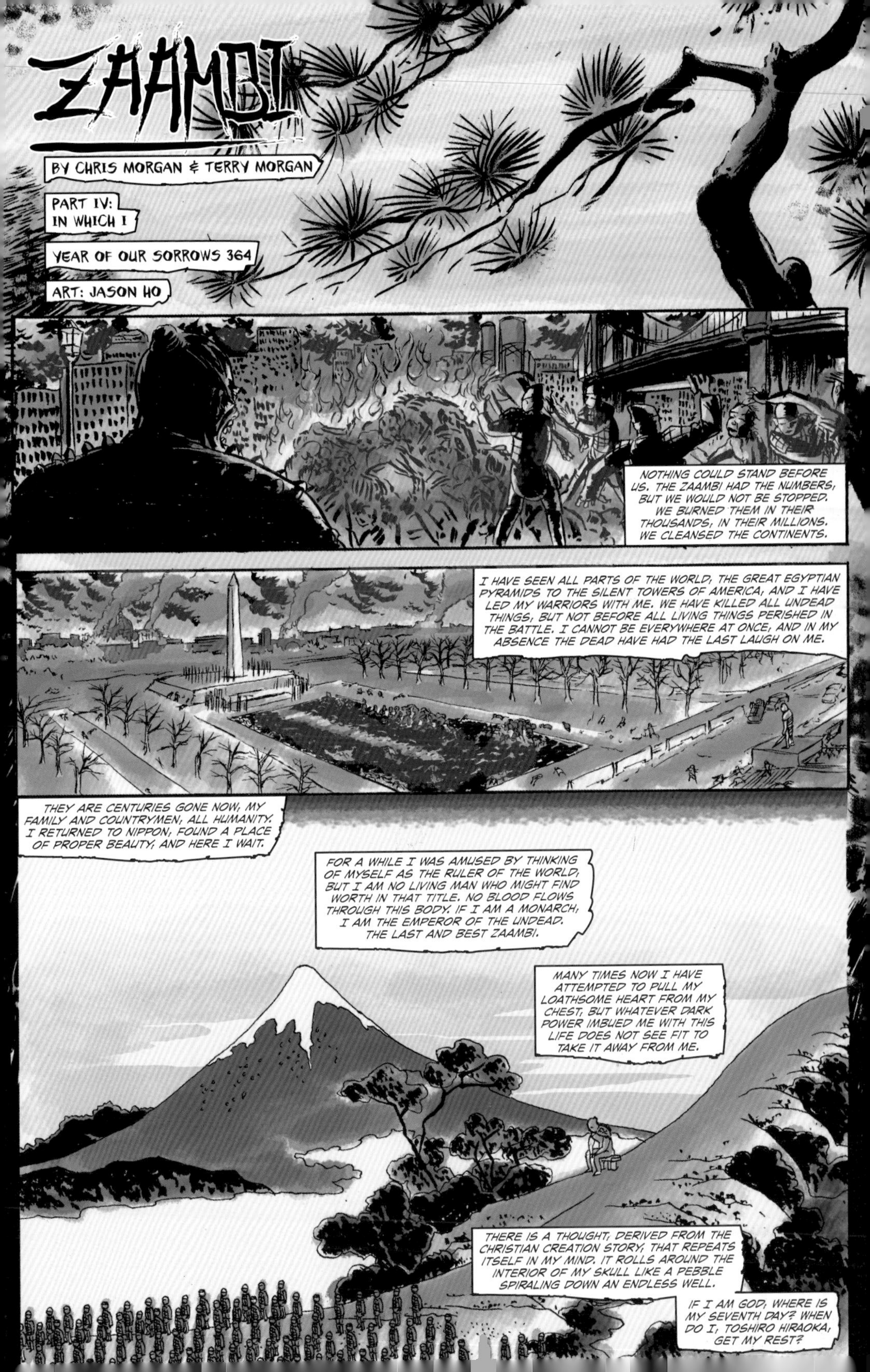
ZAAMBI
BY CHRIS MORGAN & TERRY MORGAN
PART IV: IN WHICH I
YEAR OF OUR SORROWS 364
ART: JASON HO
NOTHING COULD STAND BEFORE US. THE ZAAMBI HAD THE NUMBERS, BUT WE WOULD NOT BE STOPPED. WE BURNED THEM IN THEIR THOUSANDS, IN THEIR MILLIONS. WE CLEANSED THE CONTINENTS.
I HAVE SEEN ALL PARTS OF THE WORLD, THE GREAT EGYPTIAN PYRAMIDS TO THE SILENT TOWERS OF AMERICA, AND I HAVE LED MY WARRIORS WITH ME. WE HAVE KILLED ALL UNDEAD THINGS, BUT NOT BEFORE ALL LIVING THINGS PERISHED IN THE BATTLE. I CANNOT BE EVERYWHERE AT ONCE, AND IN MY ABSENCE THE DEAD HAVE HAD THE LAST LAUGH ON ME.
THEY ARE CENTURIES GONE NOW, MY FAMILY AND COUNTRYMEN, ALL HUMANITY. I RETURNED TO NIPPON, FOUND A PLACE OF PROPER BEAUTY, AND HERE I WAIT.
FOR A WHILE I WAS AMUSED BY THINKING OF MYSELF AS THE RULER OF THE WORLD, BUT I AM NO LIVING MAN WHO MIGHT FIND WORTH IN THAT TITLE. NO BLOOD FLOWS THROUGH THIS BODY. IF I AM A MONARCH, I AM THE EMPEROR OF THE UNDEAD. THE LAST AND BEST ZAAMBI.
MANY TIMES NOW I HAVE ATTEMPTED TO PULL MY LOATHSOME HEART FROM MY CHEST, BUT WHATEVER DARK POWER IMBUED ME WITH THIS LIFE DOES NOT SEE FIT TO TAKE IT AWAY FROM ME.
THERE IS A THOUGHT, DERIVED FROM THE CHRISTIAN CREATION STORY, THAT REPEATS ITSELF IN MY MIND. IT ROLLS AROUND THE INTERIOR OF MY SKULL LIKE A PEBBLE SPIRALING DOWN AN ENDLESS WELL.
IF I AM GOD, WHERE IS MY SEVENTH DAY? WHEN DO I, TOSHIRO HIRAOKA, GET MY REST?